utetegwi@msu.edu

Gwinyai Tichayedzi Utete

Equity Valuation and Analysis with eVal

Russell Lundholm
University of Michigan

Richard Sloan
University of Michigan

Boston   Burr Ridge, IL   Dubuque, IA   Madison, WI   New York   San Francisco   St. Louis
Bangkok   Bogotá   Caracas   Kuala Lumpur   Lisbon   London   Madrid   Mexico City
Milan   Montreal   New Delhi   Santiago   Seoul   Singapore   Sydney   Taipei   Toronto

EQUITY VALUATION AND ANALYSIS WITH EVAL

Published by McGraw-Hill/Irwin, a business unit of The McGraw-Hill Companies, Inc.,
1221 Avenue of the Americas, New York, NY, 10020. Copyright © 2004 by The
McGraw-Hill Companies, Inc. All rights reserved. No part of this publication may be
reproduced or distributed in any form or by any means, or stored in a database or retrieval
system, without the prior written consent of The McGraw-Hill Companies, Inc.,
including, but not limited to, in any network or other electronic storage or transmission,
or broadcast for distance learning.

Some ancillaries, including electronic and print components, may not be available to
customers outside the United States.

This book is printed on acid-free paper.

1 2 3 4 5 6 7 8 9 0 DOC/DOC 0 9 8 7 6 5 4 3

ISBN 0-07-281933-2

Editor in chief: *Brent Gordon*
Executive editor: *Stewart Mattson*
Editorial assistant: *Jennifer Jelinski and Timothy Matray*
Marketing manager: *Katherine Mattison*
Senior producer, Media technology: *Ed Przyzycki*
Project manager: *Natalie J. Ruffatto*
Senior production supervisor: *Rose Hepburn*
Designer: *Adam Rooke*
Supplement producer: *Matthew Perry*
Senior digital content specialist: *Brian Nacik*
Cover design: *JoAnne Schopler*
Cover image: *© 2003 Getty Images*
Typeface: *10/12 Times New Roman*
Compositor: *GAC Indianapolis*
Printer: *R. R. Donnelley*

Library of Congress Cataloging-in-Publication Data

Lundholm, Russell James.
    Equity valuation and analysis with eVal / Russell Lundholm, Richard Sloan.
        p. cm.
    Includes index.

    ISBN 0-07-281933-2 (alk. paper)
    1. Corporations—Valuation. 2. Business enterprises--Valuation. 3. Stock price
forecasting. 4. Investment analysis. 5. eVal (Electronic resource) I. Sloan, Richard G. II.
Title.
HG4028.V3L796 2004
332.63'221'02855369--dc21

                                                                                2003051003

www.mhhe.com

About the Authors

Russell J. Lundholm

Russell J. Lundholm is the Arthur E. Andersen Professor of Accounting at the University of Michigan Business School. Professor Lundholm holds a Ph.D. in Business Administration and a Masters of Science in Statistics from the University of Iowa. He has taught at the University of Michigan since 1993 and at Stanford University from 1987 to 1993.

Professor Lundholm's research interests lie at the intersection of financial accounting and financial economics. Currently he is studying models that use accounting data to value stocks. Professor Lundholm's research is published in the *Journal of Accounting Research,* the *Accounting Review, Contemporary Accounting Review,* the *Journal of Finance,* the *Review of Financial Studies,* the *Journal of Political Economy* and *Econometrica.* His research has also been discussed in *BusinessWeek, Fortune,* the *New York Times* and *The Wall Street Journal.* Professor Lundholm's principal teaching interest is in graduate level financial statement analysis, with a particular emphasis on stock valuation. He also directs an executive education class for senior investor relations professionals and regularly speaks to organizations about accounting, disclosure and valuation issues.

Richard G. Sloan

Richard G. Sloan is the Victor L. Bernard PricewaterhouseCoopers Collegiate Professor of Accounting and the Director of the Financial Research and Trading Center at the University of Michigan Business School. He received his Ph.D. at the University of Rochester and previously served for six years on the faculty of the Wharton School at the University of Pennsylvania.

Professor Sloan's research focuses on the role of accounting information in firm valuation. His research is widely published in journals such as the *Accounting Review,* the *Journal of Accounting and Economics,* the *Journal of Accounting Research,* the *Journal of Finance* and the *Journal of Financial Economics.* His research is also regularly featured in the business press in publications such as *BusinessWeek, Fortune, Forbes,* the *New York Times, The Washington Post, The Financial Times* and *Worth.*

Professor Sloan currently teaches financial statement analysis, business valuation and investment management in undergraduate, MBA, Ph.D. and executive courses at the University of Michigan Business School. He also serves as a speaker and consultant for various organizations in the investment management industry.

Brief Contents

Table of Contents

Preface

Why This Book?

We wrote this book because we saw a void between the abstract theoretical treatment of equity valuation and the practical problem of valuing an actual company using real world data. We give serious treatment to the underlying theory of financial analysis and valuation, but our main goal is to be able to arrive at a pragmatic answer to the all-important question, "What is this company really worth?" To answer this question, we adopt a very different approach from other textbooks. The key differences can be summarized as follows:

1. Our overriding focus is on generating good financial statement forecasts.
2. We provide detailed practical guidance on how to obtain and analyze relevant real-world data.
3. We demystify the mechanics of equity valuation.

We believe that good forecasts of the future financial statements are the key input to a good valuation. Most other aspects of the valuation process are mechanical and can be programmed into a computer. In fact, this text is supplied with eVal, an Excel-based computer program that takes care of these mechanical tasks. As with many other textbooks, we discuss topics like business strategy analysis, accounting quality analysis, financial ratio analysis, etc. However, we always do so with a clear view to how these analyses help us to generate better financial forecasts.

We also provide plenty of advice on where to go to obtain the most relevant raw data. eVal is supplied with historical financial statement data for over 8,000 companies and you can use eVal to access these companies' SEC filings, investor relations websites, analysts forecasts and new releases. Armed with such a rich source of data, we are able to provide you with plenty of practical examples on how to generate good forecasts using real world data and sound financial analysis.

A final goal of this book is to demystify the valuation process. In the past, we have seen students become lost in a sea of valuation formulas and inconsistent spreadsheet models. For example, students get confused as to whether they should use the DDM, DCF or RIM valuation formula and whether they need to compute a WACC or just a simple cost of equity capital. They become obsessed with learning acronyms and formulas, but flounder when asked to determine a plausible valuation for an actual company. Using eVal, we demonstrate that these different formulas are easily reconciled and refocus students on developing the best set of financial forecasts to plug into them. This reinforces our main point that the key to good valuations is good forecasts.

The eVal Software

We wrote the software because we realized that students were spending way too much time building and debugging their valuation spreadsheets and, consequently, way too little time thinking about the forecasts that they put into their spreadsheets. The tail was definitely wagging the dog. They also couldn't talk to one another because each student tackled the spreadsheet problem differently—it could take hours just to figure out why Jill's value estimate differed from Jack's value estimate. By building one "mother-of-all-spreadsheet valuation models" and making it completely transparent and completely general, we turned our students' attention back to the real problem at hand, which is forecasting the future financial statements. Thus, eVal was born. As we used the early version of the program with students, we discovered that we could use eVal to organize the entire historical analysis, forecasting and valuation process. All the pieces of the puzzle could finally be kept in one place. Later we realized that if we loaded the program with tons of company data and provided web links to even more data, eVal could become the final one-stop-shop for valuation analysis. We also found that once we had familiarized students with eVal, we could effectively teach complex valuation cases that would otherwise become bogged down in the details of the spreadsheet model.

The eVal software helps in doing valuation and it helps in *learning* valuation. There are many software products and web services today that take a few forecast inputs from you and then spit out a valuation, as if by magic, but how they arrived at the results is hidden in a black box. In contrast, this book and the eVal software that accompanies it are designed to be completely transparent at every stage of the valuation process. The software displays the valuation implications of your forecasts in both discounted cash flow models and residual income models, and it shows exactly how the flows of value from these models are linked to your financial statement forecasts.

Why Is This a Good Idea?

Besides the practical value of focusing our book in this way, we think that students find financial analysis and forecasting much more compelling when the theory of valuation is closely linked to real world applications. The abstract theory of financial statements, ratios and valuation formulas can be covered in one or two very boring lectures. What makes this topic exciting is seeing how an organized approach to studying a real company leaves you so much better informed about the firm's future. Is Dell really the highly efficient manufacturer of computers that everyone claims? The answer is yes, as you can see in their turnover statistics. Royal Caribbean Cruises wants to build six more cruise ships in the next three years but can they generate enough cash from the existing ships to pay for the new ones? A careful study of their cashflows shows that they will almost certainly be borrowing lots of money to buy these boats. Salton Inc., maker of the George Foreman grill, toils away in the very unexciting small appliance industry, but has been generating stellar earnings. With a price-to-earnings ratio of only five, are they undervalued? The answer is probably not, because their most popular products have just peaked and their earnings quality is suspect. Financial statements, accounting rules, financial ratios and valuation models are all pretty dull beasts on their own, but if we can use them to answer questions like this, then their usefulness becomes clear. By blending the theory of equity analysis with practical application we feel that students learn both better.

As a working example, the retail department store chain Kohl's is used throughout the book. It is also the default company in eVal, so you can readily see how the theory translates into real forecasts and valuation implications. Because eVal comes preloaded with data for over 8000 public companies, you can also compare Kohl's to Saks, Target, and Sears with just a few mouse-clicks.

Cases and the Website

We have posted a number of cases on the eVal website (www.mhhe.com/eval), and have included short descriptions of each at the end of the relevant chapter. Most of the cases come with data input files for eVal, and most of the cases are based on real companies. These cases are "freeware;" instructors should feel free to modify them as they wish. For most cases, we have also included the Power-Point slides from the lecture where we used the case in our MBA class. The website also includes other tidbits, such as installation instructions, notices about any changes in the URLs reference in the book or the software, and FAQs.

Acknowledgments

Before getting down to business, we would like to thank Patricia Dechow and Kai Petainen for their help debugging the eVal software. We would also like to thank the following reviewers for providing excellent suggestions on how to improve the text: Noel Addy, Mississippi State University; Ervin Black, Brigham Young University; Paul Hribar, Cornell University; Bruce Johnson, University of Iowa; Steve Monahan, University of Chicago; Sarah Tasker, University of California at Berkeley; and Peter Wysocki, Massachusetts Institute of Technology. We especially thank Sarah McVay for reading rough drafts of every chapter and giving us merciless feedback. We also thank our book team at McGraw-Hill/Irwin: Brent Gordon, Editorial Director; Stewart Mattson, Publisher; Katherine Mattison, Marketing Manager; Jennifer Jelinski and Timothy Matray, Editorial Assistants; Ed Przyzycki, Media Technology Producer; and Natalie Ruffatto, Project Manager. A special thanks goes to Stephanie Bednar at Media General Financial Services for the use of their data on eVal. Finally, we give our thanks to Patricia Dechow and Gretchen Bingea for their encouragement throughout the whole project, and we thank our colleagues at the University of Michigan Business School who listened patiently as we complained about all the work we had to do.

CHAPTER ONE

Introduction

1.1 GETTING STARTED

On a typical business day, well over 2 billion shares are traded on major U.S. stock markets. The combined market value of these trades exceeds 50 billion dollars. Most of the shares traded represent equity interests in the business activities of corporations. The prices at which these trades take place determine both the fortunes of the traders and the allocation of much of the economy's scarce capital resources. Our objective in this book is to make you an expert in determining the fair value of these equity interests. If we are successful, not only will you be in a good position to make a few dollars through trading, you will also be making the whole economy more efficient.

This book and the associated eVal software will provide you with a systematic framework for pricing equity securities. There are many books written on the topic. Our approach is unique in that we seek the best possible marriage between theory and practice. By providing you a framework that is both theoretically rigorous and readily amenable to practical implementation, we believe you will better learn both. And we are certain you will have more fun doing so. The eVal software is a flexible tool for the analysis and valuation of equity securities. It will give you hands-on experience building financial models and estimating the value of equity securities. The use of spreadsheet-based financial modeling software is found everywhere in practice. Such software can be a dangerous weapon in the hands of the inexperienced user, however. Our aim is to provide you with a firm grounding in valuation theory and a good understanding of the techniques that have evolved to facilitate practical application of the theory. The end result is that your financial models should work like well-oiled machines.

Valuing equity securities necessarily involves uncertainty. We intend to give you a solid framework for thinking about the uncertainty as well as plenty of good advice about what constitutes a reasonable forecast in an uncertain world. We also point out many sources of data that are available to aid you in forming your forecast. We are living in the middle of an information explosion. The Internet puts an ever-increasing array of financial data at our fingertips. In the spirit of practical advice, we will suggest places to find the best, juiciest tidbits of information and how to incorporate them into your analysis. All this work will eliminate some of the uncertainty in equity valuation, but plenty will still remain. No one knows exactly how the future will unfold; uncertainty is the nature of the beast.

This introductory chapter outlines our equity analysis and valuation framework. We begin with an overview of the nature of business activities. Next, we provide a brief discussion of equity valuation theory. We then explain the critical importance of the financial statements in the practical application of equity valuation theory. Finally, we outline the steps in our systematic approach to valuation that will take you through the remainder of the book and show you how eVal guides you through these steps. Throughout the book we use Kohl's as a working example. In case you haven't heard of them, Kohl's is a rapidly growing department store chain featuring clothing items and housewares. This chapter provides a roadmap for the entire equity valuation process, and we will refer back to this roadmap frequently as we walk you through each of the intermediate steps.

1.2   OVERVIEW OF BUSINESS ACTIVITIES

Equity securities represent ownership claims in the business activities of profit-seeking entities. The valuation of an equity security must therefore begin with a thorough analysis of the underlying business activities. Business activities can be divided into three broad categories to facilitate analysis: operating activities, investing activities and financing activities. Each category is described below.

Operating Activities

Businesses typically generate profit for their owners by providing customers with goods and services in return for cash or other consideration. As long as the consideration received exceeds the costs incurred in providing the goods and services, profit is generated. *Operating activities* are activities that are directly related to the provision of goods and services to customers. For example, in a restaurant business, the purchase, preparation and serving of food to customers are all examples of operating activities. Washing the dishes and cleaning the restrooms are also operating activities, since these are part of the package of services that a restaurant provides to its customers. The operating activities are clearly the bread and butter of any business and the primary means through which the owners of the business hope to profit from their investment.

Investing Activities

Nearly all businesses must make investments in productive capacity before they can begin to provide goods and services to their customers. For example, a restaurant business requires a building, furniture, and cooking equipment. Purchases and sales of resources that provide productive capacity are referred to as *investing activities*. We define investing activities with respect to the nature of the goods and services that the firm is in the business of providing. If the firm is in the business of selling cooking equipment, then the purchase of an oven is an operating activity. However, if the firm is in the business of selling restaurant meals, then the purchase of an oven is an investing activity, because it provides the productive capacity required to produce meals.

Why bother to distinguish between operating activities and investing activities? Investing activities involve resource commitments that are expected to provide benefits over long periods of time. Investments take place in anticipation of future operating activities and the profits from operating activities must ultimately provide a competitive return on the investment for the investment to have been worthwhile. Because the resources acquired in investing activities provide benefits for long periods of time, it can take a long time to find out how profitable these investments have been. In addition, the investing activities that a company makes today may be used to support operating activities of a very different scale and scope in the future. It is therefore useful to separate our analysis of the performance of a business's current operating activities from its investments in productive capacity to support future operating activities. In the long run, however, operating and investing activities are closely linked. Operating activities are made possible by a specific set of past investing activities, and the profits from operating activities should be evaluated in relation to the cost of the investing activities that made them possible.

Financing Activities

Somebody needs to pay for all of this stuff. In order to acquire the resources necessary to engage in operating and investing activities, businesses require financing. The owners of the business provide the initial source of financing in the hope that the business will provide them with a competitive return on their capital. In a corporation, these owners are the holders of the common equity securities. If a business is financed solely by its equity holders, and immediately pays the entire net cash flow generated by its operating and investing activities back to its equity holders, its *financing activities* consist of these simple transactions between the business and its equity holders. In practice, however, there are many other sources of financing. A business can issue debt, preferred stock, and warrants, to name just a few. In addition, a business need not immediately pay out all the cash generated by its operating and investing activities. Instead, the business may choose to invest this cash in financial assets, such as treasury bonds or financial securities issued by other businesses. Financing activities incorporate all such transactions.

Financing activities are distinct from operating and investing activities. A firm can finance a given set of operating and investing activities many different ways without affecting the nature of the operating and investing activities. This does not mean that the firm cannot add value through financing activities. Financing activities create the opportunity for the owners of the business to leverage the return from their operating and investing activities, to minimize taxes and transactions costs, and to take advantage of inefficiencies in capital markets. Investment bankers specialize in determining the amount and type of capital that takes best advantage of these financing opportunities, and the large fees charged by investment bankers speak to the potential value that can be created.

1.3 OVERVIEW OF EQUITY VALUATION THEORY

The basic theory of equity valuation is straightforward and well established. Equity securities are financial instruments, and as such, their value is equal to net present value of the future cash distributions that they are expected to generate. These cash distributions have traditionally taken the form of cash dividend payments, and so our first pass at the value of equity is based on the net present value of the expected future dividend payments, as shown in the following equation:

$$\text{Value}_0 = \sum_{t=1}^{\infty} \frac{\text{Cash Dividend}_t}{(1 + r)^t}$$

where

Value_0 = value of equity at time 0

Cash Dividend_t = expected amount of cash dividends to be paid in period t

r = discount rate (cost of capital)

This valuation model is widely known as the dividend-discounting model. However, dividends are not the only way that cash can be distributed to equity holders. Stock repurchases have become increasingly popular. While dividends represent routine cash payments made on a pro rata basis to all equity holders, stock repurchases involve the business buying back stock from specific equity holders. Nevertheless, both transactions involve distributing cash from the business to its equity holders. Another consideration in the valuation of equity securities is that companies often seek new cash infusions through the issuance of additional equity securities. These equity issuances can be thought of as negative cash distributions that should be netted against the positive cash distributions associated with dividends and stock repurchases in order to determine the net cash distributions to equity. So the dividend-discounting model is more precisely expressed as:

$$\text{Value}_0 = \sum_{t=1}^{\infty} \frac{\text{Cash Dividend}_t + \text{Stock Repurchases}_t - \text{Equity Issuances}_t}{(1 + r)^t}$$

where

Cash Dividend_t = expected amount of cash dividends to be paid in period t

$\text{Stock Repurchases}_t$ = expected amount of cash to be paid out via stock repurchases in period t

$\text{Equity Issuances}_t$ = expected amount of cash to be raised via equity issuances in period t

What determines the magnitude of the net cash distributions made by a business to its equity holders? Since equity holders are the owners of the business, they have the residual claim on the net cash flows available from a business's operating, investing and non-equity financing activities. In practice cash distributions to equity holders are made at the discretion of management, based on a wide variety of factors. The major factors are:

- How much cash did the business's operating activities generate?
- How much cash was used for investing activities in order to maintain or expand the scale and scope of the business's operating activities?
- How much cash is required to make scheduled payments to providers of non-equity capital, such as interest and principal payments on loans?
- How much cash should be raised (used) issuing (retiring) non-equity capital, such as debt and preferred stock?
- How much cash should be retained in the business in the form of financial assets to provide for future cash flow needs?

In the long run, the cash flows generated by a business's operating activities are the key driver of its cash distributions. The other factors listed above, however, can make the amount and timing of a business's operating cash flows very different from the amount and timing of its cash distributions. For example, profitable firms with growth opportunities will often have negative net cash distributions as they issue additional equity to invest in expanding their operating activities, all in the hope of making even greater cash distributions in the future.

In summary, while the basic theory of equity valuation is quite straightforward, the devil is in forecasting the future net cash distributions. There are many different valuation models floating around in academia and in practice. The key difference between these models is in the variables that are substituted as proxies for future net cash distributions. For example, practitioners are fond of substituting variables such as earnings, EBITDA, and NOPAT for cash distributions. These substitutions can be justified if done in a way that maintains consistency with the underlying dividend-discounting model. All too often, however, practitioners throw caution to the wind and come up with valuation models that require heroic assumptions to be consistent with the dividend-discounting model.

1.4   THE ROLE OF FINANCIAL STATEMENTS

The financial statements are the primary devices for bridging the gap between theory and practice in equity valuation. Although traditional valuation texts often criticize financial statements and their underlying accounting principles on the basis that they do an imperfect job of measuring value, these criticisms represent a basic misunderstanding of the role of financial statements in equity valuation. Financial statements are not designed to estimate equity value directly, and accounting book values rarely match market values. Instead, the role of the financial statements is to provide a detailed description of the financial implications of a firm's historical business activities. In other words, the financial statements summarize the historical operating, investing, and financing activities of a firm, and show how these activities affect the past, present, and expected future cash flows. The purpose of the historical financial statements is not to directly forecast the cash flow implications of future operating, investing, and financing activities.

Given that the historical financial statements do not directly forecast how future business activities will affect future cash flows, one might ask, What is their role in valuation? Their role is twofold:

- They provide the language for translating forecasts of future business activities into forecasts of cash flows.
- By describing the cash flow implications of past business activities, they provide a good starting point for determining the cash flow implications of future business activities.

The first role of the financial statements in valuation is to provide a language for describing how a firm's future business activities will affect its future cash flows. We cannot forecast cash flows in a vacuum. The role of the financial statements is to identify and categorize the activities of a firm that have cash flow implications. A set of financial statements tells us how the various operating, investing, and financing activities of a firm combine to produce cash flows. In order to forecast a firm's future cash flows, we first need a set of financial statements that capture the various intended operating, investing, and financing activities of the firm. We can then begin the process of forecasting the cash flow implications of each of these activities. For instance, by forecasting Sales and the change in Accounts Receivable, we can compute what the cash collections from customers will be. By constructing a complete set of forecasted financial statements we can systematically derive the cash flow forecasts.

The second role of the financial statements is to provide historical data on the cash flow implications of a firm's past business activities that may prove useful in forecasting its future cash flows. Many firms engage in similar business activities for long periods of time. Over time, these business activities are subject to changes, such as demand changes, supply changes, and technological changes. Nevertheless, these changes are rarely so drastic as to make the results of past business activities irrelevant to the prediction of future results. Thus, the most common forecasting procedure is to start with the past financial statements and then modify those statements based on changes that are anticipated to occur in the future. The effectiveness of this procedure varies widely. For firms in mature industries with established products and stable customer bases, past results can be a very good predictor of future results, and the past financial statements will be very relevant in estimating firm value. In contrast, for startup firms in emerging industries with evolving products and growing customer bases, past results can be a very poor predictor of future results. Past results will also be a poor predictor of future results for firms making significant acquisitions or significant changes to their business strategies. But we have to start somewhere, and the past is usually the best place to start when thinking about the future.

1.5   THREE STEPS TO EQUITY VALUATION

The discussion thus far indicates that the equity valuation process can be broken down into three distinct steps, which are illustrated in Figure 1.1. *Understanding the Past* is the first step. This analysis must go beyond simply looking at the firm's past financial results. You need to understand the firm's results in the context of the industry and economy in which the firm operates, and you need to look for clues about planned changes in the future business activities. Second, we need to use our analysis of the past in *Forecasting the Future*. This step is structured around forecasting the future financial statements, from which we will derive our estimates of future net cash distributions. The third step comprises *Valuation*. In this step, we convert our estimates of the future net cash distributions into a single estimate of intrinsic value. The eVal software provided with this book will guide you through each of these steps. In this section, we give an overview of the three steps and introduce you to eVal.

Understanding the Past

The first step in the equity valuation process is to examine all relevant information about the business. This step begins with the systematic collection of pertinent information, which we refer to in Figure 1.1 as *information collection.* If the equity security is publicly traded in the United States, then the usual starting point for information collection is the firm's financial filings with the Securities and Exchange Commission (SEC). However, there are a myriad of other information sources that should be investigated, ranging from press releases issued by the firm to macroeconomic data. Today, much of this information is available via the click

FIGURE 1.1   Framework for Equity Valuation

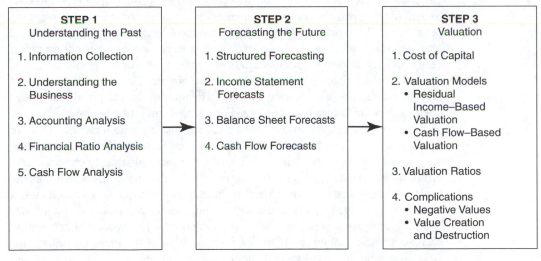

STEP 1 Understanding the Past	STEP 2 Forecasting the Future	STEP 3 Valuation
1. Information Collection	1. Structured Forecasting	1. Cost of Capital
2. Understanding the Business	2. Income Statement Forecasts	2. Valuation Models • Residual Income–Based Valuation • Cash Flow–Based Valuation
3. Accounting Analysis	3. Balance Sheet Forecasts	
4. Financial Ratio Analysis	4. Cash Flow Forecasts	3. Valuation Ratios
5. Cash Flow Analysis		4. Complications • Negative Values • Value Creation and Destruction

of a mouse. We provide a more detailed discussion of the most important information sources in Chapter 2.

Once the pertinent information has been gathered, we begin the process of analyzing it. The first task is *understanding the business.* This process is primarily qualitative and is aimed at developing a detailed understanding of the business activities in which the firm is engaged. What does the business make, how does it make it, and whom does it sell it to? Who are the main competitors, what are the industry characteristics, and how does this industry fit into the general economy? We also want to identify the elements of a firm's business strategy that are expected to make it more successful than its competitors. Just as investors strive to find securities that will provide abnormally high investment returns, managers strive to find real investment opportunities that will provide abnormally high profits. Competition among managers limits the availability of such investment opportunities. Your business analysis should leave you with a clear understanding of the firm's business plan, and some opinions about whether this plan represents a viable strategy for generating abnormally high profits. We cover the basics of business analysis in Chapter 3.

Armed with a thorough understanding of the business, we can start to scrutinize the historical financial statements. *Accounting analysis* is the first task (again see Figure 1.1). The objective here is to develop a thorough understanding of how the economic consequences of the firm's business activities are reflected in the financial statements. The financial statements report on the periodic financial position and operating performance of a business. Over long periods of time (many years), the cash consequences of a firm's operating and investing activities become known with perfect certainty, and so the economic consequences are easy to measure. But over short periods of time (a quarter or a year), the cash consequences can have little relation to the economic consequences. The difficulty arises because firms' operating and investing cycles often span many years. Firms can hold or produce inventory for long periods, they can advance credit to customers for long periods, they invest in assets that will generate benefits over long periods, and they reward employees with retirement benefits that will be paid over long periods. As a result, the net cash flows to a firm over short periods provide a very noisy signal of the long-run cash flow consequences of the firm's activities.

This is where financial accounting comes to our aid. The primary objective of accrual accounting is to provide a better indication of the long-run cash consequences of a firm's business activities. For instance, investing in a productive asset is not merely a cash outflow; the accrual accounting system records the store of future benefits that this investment represents by recording an asset on the balance sheet. But while the accrual accounting process undoubtedly creates useful information, it is also fraught with distortions. The distortions are sometimes the benign errors that come from estimating uncertain events, and they are sometimes intentionally created by management manipulation of the reported results. Accounting analysis is concerned with understanding a firm's accrual accounting policies and their implications for the interpretation of the financial statements. A solid accounting analysis will help you understand the key strengths and weaknesses of a firm's financial statements, help you identify where management may have attempted to mislead you, and help you draw informed conclusions about the economic consequences of the firm's past business activities. Accounting analysis is the subject of Chapter 4.

Once you have a solid understanding of the firm's financial statements, you are set to use the financial statements to evaluate the financial performance of the firm. Chapter 5 develops a systematic *financial ratio analysis* framework to facilitate this task. This analysis shows us how the components of a firm's financial statements interact to produce overall financial performance. What margin does the firm earn on its sales, how efficiently does it manage its assets to produce those sales, and how much leverage does it apply to finance the acquisition of its assets? The analysis enables us to quickly identify the key drivers of financial performance and spot any irregularities. When combined with accounting analysis, financial ratio analysis provides the basis for evaluating the economic consequences of a firm's past business activities and the success of its business strategy.

Ratio analysis focuses almost exclusively on a firm's accrual accounting statements—the income statement and the balance sheet. In order to remain solvent, however, to fund new business opportunities, and ultimately to make cash flow distributions, a firm must also carefully manage its cash. A firm's cash flows are described in the statement of cash flows and the analysis of this information is the topic of Chapter 6. *Cash flow analysis* is concerned with understanding the articulation of the cash flows between a firm's operating, investing, and financing activities. A sound business strategy should anticipate the cash flow requirements associated with operating and investing activities and provide for their timely and efficient financing. Also, firm value is ultimately dependent on the distribution of cash flows to equity holders. Unfortunately, some firms choose to invest surplus cash flows in wasteful ways rather than to make timely distributions to equity holders. These and other related issues are discussed in more detail in Chapter 6.

Forecasting the Future

Once you understand the past, you are ready to forecast the future. The tasks involved in this step are summarized in the second box of Figure 1.1. Our goal in this step is to forecast the future financial statements. Recall from our earlier discussion that the financial statements represent the language for converting forecasts of future business activities into forecasts of future cash flows. In Chapter 7 we introduce *structured forecasting*—the systematic way that we go about developing forecasts. Rather than attempt to forecast each line item of the financial statements in isolation, we frame the forecasting problem using the same types of ratios that you will study in Chapter 5. You express your assumptions about the firm's operating, investing, and financing activities using these ratios, and then derive the implied values for the underlying financial statement line items.

In Chapter 7, we also discuss earnings-per-share (EPS) forecasts. EPS forecasts are probably the most widely followed financial metrics on Wall Street. On the surface this computation might seem simple—take the forecasted earnings and divide by the number of shares. But what number of shares should you use? Our forecast of the future number of shares outstanding depends on both our forecast of the amount of new equity that is expected to be issued/repurchased between now and the forecast date and the stock prices at which the issuances/repurchases are expected to occur. While our pro forma financial statements will provide us with dollar forecasts of issuances and repurchases, they do not provide us with forecasts of future issuance and repurchase prices. Thus, per-share analysis turns out to be quite a complex topic involving some thorny issues.

The eVal software requires a number of specific forecasting assumptions. In Chapter 8 we give you advice concerning *forecasting details*. The process begins with the very first line on the income statement, the Sales forecast. Most firms have business models that center around providing goods and services to customers in return for sales revenue. The sales forecast is the single most important forecast; it represents the key driver of most other business activities. For example, the remaining lines in the income statement capture the costs that are incurred in the firm's operating activities, and many of these costs depend on the level of business activity, as described by the sales forecast. But the costs also depend on the efficiency with which the business is run and the prices at which the inputs for the business (such as materials and labor) are purchased, so forecasting these costs is not as simple as taking a fixed percentage of sales.

Income statement forecasts concern operating activities. Balance sheet forecasts concern the impact of the operating, investing, and financing activities on the financial resources and obligations of a firm. The forecasting of the balance sheet can be divided into two distinct tasks. First, we must forecast the resources and obligations necessary to sustain the operating activities that we forecast on our income statement. Operating activities typically require investments in working capital (for instance, inventory) and long-term capital (property, plant, and equipment) and can also result in obligations (such as accounts payable and pension benefits for employees). The forecasted amount of operating resources and obligations depends on both the forecasted level of operating activity and the efficiency with which the firm is forecasted to conduct its operations. The second distinct task is to forecast the resources and obligations associated with the firm's financing activities. Most firms hold some financial resources (cash and marketable securities) and use some non-equity financing (debt and preferred stock). The forecasting of the individual financial resources and obligations on the balance sheet provides a systematic process for determining the amount and mix of financing that is used to support the firm's operating and investing activities.

The next task is to create cash flow forecasts. As we discussed earlier, the financial statements provide the language we use to describe the economic consequences of business activities. Ultimately, these economic consequences are represented by cash flows and the statement of cash flows reports these cash consequences. Contained within the cash flow forecasts are implied forecasts of the net cash distributions to equity holders, a key input for equity valuation, so this is an important step. Fortunately, cash flow forecasting is quite straightforward. As you may recall from your accounting classes, we can derive a statement of cash flows from an income statement and the beginning and ending balance sheets. So, we simply use our income statements and balance sheet forecasts to construct our cash flow forecast, and the eVal software handles this step for us.

The forecasted financial statements are often referred to as "pro forma" financial statements ("pro forma" is Latin for "a matter of form"). The last step is to apply the same ratio analysis and cash flow analysis that we discussed in Chapter 5 to the pro forma financial statements. This final step provides a reality check on the plausibility of our forecasts. For example, we may find that our forecasting assumptions imply a level of profitability for a firm that far exceeds the historical industry average. Such performance may be justified through some unique feature of the firm's business strategy. If we do not see anything particularly unique, however, we should probably revise the forecasting assumptions to bring profitability back to more reasonable levels. Similarly, our pro forma cash flow analysis may reveal that our forecasting assumptions imply that a firm must raise substantial additional capital. If the firm has no plans to raise new capital, or would have difficulty accessing capital markets on favorable terms, we should revise our forecasting assumptions accordingly.

Valuation

With your forecasts of the future under your belt, you are ready for step three, *valuation.* The tasks involved in the valuation step are summarized in the third box of Figure 1.1. First you need to decide on the necessary valuation parameters. The most important of these is the *discount rate* or *cost of capital,* which enters the denominator of our equity valuation model. Unfortunately, there is much disagreement concerning the selection of an appropriate discount rate. In Chapter 9, we will discuss some of the most popular techniques for computing the discount rate and provide some general advice on how to handle this issue.

The remaining tasks consist of the equity valuation computations themselves. The good news here is that eVal does all the work for you. eVal provides computations using both a Residual Income Valuation Model (RIM) and a Discounted Free Cash Flow Model (DCF) model. Why do we need two valuations? Actually we don't, and it turns out that both these valuations will give you exactly the same answer. These are simply two different algebraic formulations of our basic dividend-discounting model. Regardless of the formula used, it is your forecasts of the future financial statements, along with your valuation parameters, that ultimately determine the value of the equity. The only issue here is whether you would like to look at computations based on earnings or cash flows. Making use of both sets of computations, you will be able to effectively communicate your equity valuation work to fans of either model.

A second issue in constructing the valuation models is whether we choose to discount the cash distributions directly to equity holders using the cost of equity capital, or whether we discount cash flows to all providers of capital (common equity plus preferred stock and debt) using a weighted average cost of capital, and then subtract the value of the non-equity capital to derive equity value. Again, eVal does the valuation both ways, both ways give the same answer, and the choice between the two approaches is largely a matter of taste. Chapter 10 provides a detailed explanation of the valuation gymnastics involved in these alternative *valuation models*.

Financial analysts often communicate their beliefs about the value of the firm in terms of *valuation ratios*. Some of these ratios are quite straightforward, such as the market-to-book ratio, defined as the price divided by the book value. Others are much more complex, like the PEG ratio (don't ask). In Chapter 11 we discuss some of these ratios, what they represent, and how they can be used to spot underpriced or overpriced stocks. These ratios are commonly used shortcuts but they are just that; they are no substitute for a full-blown valuation analysis.

The final step in the equity valuation process is to consider some *complications*. If you are lucky, none of these complications will apply to the equity securities you are valuing. However, one or another of these monsters often rears its ugly head. We mention them here briefly only to alert you to their existence; Chapter 12 provides more detailed coverage.

The first complication concerns negative equity values. Stock prices cannot be negative in practice, but models can be constructed in eVal that generate negative equity values. If you find yourself with a negative equity valuation, then you should read Chapter 12. A second and related complication concerns the abandonment option. If you come up with a positive equity valuation, but your sensitivity analysis reveals that negative valuations are also reasonably likely, then you need to consider the abandonment option.

A third complication arises when we introduce the possibility that a firm may create or destroy value through transactions in its own mispriced securities. For example, if a firm's stock is overpriced relative to its intrinsic value, it can create value for its existing equity holders by issuing additional shares of the overpriced stock. Thus, not only do we have to correctly determine the intrinsic value of a firm's operating and investing activities, we also have to forecast how much additional value will be created or destroyed through the firm's financing activities. A final and related complication concerns contingent equity claims. Contingent equity claims provide their holders with the option, but not the obligation, to purchase shares of common stock for a prespecified exercise price. Firms issue contingent claims on their equity for a variety of reasons. For example, firms can raise capital by issuing warrants, firms can reduce the interest rate paid on debt by issuing convertible debt, and firms can compensate employees using employee stock options. Because the holders of contingent claims only have to exercise their claims when it is profitable to do so, the claims themselves will have value as long as there is some probability of a profitable future exercise. These claims can therefore result in equity securities being issued for consideration less than fair value.

1.6   THE ROLE OF eVal

We are now at an ideal point to introduce eVal, our Excel-based financial modeling software (see Appendix A for instructions on how to install eVal on your computer). Remember that you MUST enable macros for eVal to work. We promise that we haven't programmed anything evil, so click "Enable" when prompted. Each time you start a new model in eVal you will be greeted by the eVal introductory screen, shown in Figure 1.2. This screen contains some boilerplate legal notices, and after acknowledging them you simply hit the OK button to start using eVal. Clicking the OK button takes you to the User's Guide worksheet, shown in Figure 1.3.

The User's Guide worksheet is eVal's control center, and you will use this worksheet to guide you through the construction of your financial models. Note that this worksheet is organized around the same three steps that we outlined in the equity valuation framework. The worksheet consists of a series of ordered buttons. Clicking a button takes you to another worksheet, where you will either input required valuation data or view financial data prepared by eVal. Each sheet that you are taken to will have a Go To User's Guide button in the top left corner. When you have finished with a sheet, click this button to take you back to the User's Guide worksheet. While we have organized the buttons so as to systematically walk you through the entire equity valuation process, you are free to skip between buttons and worksheets as you wish while you build your model.

Figure 1.4 summarizes the role played by eVal in each of the three steps of our valuation framework. The first box in Figure 1.4 summarizes how eVal assists you in step one, *Understanding the Past.* eVal begins by importing the firm's historical financial data into a standardized spreadsheet format and provides you with a variety of links to company data. Next, eVal performs systematic financial ratio analysis and cash flow analysis on the firm's historical financial statements. These

FIGURE 1.2   **eVal Splash Screen**

FIGURE 1.3 eVal User's Guide

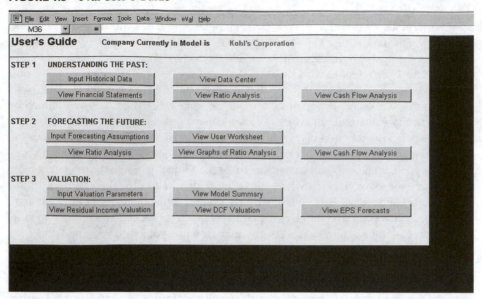

repetitive and tedious data input and data manipulation tasks are done for you automatically. There is no escaping the inevitable fact that you must perform the vast majority of the work in this first step yourself, however. A thorough understanding of all the relevant information concerning a business can only be achieved through your own detailed information collection and analysis.

The second box in Figure 1.4 summarizes how eVal helps you in step two, *Forecasting the Future.* eVal will initially prompt you for a forecast horizon. It will then generate a forecasting template and prompt you for the individual forecasting assumptions required to build the forecasted financial statements. The structure in eVal is designed to simplify an otherwise daunting task, yet remain sufficiently flexible to hit any desired set of financial results. eVal also provides default forecasting assumptions that are reasonable for the average firm in the average industry in the average year. You should avoid relying too heavily on these defaults. We are not licensed soothsayers; our defaults are simply based on the naïve extrapolation of past data. You should use your detailed information analysis from step one to provide more accurate forecasting assumptions. Once you have updated the assumptions, eVal will prepare the pro forma financial statements implied by these assumptions and will perform a detailed financial ratio analysis and cash flow analysis on the pro forma financial statements.

The third box in Figure 1.4 summarizes how eVal helps you in step three, *Valuation.* You have already done most of the hard work in steps one and two, leaving eVal to do most of the work in step three. eVal begins by presenting detailed valuation calculations using both the residual income (RIM) and discounted free cash flow (DCF) valuation models. You can use the formulas in the valuation

FIGURE 1.4   **The Role of eVal in Application of the Equity Valuation Framework**

STEP 1 Understanding the Past	**STEP 2** Forecasting the Future	**STEP 3** Valuation
What You Do: Obtain and analyze financial and non-financial information on the business **What eVal Does:** Imports historical financial data using **eVal's** standardized format Provides links to company data Performs systematic ratio analysis on historical data Performs systematic cash flow analysis on historical data	**What You Do:** Select forecast horizon Modify **eVal's** default forecasting assumptions based on the insights from your analysis in STEP 1 **What eVal Does:** Creates forecasting template and prompts you for key forecasting assumptions Provides historic values and suggests default values for forecasting assumptions Prepares pro-forma financial statements from forecasting assumptions Performs ratio and cash flow analysis on pro-forma financials	**What You Do:** Provide cost of equity capital and other valuation parameters **What eVal Does:** Performs residual income valuation to both common equity holders and all capital providers Performs discounted cash flow valuation to both common equity holders and all capital providers Maintains internal consistency between the two valuation models Provides EPS forecast schedule Provides model summary and sensitivity analysis

spreadsheets to trace all of the amounts entering the valuation calculations back to the pro forma financial statements prepared in step two. eVal will also ensure that the valuations obtained using the RIM and DCF models are identical. While this feature is simply a reflection of the consistent application of the dividend-discounting valuation model in both cases, it is important from a practical perspective. One of our strongest motivations for creating eVal was the hundreds of hours that we spent trying to reconcile the inconsistent valuation models of students. eVal also provides a detailed analysis of the earnings-per-share (EPS) implications of your pro forma financial forecasts, which helps you to benchmark your forecasts with those of Wall Street analysts. EPS is the most closely tracked summary measure of firm performance and EPS surprises are a big catalyst for stock price changes. If your EPS forecasts are more accurate than the consensus forecasts of Wall Street analysts, the differences between your forecasts and the consensus should provide the basis for a lucrative investment strategy. Finally, eVal provides a summary of the key inputs in your valuation model and a sensitivity analysis tool that allows you to determine the sensitivity of your valuation estimate to changes in the key assumptions. These features of eVal are particularly useful for sharing the key ingredients of your valuation model with others.

1.7 CLOSING COMMENTS

In this chapter, we provided you with an overview of the theory and practice of equity valuation and introduced our framework for equity valuation. We also highlighted the role played by the eVal financial software in helping you to apply this framework more efficiently and to communicate the key ingredients of your analysis more effectively. If you have a reasonable background in accounting and finance, this overview is probably enough to get you up and running with eVal. However, the "garbage-in, garbage out" maxim rules the day. Even software such as eVal cannot protect you from your own bad forecasting assumptions. In the chapters that follow, our main purpose is to provide you with a framework for deriving the best possible forecasting assumptions from the available information. Let's face it, valuation software like eVal costs just a few dollars. It stands to reason that such a tool by itself cannot give you the edge in the competitive world of Wall Street. So for those of you who want to make it big in the investment world, there are still 11 more chapters and a lifetime of diligent work ahead of you.

CHAPTER TWO

Information Collection

2.1   INTRODUCTION

The heart of a good valuation is a good forecast, and a forecast is only as good as the information that is used to support it. So the more relevant information you collect, the more accurate your forecast will be. You may be thinking that information collection is time consuming and costly, and that our "more is better" advice ignores this aspect of the trade-off. But our advice comes from years of experience watching students and practitioners underinvest in information collection. The chapters that follow talk in more detail about how to interpret the specific information you collect. This chapter focuses on describing the most important sources of information and how eVal can help you obtain and process this information. By focusing your information collection effort where it yields the highest returns, and using tools such as eVal to leverage your data collection and processing abilities, you will maximize the payoff to information collection.

We begin by identifying the key sources of company-specific data. Filings with the Securities and Exchange Commission (SEC) are the most important source of company-specific information. We identify the most important filings and describe their contents. We then discuss other data sources, such as company websites, company press releases, new stories, and analysts' reports. Next, we identify and briefly discuss the key sources of industry and macroeconomic data. Finally, we explain the various options for importing historical financial statement data into eVal.

Throughout this chapter we will give you links to sources of information on the Internet. We simply name the site in the text and, in the last section of the chapter, give you the URL that gets you to the site. Many of the company-specific links can be found on the Data Center sheet in eVal. The more general links can be found under the eVal menu.

2.2   COMPANY DATA

You should spend most of your time collecting company-specific data. Two-thirds of the variation in a typical stock's price is company specific and unrelated to market or industrywide movements. We recommend that you spend at least two-thirds of your time on the analysis of company-specific data. The major sources of company-specific data are explained below.

17

SEC Filings

Public companies in the United States are required to file a number of detailed financial reports with the Securities and Exchange Commission (SEC), which in turn makes the reports available to the public. These SEC filings represent the most important source of company-specific information and provide the natural starting point for the collection of company data. A summary of the most important SEC filings is provided in Figure 2.1. A more detailed description of SEC forms is available on the SEC's website.

Listed first in Figure 2.1 is the annual Form 10-K, the most useful SEC filing. All domestic publicly traded companies are required to file this form within 90 days of their fiscal year end (the filing deadline will be reduced to 60 days by

FIGURE 2.1 **Guide to Common SEC Filings**

Filing	Description
Form 10-K	This is the annual report filed by most companies. It provides a comprehensive overview of the company's business (see Figure 2.2 for details). It must be filed within 90 days of the close of the fiscal year (60 days by 2005).
Form 10-Q	This is the quarterly financial report filed by most companies. It includes unaudited financial statements and provides a continuing view of the company's financial position during the year. It must be filed within 45 days of the close of the quarter (35 days by 2005).
Form 8-K	This is the "current report" that is used to report the occurrence of any material events or corporate changes which are of importance to investors and have not been previously reported.
Proxy Statement (Form DEF 14A)	Proxy statement providing official notification to designated classes of shareholders of matters to be brought to a vote at a shareholders' meeting.
Schedule 13D	Filing required by 5% (or more) equity owners within 10 days of acquisition event.
Schedule 13E	Filings required by persons engaging in "going private" transactions in company's stock or by companies engaging in tender offers for their own securities.
Schedule 13F	Quarterly report required of the equity holdings of all institutional investors with equity assets of $1 million or more.
Schedule 13G	Similar to Schedule 13D, but only available in special cases where control of issuer is not compromised.
Schedule 14D	Filings required pursuant to a tender offer.
Form 3, Form 4 and Form 5	Statement of ownership filings required by every director, officer or 10% owner. Form 3 is initial ownership filing, Form 4 is for changes and Form 5 is the annual filing.
Registration Statements (Forms S-1, S-2 and S-3)	Filings that are used to register securities before they are offered to investors. Form S-1 is typically the initial public offering and Forms S-2 and S-3 are for seasoned offerings of small and large companies, respectively.
Prospectus (Form 424B4)	Document that is made available to investors in a security offering.

2005). If you were going to read only one document about the company before starting your valuation, this would be the one. This can be quite a lengthy document, but it follows a standardized format and familiarizing yourself with this format will improve your ability to process the contents efficiently.

The basic format of a Form 10-K is summarized in Figure 2.2. The first item, the description of business, provides a detailed discussion of the company's past and expected future business activities. Companies are required to provide a

FIGURE 2.2   **Items of Disclosure Contained in Form 10-K**

Item	Description
Cover Page	Lists fiscal year end, state of incorporation, details for each class of publicly traded securities and other descriptive information.
Item 1—Business	Identifies principal products and services of the company, principal markets and methods of distribution and other key attributes and risks of the business.
Item 2—Properties	Location and character of key properties.
Item 3—Legal Proceedings	Brief description of material legal proceedings pending.
Item 4—Submission of Matters to Vote	Information relating to the convening of a meeting of shareholders, whether annual or special, and the matters voted upon.
Item 5—Market for Common Stock	Principal market in which voting securities are traded with high and low sales prices for each quarter during the last two years, dividends paid during last two years and future dividend plans.
Item 6—Selected Financial Data	Five-year selected summary financial data including net sales and operating revenue, income from continuing operations, total assets and long-term obligations.
Item 7—Management's Discussion and Analysis	Discussion of liquidity, capital resources and results of operations; trends and significant events or uncertainties; causes of any material changes, effects of inflation and changing prices and critical accounting policies.
Item 7A—Information about Risk	Provides qualitative and quantitative disclosures about market risk (e.g., interest rate, exchange rate and commodity price risk). The disclosure requirements apply to financial instruments and commodity instruments.
Item 8—Financial Statements	Two-year audited balance sheets, three-year audited statements of income, three-year audited statements of cash flows statement plus supporting notes and schedules.
Item 9—Changes/ Disagreements with Accountants	Description of any changes in and disagreements with accountants on accounting and financial disclosure.

long list of information on things such as the principal products sold, sources and availability of raw materials, key patents, trademarks and licenses, seasonalities, key customers, competitive conditions, and important government regulations. The SEC designed this item to be a thorough and objective overview of a company's business activities, and it is a great starting point for getting to know a company.

The next three items in Form 10-K provide information about other aspects of the company that regulators decided were worth singling out. Item 2 requires a description of the property of the company, Item 3 requires a description of any material pending legal proceedings against the company, and Item 4 requires a description of any matters submitted during the fourth quarter to a vote of security holders. You should scan this information for anything important, but there isn't usually too much here. Item 5 requires summary information concerning recent stock price and dividend activity and Item 6 provides summary financial data for the last five years. You can obtain the information in Items 5 and 6 in more detail from other sources, but since it provides a convenient summary, you may want to scan through it.

Item 7 contains management's discussion and analysis of financial conditions and results of operations. Referred to as the MD&A, this is a "must read." The discussion and analysis of financial conditions requires management to identify any factors that might cause the company's liquidity to change. It also requires a description of the company's material capital expenditure commitments, the purpose of such commitments, and the anticipated sources of funding for the commitments. Finally, the company is required to discuss any pending changes in the company's capital structure. The discussion and analysis of results of operations require management to walk the reader through the line items in the company's income statement, identifying any unusual or non-recurring items and explaining any significant changes from previous years. A recent SEC proposal also requires firms to identify and describe their critical accounting policies in the MD&A. Lastly, because much of the material in the MD&A is forward-looking, it normally finishes with a long list of all the risk factors that add uncertainty to these forecasts. As you can see, the management discussion and analysis requires management to divulge a wealth of information that is useful in forecasting. Moreover, the company's auditor is required to perform a reality check on the information in the MD&A. So read the MD&A.

Following the MD&A is Item 7A, requiring disclosures about the company's exposure to certain market risks, such as interest rate risk. This item is important for financial services companies and other companies holding large amounts of financial instruments or engaging in significant hedging activities. Next is the all-important Item 8. Item 8 contains the company's financial statements and supplementary data. This item includes annual balance sheets for the last two years and annual income statements, statements of cash flows, and statements of changes in stockholders equity for the past three years. These financial statements must also include a detailed description of significant accounting policies, detailed supporting notes and schedules, and an auditor's opinion. The analysis of these financial statements is one of our most important tasks, and is the subject of Chapters 4, 5, and 6.

Finally, Item 9 contains information about changes in and disagreements with accountants on accounting and financial disclosure. Item 9 basically requires disclosure if the company's auditor either resigned or had a major accounting disagreement with management in the past two years. Most of the time you will find nothing in this section, but you should always check it out just to be sure. It takes a whopper of a disagreement for the company and auditors to get to the point of hanging out their dirty laundry in Item 9.

To summarize, Form 10-K is the most important SEC filing and your starting point for analyzing a company. The most important parts of Form 10-K are the description of business in Item 1, the MD&A in Item 7, and the financial statements in Item 8. The main drawback of Form 10-K is that it is made available only once a year. Our main interest in the other SEC filings in Figure 2.1 is to access more timely information.

The second filing listed in Figure 2.1 is the Form 10-Q filing. This is the quarterly version of Form 10-K; it must be filed within 45 days of the end of the quarter (reduced to 35 days by 2005), for each of the first three quarters of the fiscal year (the annual 10-K filing handles the fourth quarter). These filings are not as detailed as the 10-K, nor do they give you the general description of the business and much of the other information that comes with the 10-K. But, obviously, they are more current. They typically contain a summary version of the MD&A and abbreviated, unaudited financial statements. You should plan on reviewing all Form 10-Qs filed since the most recently available Form 10-K. You should also make sure you are familiar with the information in the 10-K before attempting to read a 10-Q, since the 10-K provides the necessary context to understand the information in the 10-Q.

The third filing listed in Figure 2.1 is the Form 8-K filing. This filing is used to report significant current events on a timely basis. Examples of events that warrant a Form 8-K include a change in control of a company, the acquisition or disposition of a significant portion of the company's business operations, bankruptcy, change in auditors, and the resignation of key directors or officers. The Form 8-K filing must generally be made within 15 days of the event being reported. (Note: At the time of this writing the SEC has proposed to add many new events to the list that require an 8-K filing and to reduce the number of days within which the report must be filed.)

There are lots of other forms that a firm must file with the SEC; the most common ones fill out the rest of Figure 2.1. Most of these other filings aren't as relevant for our purposes as the 10-K, 10-Q and 8-K, but here are a few of the more interesting ones. Whenever shareholders are required to vote on something, which is at least once a year at the annual meeting, the firm must file a proxy statement. This statement gives spicy details about management compensation. So if you think management is skimming too much off the top, this is the place to see just how much they are taking. There are a few different filings related to proxy statements, but the most common one is filed under the designation DEF 14A. Insider trades (i.e., trades by management in the company's stock) are reported on Forms 3, 4 and 5. Note that these forms are filed directly by the managers themselves, rather than under the name of the company. Finally, if a company issues new securities, it will typically file a Form S-2 or S-3 to register the securities and a Form 424B4 for the final prospectus.

All these filings can be accessed directly from the EDGAR database on the SEC's website. This site is not the world's best example of a user-friendly web interface. To assist you in tracking down SEC filings, eVal includes direct links to each company's Form 10-K and Form 10-Q filings, as well as the complete list of all SEC filings. To use this feature, click the Data Center button on the User's Guide sheet in eVal. This will take you to the Data Center sheet shown in Figure 2.3.

This sheet contains a listing of all companies with financial statement data available from Media General and covers over 8,000 U.S. companies. To find a specific company in the list, use the Search button at the top of the screen. The company, sector, and industry tickers on the left-hand side of the screen allow you to import financial statement data into eVal, and we discuss these data import functions later in the chapter. The company links on the right-hand side of the screen allow you to link directly to a variety of company-specific information sources on the web. You must be connected to the Internet to use these links. The first three links are the 10-K link, the 10-Q link, and the link to all SEC filings.

FIGURE 2.3   **eVal Data Center Worksheet**

	Company Name	Ticker	Industry	Sector	Links to SEC filings, Company Websites, News and An:				
	Data Center				Annual Financial Data is originally from April				
	Go To User's Guide		Go	Search	Click Here for an annual update				
	To import historical data double-click any cell or enter ticker above								
			Industry Code LookUp						
6	1-800 CONTACTS INC	CTAC	MG520	MG5	Form 10-Ks	Form 10-Qs	All Filings	Home Page	Investor Relatic
7	1-800-FLOWERS.COM CL A	FLWS	MG852	MG8	Form 10-Ks	Form 10-Qs	All Filings	Home Page	Investor Relatic
8	1ST CENTENNIAL BANCORP	FCEN	MG411	MG4	Form 10-Ks	Form 10-Qs	All Filings	NA	NA
9	1ST COLONIAL BANCORP	FCOB	MG411	MG4	Form 10-Ks	Form 10-Qs	All Filings	NA	NA
10	1ST NET TECHNOLOGIES INC	FNTT	MG826	MG8	Form 10-Ks	Form 10-Qs	All Filings	NA	NA
11	1ST SOURCE CORP	SRCE	MG414	MG4	Form 10-Ks	Form 10-Qs	All Filings	Home Page	Investor Relatic
12	1ST STATE BANCORP INC	FSBC	MG419	MG4	Form 10-Ks	Form 10-Qs	All Filings	NA	NA
13	21ST CENTURY HOLDING CO	TCHC	MG432	MG4	Form 10-Ks	Form 10-Qs	All Filings	Home Page	Investor Relatic
14	21ST CENTURY INSURANCE	TW	MG430	MG4	Form 10-Ks	Form 10-Qs	All Filings	Home Page	Investor Relatic
15	21ST CENTURY TECHNOLOGIE	TFCT	MG316	MG3	Form 10-Ks	Form 10-Qs	All Filings	NA	NA
16	24/7 REAL MEDIA INC	TFSM	MG852	MG8	Form 10-Ks	Form 10-Qs	All Filings	Home Page	Investor Relatic
17	24HOLDINGS INC	TFHD	MG826	MG8	Form 10-Ks	Form 10-Qs	All Filings	NA	NA
18	3CI COMPLETE COMPLIANCE	TCCC	MG637	MG6	Form 10-Ks	Form 10-Qs	All Filings	Home Page	Investor Relatic
19	3COM CORP	COMS	MG814	MG8	Form 10-Ks	Form 10-Qs	All Filings	Home Page	Investor Relatic
20	3D SYSTEMS CORP	TDSC	MG820	MG8	Form 10-Ks	Form 10-Qs	All Filings	Home Page	Investor Relatic
21	3DO COMPANY	THDO	MG820	MG8	Form 10-Ks	Form 10-Qs	All Filings	Home Page	Investor Relatic
22	3M COMPANY	MMM	MG210	MG2	Form 10-Ks	Form 10-Qs	All Filings	Home Page	Investor Relatic
23	3SI HOLDINGS	TSIH	MG850	MG8	Form 10-Ks	Form 10-Qs	All Filings	Home Page	Investor Relatic
24	3TEC ENERGY CORPORATION	TTEN	MG123	MG1	Form 10-Ks	Form 10-Qs	All Filings	NA	NA
25	4-D NEUROIMAGING	FDNX	MG521	MG5	Form 10-Ks	Form 10-Qs	All Filings	Home Page	Investor Relatic
26	4KIDS ENTERTAINMENT INC	KDE	MG763	MG7	Form 10-Ks	Form 10-Qs	All Filings	Home Page	Investor Relatic
27	4NET SOFTWARE INC	FNSI	MG210	MG2	Form 10-Ks	Form 10-Qs	All Filings	Home Page	Investor Relatic
28	5B TECHNOLOGIES CORP	FIVE	MG826	MG8	Form 10-Ks	Form 10-Qs	All Filings	NA	NA
29	7-ELEVEN INC	SE	MG734	MG7	Form 10-Ks	Form 10-Qs	All Filings	Home Page	Investor Relatic

User's Guide Data Center Financial Statements Ratio Analysis Cash Flow Analysis Forecasting Assumpt

Ready

Clicking on these links will take you directly to the corresponding company filings on the SEC's EDGAR database. Another useful website for accessing SEC filings is the PricewaterhouseCoopers EDGARSCAN website. This site provides a nicer user interface than EDGAR and also performs some useful processing and formatting of the data. Finally, MSN Money provides brief but standardized financial statement data that you can cut-and-paste into eVal.

Even after visiting the above sites, it can sometimes be a challenge to find the exact filing you are looking for. Companies frequently file one form and then later file an amendment to the form (appending a "/A" to the form name). They also incorporate information in a required filing by referencing another filing. But be persistent, especially when seeking the 10-K and 10-Q. They must be out there somewhere.

Company Website

You can learn much about a company's business by surfing its website. Most companies have a dedicated Investor Relations section of their website providing financial information about the company. In fact the development of the Internet along with the passage of Regulation FD (Fair Disclosure) by the SEC have proved to be a boon to small investors. Regulation FD was introduced by the SEC in October 2000 and basically prohibits companies from selectively disclosing non-public information to a few individuals, such as portfolio managers or Wall Street analysts. In order to comply, most companies put out any information that they have disclosed to other investors on their website. The Data Center sheet in eVal provides links to each company's main homepage and investors relations homepage.

One "must read" in the company website is the press release section. Company press releases often provide more timely information than SEC filings. However, you should also remember that the information in these press releases is not subject to the same standards as the company's SEC filings. Good examples are press releases related to quarterly earnings announcements. These press releases are made days or even weeks ahead of the corresponding Form 10-Q filing. However, companies often make up their own pro forma measures of earnings in their press releases and typically emphasize good information and downplay bad information. So always read these press releases with a grain of salt. Another document you will often find on the website is the annual report to shareholders. Be careful not to confuse the firm's annual report with its official Form 10-K filing. There are far fewer required disclosures in the annual report than in the 10-K and for many companies the annual report is little more than a marketing document. You will see lots of fancy graphs and photographs of happy employees and customers all designed to convince you that the company is financially healthy, very profitable, an exemplary global citizen, and especially kind to animals and small children.

If you check out the company's website shortly after an earnings announcement you will frequently find an audio file that replays the conference call that management had with analysts to discuss the quarter's results. These can be rich sources of information, but they have a short half-life; most companies remove them from the website after a week or two. After listening to a few of these you will notice that they are very short sighted and long winded. Most analysts are interested in forecasting only the next quarter's results, and most CEOs are counseled to refrain from expressing opinions about what the future may hold any further down the line.

News on the Wire

The company isn't the only one talking. A very active financial press scurries about trying to uncover interesting, and sometimes scandalous, facts about the company. The company will not rush to write a press release about their own questionable accounting practices, but the financial press will not hesitate to do so. And the company will not generally compare itself to other firms in the same industry, but a good news article frequently does this. The only word of warning we offer is that writers for the financial press are paid to write exciting stories that people will be drawn to read; being accurate is desirable but not paramount. Frequently the financial press is the first to call attention to a firm's questionable accounting practices but, in our experience, only about half the time does the accounting really turn out to be bad.

Most of the major financial portals on the web have links to recent news stories, along with the firm's press releases. The Data Center sheet in eVal provides you with a link to each company's news page on the Yahoo! Finance portal. This link follows immediately after the investor relations link. Other free sites that we recommend include Multex Investor and MSN Investor. If you want to join the professionals, then a real-time subscription to the Dow Jones Newswire Service will give you access to the most comprehensive newswire service.

Lots of regional newspapers also write about companies in their own backyard, and the major wire services may not pick up these stories. One way to be sure you haven't missed something big—and we hesitate to recommend this—is to check out the investment message boards for the company. Yahoo, AOL, MSN and several other sites sponsor boards where investors exchange views about particular stocks along with insults about one another's intelligence. The analysis offered by the average user of these boards is suspect, but you can benefit from the board's collective eyes and ears. If a great story about the company appeared in a local newspaper, or some other source you have overlooked, the odds are high that somebody on the message board has posted something about it. Look for message titles with headlines like "Did anyone else see the article on Hurricane Corporation in the *Miami Herald?*"

Analyst Research Reports

One final source for company-specific information is the research distributed by analysts working for the research departments of brokerage houses. Analysts working for brokerage houses are referred to as "sell-side" analysts to distinguish them from the "buy-side" analysts working for institutional investors. Buy-side research is used internally by the institutional investor and is not typically available to other investors. Sell-side research is primarily produced for brokerage clients, but a number of services now collect and redistribute these research reports. Two of the largest such services are Multex and Investext. Both are subscription-based services.

Sell-side research reports generally provide very precise and confident forecasts based on a rudimentary analysis of a company. Our experience suggests that students and other neophyte investors are often taken in by the apparent confidence with which these reports are written and their association with prestigious investment houses. Historically, however, the recommendations and price targets contained in these reports have been unreliable. Moreover, sell-side analysts rarely charge a direct fee for the research they issue to clients. Instead, they generate revenue from two indirect sources. First, they help their brokerage house to generate brokerage commissions by attracting clients and encouraging them to trade. Second, the analysts typically work for brokerage houses that are affiliated with investment banks. By issuing positive research on current and potential investment banking clients, sell-side analysts help to generate investment-banking business. As you can imagine, the fact that sell-side analysts generate revenue through these indirect sources poses a serious conflict of interest. One strategy we recommend is to zero in on the research report of the analyst issuing the least favorable recommendation on a stock. This way, you are more likely to find solid analysis rather than superficial hype.

Given the limitations of sell-side research discussed above, we encourage you to read this research with a healthy dose of skepticism. However, sell-side research does have its redeeming features. First, sell-side analysts tend to be industry specialists. A sell-side research report may give you some deep industry insights that you missed in your own industry analysis. Second, sell-side analysts are usually up to date on recent company news and guidance. They can be a good place to check that you have all the latest and greatest company-specific information. Third, sell-side research almost always contains earnings forecasts for the next year or so. One of the strongest catalysts for a stock price change is an earnings surprise, whereby a company announces earnings that differ from the consensus forecast of sell-side analysts. A number of services collect sell-side analysts forecasts and construct consensus earnings estimates from these forecasts. The leading services are First Call and Zacks. The Data Center sheet in eVal provides you with a link to each company's First Call consensus earnings estimates on the Yahoo! Finance portal. The MSN Investor portal provides the Zacks consensus, so it is worth checking both sites.

2.3   MACROECONOMIC AND INDUSTRY DATA

Careful analysis of company-level data is where you are most likely to generate the best insights. However, a good understanding of industry and economywide factors is crucial for the interpretation of past company data and forecasting of the future. We have had many experiences where students have become excited about stocks that look "cheap" relative to past fundamentals, only to learn that the student overlooked some key macroeconomic shifts. Examples include "cheap" oil services stocks in periods following dramatic declines in the price of crude oil and "cheap" banking and home construction stocks following dramatic rises in interest rates. You don't have to be an expert macroeconomist to do sound equity analysis and valuation. But you do need to have a good idea of the macroeconomic factors that impact the industry and company you are analyzing, and you need to know the consensus view of where these macroeconomic factors are heading. Macroeconomic and industry analysis is covered in Chapter 3. In this section, we provide you with a taxonomy for organizing your data collection and describe the key sources of data.

The Global and Domestic Economy

The generally accepted approach to conducting macroeconomic and industry analysis is provided in Figure 2.4. At the broadest level we have the global economy. As the economies of the many countries in the world become increasingly integrated, the health of domestic economies is increasingly linked to the health of the global economy. Global economic trends are measured by summing the trends in domestic economies. Countries with the largest domestic economies, such as the United States, Japan, and the U.K., tend to dominate global economic trends. However, economic crises in smaller countries, such as those in the Middle East and Latin America, can have a material impact on the global economy. There are a number of paid subscription services that track trends in the global economy. One example is Cornell's Global Economic Trends, which also offers a

FIGURE 2.4
Taxonomy for Conducting Macroeconomic and Industry Analysis

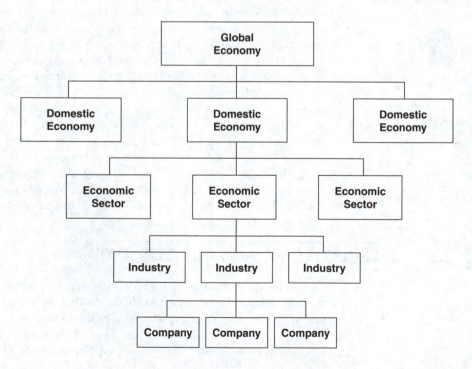

bit of free information. Absent a paid subscription service, it is up to you to track the health of the global economy by closely following the progress of the countries with the largest domestic economies (Canada, France, Germany, Italy, Japan, United Kingdom, United States) and keeping an eye out for major developments in the economies of the remaining countries. One good source of free data that provides economic profiles for most countries as well as international economic news and exchange rates is the Yahoo! International Finance Center.

Armed with data on the global economy, you should next collect data on the domestic economy. The operations of most businesses are concentrated in a particular country and the health of this country's domestic economy is a key driver of profitability. Our discussion focuses on the U.S. economy. There is a wealth of free data available on the domestic U.S. economy, most of it made available courtesy of the U.S. government. Four good portals are

- FreeLunch
- Economagic
- FedStats
- White House Economic Statistics Briefing Room

The underlying sources for most of this information are government bureaus, where you can find even more juicy details. The U.S. Census Bureau provides information on the population and how it is changing. It also conducts an economic census, which contains a wealth of data on consumer spending habits by industry, and collects "e-stats," which are e-commerce statistics such as web-generated sales by industry. The Bureau of Economic Analysis provides three main types of data. They report GDP data and its components, by industry and by state. They also report Input-Output statistics, which document the flow of goods between industries. Finally, their Fixed Asset Surveys report the new investment, net holdings, and average age of major classes of assets. For example, it gives the amount the electrical machinery industry spent on metalworking machinery (lots) versus farm tractors (very little). The Bureau of Labor Statistics reports many labor-related statistics, and also conducts an annual consumer expenditure survey. This is a great source of information about the buying habits of American consumers, including data on their expenditures, income, and consumer unit (families and single consumers) characteristics. The Federal Reserve is a good source of information for industrial capacity statistics and periodic releases on consumer, real estate, and business credit. If you take an evening and peruse these links you will no doubt be left with the following two thoughts: (1) there is an unbelievable amount of economic information available on the web and (2) our government spends way too much time collecting all of it.

As we discuss in the next chapter, the success of many companies is tied to the success of the U.S. economy. While the previous links describe the past very well, what you are really interested in is how the future economy will evolve. Two good sources for forecasts of future Gross Domestic Product in the United States are the Conference Board and the Congressional Budget Office.

Finally, you should keep track of major economic announcements by following an economic calendar of events. The Yahoo! Economic Calendar provides a good free economic calendar that includes detailed descriptions and additional links for many economic statistics. We'll give you a framework for interpreting all this domestic economic data in Chapter 3.

Sectors and Industries

Economic sectors and industries are the next two levels in our taxonomy. Before we can discuss sources of data for analysis at this level we need to define what we mean by "sector" and "industry." An economic sector consists of a group of industries that are similarly affected by key macroeconomic factors, such as the demand for energy, the need for health care, or sensitivity to consumer spending. For example, "consumer goods" defines an economic sector consisting of firms in industries that supply discretionary goods to consumers (as opposed to other businesses). Firms in this sector are particularly sensitive to macroeconomic factors that influence consumer spending, such as the GDP growth rate, consumer confidence, and interest rates. Examples of industries included in this sector are auto manufacturers and beverage manufacturers. The production technologies are very different across these two industries, but it is their common sensitivity to discretionary consumer spending that places them in the same economic sector. Macroeconomists frequently make "sector allocation" recommendations based on their forecasts of major macroeconomic trends.

Within each sector are many industries. Industries are defined by the nature of the good or service that is provided by the business. Firms in the same industry provide similar goods and services and will typically use similar inputs and production technologies. Because of these similarities, the techniques of analysis are very similar for firms in the same industry. Also, because firms in the same industry typically compete for market share, analysis of the competitive structure of input and output markets is usually conducted at the industry level. While the macroeconomic and sector level analysis provides necessary background, the industry level is where we really get to understand the operating characteristics and competitive environment facing a company.

There are several competing classification systems for allocating firms to sectors and industries. Two of the most frequently used are the Standard & Poor's GICS system and the Media General system. To make matters more confusing, the U.S. government has its own system, the North American Industrial Classification System (NAICS). Since the data in eVal is supplied by Media General, we use their classification system. While the similarities between these systems outnumber their differences, it is important to use a single classification system consistently, otherwise you can end up double counting some companies and missing others altogether. Figure 2.5 provides an overview of the Media General sector and industry classification system.

There are 9 sectors and over 200 industries in the Media General classification system. Media General has a numeric code for each sector and industry; some are shown in Figure 2.5 and a complete list is given in Appendix B. In addition, listed next to the name and ticker symbol for each company on the Data Center work-

FIGURE 2.5

The Media General Sector and Industry Classification Scheme The Sector Weights are Based on Market Capitalizations for the Firms in the S&P Supercomposite Index on April 4, 2002.

Sector (industry codes)	Sector Weight	Major Industries (industry codes)
Basic Materials (MG110-MG136)	10%	Chemicals (MG110-MG113) Energy (MG120-MG125) Metals & Mining (MG130-MG136)
Conglomerates (MG210)	5.4	Conglomerates (MG210)
Consumer Goods (MG310-MG351)	10	Consumer Durables (MG310-MG318) Consumer Non-Durables (MG320-MG327) Automotive (MG330-MG333) Food and Beverage (MG340-MG348) Tobacco (MG350-MG351)
Financial) (MG410-MG449	18.9	Banking (MG410-MG419) Financial Services (MG420-MG427) Insurance (MG430-MG434) Real Estate (MG440-MG449)
Healthcare (MG510-MG528)	13.0	Drugs (MG510-MG516) Health Services (MG520-MG528)
Industrial Goods (MG610-MG637)	2.5	Aerospace/Defense (MG610-MG611) Manufacturing (MG620-MG628) Materials and Construction (MG630-MG637)
Services (MG710-MG716)	18.4	Leisure (MG710-MG716) Media (MG720-MG729) Retail (MG730-MG739) Specialty Retail (MG740-MG745) Wholesale (MG750-MG759) Diversified Services (MG760-MG769) Transportation (MG770-MG776)
Technology (MG810-MG852)	18.3	Computer Hardware (MG810-MG815) Computer Software (MG820-MG827) Electronics (MG830-MG837) Telecommunications (MG840-MG846) Internet (MG850-MG852)
Utilities (MG910-MG914)	3.5	Utilities (MG910-MG914)

sheet in eVal is the numeric code for the company's sector and industry. Clicking the Industry button on this worksheet allows you to sort firms by industry in order to easily identify the individual firms in each industry. You can also import financial data into eVal that is averaged across all available firms in that sector or industry by double clicking on a sector or industry code. eVal averages all the company data in the industry or sector and then treats this average as if it was a single firm. This is a great way to assess what the typical firm in the industry or sector looks like—how big it is, how profitable it is, and how rapidly it is growing. We describe how you can use these sector and industry aggregates as part of your financial analysis in Chapter 5.

Beyond the Media General data, the very best starting point to begin analyzing a new industry is the pertinent *Standard & Poor's Industry Survey*. Unfortunately, these surveys are available only on a subscription basis. If you work for a large organization, however, you may find that you have them available to you on the Internet through a subscription to Standard and Poor's NetAdvantage service. There is also a wealth of industry-specific information available on the web. A good portal for accessing this information is Polson Enterprises Industry Portals.

In closing this section, we offer a final word of advice. The list of information given above may seem quite daunting. You may be asking, Do I really need to gather and read all of this every time I want to value a company? The answer is probably Yes if this is the first time you have ever studied the company and you know nothing about it, the economy, or the industry in which it resides. But a more typical situation is that you already have a good knowledge of general macroeconomic trends and may have good industry knowledge from following other companies operating in the same industry. Also, with experience you become much quicker at identifying what is relevant and what is irrelevant, and you can zoom right in on the important details that will yield you a better forecast.

2.4 INPUTTING HISTORICAL DATA INTO eVal

When you are ready to start building a valuation model, the first step is to obtain the company's historical financial statement data. This data will provide the foundation on which you will build your forecasts of the future financial statements. eVal provides a number of options that simplify the process of importing historical financial statement data into eVal's standardized spreadsheet format. The very first button in eVal's main User's Guide sheet is the Input Historical Data button. Clicking this button will provide you with three data input options, as shown in Figure 2.6. Most of the time, you will want to choose the first option, Import Media General Data, but there are times when you may want to use one of the other two choices, as we discuss below.

eVal uses up to five years' worth of historical data, but will operate effectively with as few as two years. The basic data input requirements for eVal are the historical income statement, the historical balance sheet, historical dividends, and the number of shares outstanding at the most recent fiscal year end. All these data items can be readily obtained from a company's annual financial statements. Unfortunately, companies do not create their financial reports using a standardized template; rather, each company chooses its own line items. This disparity in company financial reports has given rise to services such as Media General that

FIGURE 2.6
eVal Data Input
Options

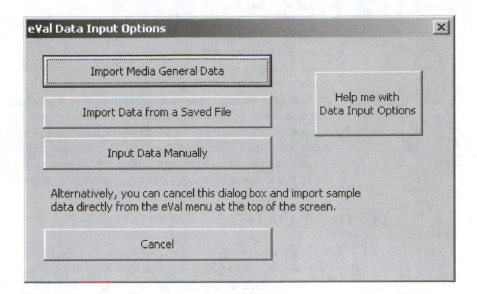

standardize the financial data, making it usable in computerized applications. The standardization process ensures that every line item appearing on a firm's income statement and balance sheet is included as part of a line item in eVal's standardized financial statements. The process by which all the various line items that can be reported in a firm's actual financial statements is mapped to a standardized line item in eVal is described in more detail in Appendix C.

This standardization process has important advantages and disadvantages. The most important advantage is that it provides a common and familiar framework for analyzing and valuing companies. The most important disadvantage is that some of the detailed information in individual line-item titles does not appear in eVal. For this reason, you *must* have a copy of the company's financial statements on hand so that you can figure out how the line items on those financial statements relate to the standardized financial statements in eVal (as noted above, links to the actual financial statements in the 10-K filings are available on the Data Center sheet).

2.5 IMPORTING MEDIA GENERAL DATA

Included with the eVal software is the standardized financial data from Media General for over 8,000 publicly traded U.S. companies. To import the data for a specific company into eVal hit the Import Media General Data button in the Input Options dialog box. This will take you to the Data Center sheet where you will find a list of all the available companies. If you know the ticker of the company whose data you are after, enter it in the input box at the top of the screen and click the adjacent Go button. The company's data will load into eVal, and you will be returned to the User's Guide worksheet.

If you do not know the company's ticker you can sort the list by company name, ticker, industry code, or sector code and then scroll through it to find the company you are looking for, or you can use the search function. To search the list click the Search button at the top of the screen, enter the company name (or some fragment thereof) in the input box of the resulting dialog box and click the Find Next button. To import the data, either double click on the company name or type the ticker into the input box at the top of the sheet and hit Go. The list also includes sector and industry financial statement averages, named using the industry and sector codes listed in Appendix B. These averages can be imported just like a regular company by either double clicking on them or typing in the code in the input box at the top of the page and clicking the Go button.

2.6 IMPORTING DATA FROM A SAVED FILE

In addition to providing immediate access to Media General data, eVal is able to use data from standardized financial statement templates created by other data providers, such as Thomson Research (formerly Global Access) and WRDS (Wharton Research and Data Services). We have also designed generic spreadsheet templates to allow for the importing of COMPUSTAT and Media General data that were saved from a source outside eVal. If you have access to any service that allows you to download COMPUSTAT or Media General data into a spreadsheet, then you can use our generic spreadsheet templates to import this data. Given that Media General data is supplied with eVal, you will need to use this option only in special circumstances. For example, an instructor might give you a historical data file for a case. Alternatively, new financial statement data may have been released since you purchased eVal and you want to import the updated data.

If you choose to use one of these other data import options, inputting the historical data is a two-step process. First you access the data from the third party source and save it in the particular format that we describe in Appendix D. This step does not involve eVal directly, although we provide you with some basic guidance in the appendix. Second, you import the data into eVal by clicking the Import Data From a Saved File button in the data input options dialog box and selecting the database option that matches your data source.

2.7 INPUTTING DATA MANUALLY

Manual input is somewhat tedious, but it is sometimes the only option. If you are studying a private company, or a division of a company, then you won't find standardized financial data. This option, however, does have two redeeming features. First, since it requires that you manually map data from the published financial statements to eVal's standardized format, you will develop a detailed knowledge of the underlying line items listed in the published statements. This will help you conduct a more informed analysis. Second, standardized financial data is gradually becoming available for free on the web, and it is usually the most current data available. It is already possible to simply cut and paste standardized data from the web into eVal using the manual input option. One free and respectable web-based source of historical financial statement data is MSN Money, which provides data sourced from Media General Financial Services.

Clicking the Input Data Manually option in eVal will take you to another dialog box that gives you two choices. The first option takes you to the Financial Statements worksheet with a completely empty set of financial statements. You can enter your company's historical financial information in the yellow cells. All other cells in the worksheet are write-protected to prevent you from accidentally changing them. You can enter a maximum of five years of income statement and balance sheet data, but you don't have to complete the whole spreadsheet to use eVal. The minimum amount of data that we recommend is the company name, the number of shares outstanding, the most recent fiscal year end, and the financial statement data for each of the two most recent fiscal years. The second option moves whatever data that is currently in the financial statements back one year and empties out the most recent year. This is a useful option if you need to update the Media General data.

You should enter all dollar and share amounts in thousands. You also need to make sure that you follow eVal's conventions for positive and negative numbers. All amounts that increase net income, assets, liabilities, or equities are entered as positive amounts, while all amounts that decrease net income, assets, liabilities, or equities are entered as negative amounts. For example, costs and expenses such as Cost of Goods Sold are entered as negative numbers, even though they are usually shown as positive numbers in firms' actual financial statements. You can check your signing decisions by making sure that the subtotals of various line items computed in eVal are the same as the corresponding subtotals in your firm's actual financial statements.

You will have to exercise some judgment in mapping line items from the as-reported financial statements to the standardized line items in eVal. Many line items will have different names from the names that we have used in eVal. For example, some firms refer to Cost of Goods Sold as Cost of Sales. Also, many companies report detailed line items that you will have to aggregate into a single line item in eVal. For example, some firms report marketing expenses and administrative expenses as separate line items, while eVal aggregates these expenses into the single line item SG&A Expenses. We provide detailed guidelines concerning the definitions for each of eVal's standardized line items in Appendix C. However, it is not critical that you follow these guidelines to the letter. The most important thing is that you find a home for every single line item appearing on the as-reported financial statements. As you are doing this, remember the nature of the as-reported line items underlying each eVal line item, so that you can interpret ratios computed using the line item and generate meaningful forecasts.

eVal has built-in alerts to warn you if your data input decisions seem unreasonable. For example, the message "Error! -Exp?" indicates that you have entered an expense as a positive number, when expenses should be entered as negative numbers. In some cases you may actually mean to do this; for instance, if interest revenue and interest expense are netted together and the revenue exceeds the expense, then the amount of net interest expense should be entered as a positive amount. But generally the expense lines will be negative. The message "Error! A=L+E?" means that your balance sheet does not balance. This error is less forgivable—the entire financial analysis in eVal is suspect if this error is present. In sum, eVal will pick up some, but not all, data input errors, so you should exercise care and make sure that all the financial statement totals in eVal are the same as the corresponding totals in the as-reported financial statements.

2.8 LINKS AND REFERENCES

Cases

The case "Will the Real GE Financial Statements Please Stand Up?" illustrates the many pitfalls that can arise in the seemingly obvious task of translating a set of as-reported financial statements into a standardized format. The case shows how three different services arrived at remarkably different answers. This case is available at the eVal website.

Links to Company-Specific Information

- SEC website—http://www.sec.gov

  The Security and Exchange Commission's official site.

- Description of SEC forms—http://www.sec.gov/info/edgar/forms.htm

  A company files many forms with the SEC. Here is the guide to help you find the interesting ones.

- EDGAR database—http://www.sec.gov/edgar/searchedgar/webusers.htm

  This is where the SEC keeps the official financial statement filings for all the companies that are registered in the United States. The statements are not formatted very nicely on this site but sometimes this is the only place you can find them.

- EDGARSCAN website—http://edgarscan.pwcglobal.com/

  A free service provided by PriceWaterhouseCoopers that gives the SEC filings in a much nicer format.

- MSN Money—http://moneycentral.msn.com/investor/invsub/results/statemnt.asp

  A link within the MSN Investor site, it provides brief but standardized financial statements.

- Yahoo! Finance—http://finance.yahoo.com

  Our favorite general-purpose financial portal. Also a good source for FirstCall analyst forecasts (but not the full reports). Hit the Research link.

- Multex Investor—http://www.multexinvestor.com/home.asp

  Another great financial portal. Requires registration for full access, but registration is free.

- MSN Investor—http://moneycentral.msn.com/investor/
  Yet another financial portal. A good source for Zacks analyst forecasts (but not the full report).
- Dow Jones Newswire Service—http://www.djnewswires.com/
  A subscription service for news used by the professionals.
- Investext—http://www.investext.com/
  A subscription service for analyst reports.
- Multex—http://www.multex.com
  Another subscription service for analyst reports.
- First Call—http://www.firstcall.com/
  A service that collects analyst forecasts. Get the consensus forecast for free from MSN Investor.
- Zacks—http://www.zacks.com/
  Another service that collects analyst forecasts. Get the consensus forecast for free from Yahoo!Finance.

Links to Global Macroeconomic Information

- Cornell's Global Economic Trends—http://www.getrends.com/
  Mostly a paid subscription service but offers a small amount of free information.
- Yahoo! International Finance Center—http://biz.yahoo.com/ifc/
  The best free source of international data. This site also gives great country profiles.

Links to U.S. Domestic Macroeconomic Information

- FreeLunch—http://www.economy.com/freelunch
  A great portal to many economic statistics. Requires registration but is free.
- Economagic—http://www.economagic.com/
  A clunkier portal of economic statistics, but a good backup to freelunch.
- FedStats—http://www.fedstats.gov/
  A comprehensive collection of government statistics, but not always described very well. You really need to use its search engine to find anything. But, if diligent, you can find the amount spent on fish consumption for each state in the United States in 1992. Cool?
- White House Econ/Stat Briefing Room—http://www.whitehouse.gov/fsbr/esbr.html
  Great graphs but not as comprehensive as the other portals.
- U.S. Census Bureau—http://www.census.gov
  Contains juicy details about the changing demographics of the U.S. population. Also has a consumer expenditure survey and e-stats documenting how e-commerce is evolving.

- Bureau of Economic Analysis—http://www.bea.gov

  Lots of statistics on the components of the gross domestic product, on transfers between industries, and on the stock of fixed assets in the United States.

- Bureau of Labor Statistics—http://www.bls.gov

  Good source for labor statistics (obviously) but also conducts a massive biennial Consumer Expenditure Survey that documents changing spending habits of the American household.

- Federal Reserve—http://www.federalreserve.gov

  Good source for industrial capacity statistics and releases on consumer, real estate, and business credit.

Links to Gross Domestic Product Estimates and Announcements

- Conference Board—http://www.conference-board.org/economics

  Offers free estimates of future gross domestic product. A subscription gets you many more juicy forecasts.

- Congressional Budget Office—http://www.cbo.gov/

  This is the government's official estimate of future gross domestic product. It also goes farther into the future than the conference board.

- Yahoo! Economic Calendar—http://biz.yahoo.com/calendar/

  A good list for what macroeconomic statistic will get announced when.

Links to Industry Information

- Standard & Poor's Industry Survey—http://www.standardandpoors.com/ProductsAndServices/InvestmentServices/IndustrySurveys/index.html

  A subscription service with great industry surveys.

- Standard and Poor's NetAdvantage—http://www.netadvantage.standardandpoors.com/

  A common package of services that contains the S&P industry surveys.

- Polson Enterprises Industry Portals—http://www.virtualpet.com/industry/mfg/mfg.htm

  A free portal organized by industry with links to many industry-specific data sources.

Other Links

- eVal website—http://www.mhhe.com/eval

CHAPTER THREE

Understanding the Business

3.1 INTRODUCTION

After collecting the wealth of data described in Chapter 2, your next task is to weave it together in a meaningful way. Your goal is to develop a thorough knowledge of the macroeconomic environment, the industry structure, and the operations and strategies of the particular business you are studying. We encourage you to adopt a "top down" approach. First, you should consider the general macroeconomic conditions. This will help you to understand how the current economic climate affects the performance of each of the industries that the business operates in. Next, you should consider each of the industries in which the business operates. Most professional analysts concentrate on just one or two industries, and they know these industries like the back of their hand. So if you are going to produce work of similar quality, you will also need to develop a thorough knowledge of the industry. The final stage is a detailed analysis of the operations and strategy of the business. What is the company's plan for success in each of the industries in which it operates, and what are the synergies between the different areas? We briefly review each of these steps below and refer you to the appropriate texts for a more detailed treatment.

Before you devote the next month to poring over macroeconomic data and reading strategy textbooks, we encourage you to use a healthy dose of economic intuition and common sense in your analysis. Macroeconomic and industry statistics are only useful if you can draw a link between them and the particular firm you are studying and you can generate good forecasts of where they are going in the future. The strategy literature has seen many fads over time—remember the "new economy"? Don't just join the herd and assume that any firm that pours resources into implementing the latest fad will have stellar growth and staggering profitability for the foreseeable future. Your goal at this stage is to develop a working understanding of the business you are studying and how it fits into the larger economy.

Rather than repeat all the links to data sources here, we simply remind you that Chapter 2 describes sources for all the macroeconomic, industry, and firm-specific factors we will discuss and gives the links at the end of the chapter.

3.2 MACROECONOMIC FACTORS

A top down approach to understanding a business must start with the global economy. Most domestic businesses have direct exposure to the global economy through their product markets, input markets, or foreign operations. Even businesses without direct exposure to global markets are sensitive to the global economy because the U.S. economy as a whole has becoming increasingly sensitive to global economic conditions. You need to understand the state of the global economy and the consensus opinion among experts about where it is headed. You should also be aware of the state of the individual domestic economies that your business is exposed to and their individual sensitivities to the global economy. In particular, you should be aware of the expected economic growth rates, political risks, and currency risks in each of the domestic economies that the firm operates in. These factors can vary widely across countries. For example, expected growth is relatively low in large, mature economies, such as the U.S. and European markets. Expected growth rates are much higher in emerging markets, such as Asia and South America, but these economies also tend to have the greatest political risks and currency risks.

Armed with a basic understanding of the global economy and your firm's exposure to particular countries, you should next focus on the current state and future prospects for the U.S. economy. For most U.S. firms, operations and customers are concentrated in the United States and, consequently, the U.S. economy is a key driver of the firm's profitability. The state of the domestic economy and its future prospects can be summarized by a few key economic statistics. We review these below.

Gross Domestic Product

Gross domestic product (GDP) is the most widely used measure of macroeconomic performance. It measures the market value of final goods and services produced domestically. Figures for GDP are released quarterly by the Commerce Department. These figures are typically expressed in real (inflation-adjusted) terms as an annualized quarter-to-quarter percentage change, which is referred to as the real GDP growth rate. The overall rate at which the economy is growing is an important determinant of the rate at which many businesses can grow, which explains why the GDP growth rate is such a closely watched statistic. Over the last 40 years, the real GDP growth rate has averaged about 3–4 percent, reaching highs of over 10 percent and lows of less than −5 percent. The most commonly used definition of an economic recession is two consecutive quarters of negative real GDP growth. Economists carefully monitor many leading indicators of GDP growth in an attempt to predict its future movements. Common leading indicators include unemployment insurance claims, consumer spending, consumer confidence, business orders, business productivity, and housing and construction activity.

Interest Rates

Interest rates reflect the cost of borrowing money and affect business performance in two important ways. First, interest rates determine the price that a firm must pay on its own borrowings. Other things equal, lower interest rates mean less interest expense and higher profits. Low interest rates also reduce the cost of current consumption relative to future consumption for customers. For example, you have a greater incentive to buy a new car today if the amount of interest you will earn by saving your money declines. A decline in interest rates tends to spur consumer spending, thereby increasing sales growth for many businesses. It is important to note that it is *changes* in interest rates that cause changes in consumer spending. If interest rates are low today, but have been low for many years, then consumers are not going to suddenly rush out today to increase their current consumption. If interest rates have been running at high levels in recent years, however, and suddenly drop to more moderate levels, we will see an increase in consumption as the relative cost of current versus future consumption falls. Interest rates reflect not only the cost of current versus future consumption, but also expected inflation and credit risk. We can abstract from the credit risk portion of interest by examining the interest rate on low credit risk borrowings, such as the federal funds rate or the yields on the bills, notes, and bonds issued by the U.S. Treasury. Over the past 40 years, nominal (that is, not inflation-adjusted) interest rates on low risk borrowings have ranged from less than 2 percent to over 15 percent, with an average of about 7 percent.

Inflation

Inflation is defined as a general rise in price levels. Inflation creates the gap between real and nominal economic effects. In times of high inflation, businesses will generally find that they are better off in nominal terms because they are selling their goods for higher prices. But if those incoming dollars buy fewer goods and services, the businesses may actually be worse off in real terms. Armed with the inflation rate, it is possible to adjust nominal dollars into real dollars and get a clearer picture of economic performance. Inflation has other more pernicious effects. In times of high and uncertain inflation, the risk from investing in financial assets increases and the credibility of the domestic currency is undermined in the global currency market. Faced with such risk, investors will take their capital to countries without such uncertainty or invest directly in commodities such as gold that provide a hedge against inflation. The inflation rate is most commonly measured using the rate of change in the Consumer Price Index (CPI), published monthly by the Bureau of Labor Statistics. The CPI measures the price of a fixed basket of goods bought by a typical consumer. Over the past 40 years, the annual rate of inflation, as measured by the CPI, has ranged from less than 0 percent to over 12 percent, and has averaged around 4 percent.

Foreign Exchange Rates

Foreign exchange rates describe how many units of one currency can be bought with a unit of another currency. Many of the inputs bought and outputs sold by domestic businesses are in transactions with foreign entities. As the relative value of the $US rises, the cost of foreign inputs decreases and the revenue from foreign sales also decreases. Thus, the impact of foreign exchange rate fluctuations on a business depends not only on whether the rates go up or down, but also on whether the firm is a net importer or exporter in a particular currency. Foreign exchange rates are driven by a complex variety of factors, including the relative productivity of capital and labor, relative inflation rates, and relative real interest rates.

Oil Prices and Other Key Commodity Prices

Commodity prices affect the costs of all businesses. The most important commodity price at the macro level is the price of oil. Oil is key to the successful functioning of an industrialized economy. Oil prices tend to be volatile because of the concentration of a large proportion of the world's oil reserves in a small number of countries. Increases in oil prices lead to increases in transportation and energy costs that affect nearly all businesses. Increases in oil prices also reduce the amount of income that consumers have to spend on other products. Other important commodity prices include natural gas and various metals. Obviously, different industries have different key commodity inputs—the price of leather is important for the shoe industry and the price of palladium is important for the semiconductor industry. Make sure you identify the commodities that are key to the industry you are studying

Aside from the economic indicators above, other important factors to consider in your macroeconomic analysis are corporate hedging activities and the business cycle.

Hedging

A firm can effectively hedge its exposure to interest rates, foreign exchange rates, and most commodity prices. Consequently, two firms in exactly the same business may have completely different exposures to these factors. For instance, one gold-mining firm may sell its entire production forward, so that its profits are unaffected by changes in gold prices, while another firm may retain the right to all the gold it produces, in which case the value of its production varies directly with the price of gold. Similarly, financial institutions can change their exposure to changes in interest rates by entering into various interest rate derivative contracts. Firms can also form natural hedges by the way they structure their business. For instance, a firm that expects a large increase in receivables denominated in a foreign currency can arrange its operations in such a way that it also has a large increase in payables denominated in the same currency. The currency gains or losses on receivables will be exactly offset by the gains or losses on the payables. The point is that, even if a firm's underlying business is exposed to changes in interest rates, foreign exchange rates, or commodity prices, you won't know for sure what the true exposure is until you understand how they structure their business. You should read the firm's SEC filings to discover the extent of their hedging activity. Recall from Chapter 2 that Item 7A of Form 10-K requires disclosure of exposures to macroeconomic risks.

The Business Cycle

The "business cycle" is an important concept for understanding the current state and future prospects of the domestic economy. Historically, domestic economies have exhibited systematic periods of expansion (characterized by high GDP growth, low unemployment, and high consumer confidence) and contraction (characterized by low GDP growth, high unemployment, and low consumer confidence). While there is no guarantee that these cycles will continue, many macroeconomists believe that they are a permanent feature of the economy. Hence, you should have a good sense of the current state of the business cycle and when and how it is most likely to change. The profitability of some sectors is much more sensitive to movements in the business cycle than others, as we will discuss below.

A Realistic Goal for Macroeconomic Analysis

If you set out to become an expert in all the factors that influence the global and domestic economies, you may never get to the point of analyzing your particular firm. You goal should be to understand what the general consensus is about these major factors. You don't need to develop your own independent forecasts of future GDP or interest rate movements, but you should understand what the experts are saying about these factors and how that might influence your firm's performance in the future.

3.3 INDUSTRY FACTORS

Before considering the details of a particular firm, it is important to think about the industry the firm is in. Professional analysts tend to specialize in particular economic sectors and industries to achieve efficiencies in business analysis. There are three main objectives when studying an industry:

- To understand the sensitivity of the industry to key macroeconomic factors.
- To understand how the industry operates and the key performance metrics for businesses operating in the industry.
- To understand the competitive structure of the industry.

We discuss each of these objectives in more detail below.

Sector Sensitivities to Macroeconomic Factors

Recall from Chapter 2 that economic sectors represent groups of industries that have similar exposures to key macroeconomic factors. Figure 3.1 provides an overview of the sensitivities of each economic sector to three key macroeconomic factors—the GDP growth rate, interest rates, and oil prices.

FIGURE 3.1
Sensitivity of Sector Profitability to Key Macroeconomic Factors.

Sector	Macroeconomic Factor		
	GDP	Interest	Oil Price
Basic Materials	+ +	−	−
Capital Goods	+ +	− −	−
Conglomerates	+	−	−
Consumer Goods	+ +	− −	−
Energy	+ +	−	+ +
Financial	+	− −	−
Healthcare	+	−	−
Services	+	−	−
Technology	+ +	− −	−
Utilities	+	−	− −

Key: + + = strong positive relation; + = positive relation; − = negative relation;
− − = strong negative relation.

The GDP growth rate is a key driver of profitability for all sectors of the economy. Some sectors are much more sensitive to this driver than others, however. For example, the basic materials, capital goods, energy, and technology sectors all provide the raw inputs required to fuel GDP growth, and these sectors are also characterized by high operating leverage (that is, they have high fixed costs and low variable costs). It takes a relatively high level of activity to cover the fixed costs in these sectors, but once the activity level exceeds some threshold they make healthy profits. When GDP growth is high there is sufficient activity to drive these sectors into the high profit region, but when GDP growth is low they can't cover their fixed costs and they lose money. The consumer goods sector is also very sensitive to GDP growth because this sector produces goods that are highly sensitive to consumer spending, which is itself closely tied to the GDP growth rate.

Increases in interest rates tend to have a negative effect on the profitability of all sectors, but some sectors are affected more than others. The capital goods, consumer goods, and technology sectors are particularly sensitive to the reductions in corporate capital expenditures and consumer spending that accompany increases in interest rates. The financial sector also suffers directly from the reduced borrowing activity associated with higher interest rates.

Increases in oil prices also tend to have a negative effect on the profitability of all sectors. The one obvious exception is the energy sector, which consists largely of companies involved in the exploration, production, transportation, refining, and marketing of oil. A sector that is particularly hard hit by oil price increases is utilities, where oil and related energy products are the major raw materials.

Industry Operation and Key Industry Ratios and Statistics

Firms in the same industry generally produce similar goods and services using similar production technologies. You should begin your industry analysis by figuring out how the industry operates. This involves finding the answers to questions such as, What is the nature of the production process that takes place in the industry? What are the key inputs in the production process? What is the nature of the marketing and distribution process? Is service after the sale a significant factor?

Once you understand how the industry operates, you should identify the key ratios and statistics that capture the financial health of the industry and firms within the industry. The particular metrics vary widely based on the nature of the industry's operations. In the oil and gas production and marketing industry, for example, key statistics include the prices of oil, gas, and refined products, the current demand for oil and gas, crude oil, and natural gas storage figures, oil refinery capacity utilization rates and oil services equipment utilization rates. In contrast, in the semiconductor industry, key ratios and statistics include the semiconductor industry monthly global sales report, the semiconductor equipment book-to-bill ratio, wafer fabrication plant utilization rates, the purchasing managers index, and business capital spending.

Industry Competition

Your study of the industry should include an assessment of how intensely firms compete with one another. As a benchmark, recall the old microeconomic concept of perfect competition. In a perfectly competitive market, there are many firms using the same production technology and facing the same input and output prices. In equilibrium, just enough firms enter the market to ensure that the equilibrium price provides a "normal" return on the invested capital to all firms in the market. In such a market, valuation is easy. In expectation, each firm simply generates a normal return on its invested capital. Thus, if we know the magnitude of the invested capital and the normal rate of return, we simply multiply the two together to forecast the expected profit. Indeed, this is exactly the logic that is applied to securities markets by efficient market theorists—in an efficient market, all investors are simply expected to earn a normal return on their investments. It is generally accepted, however, that there are inefficiencies in the market for real assets. Firms in certain industries have been known to generate abnormally high returns for extended periods of time. Coke and Pepsi have both sustained high profitability over prolonged periods, and they do so selling sugared water (with a touch of addictive caffeine)! When studying the industry you should look for characteristics that might allow firms to generate abnormal profits over a prolonged period of time.

Famed strategist Michael Porter highlights five forces that determine the degree of competition in an industry. The first three forces relate to sources of direct competition. They are the rivalry among existing firms, the threat of new entrants, and the availability of substitute products. Let's apply these three forces to the restaurant industry, focusing particularly on chains of fast-food restaurants. Clearly there is intense rivalry among existing firms—next to every McDonald's is a Burger King, with Wendy's, Taco Bell, and Subway just around the corner. Similarly, new entrants face relatively low barriers to entry—patents are not available for food items, capital expenditures are relatively minor, and franchising can help fund investments. The competitive pressure from substitute products depends entirely on how narrowly you define the industry. Customers of fast-food restaurants could switch to full-service restaurants at low cost. However, if the industry is defined as simply "restaurants," then the substitute product is cooking food in the home. The switching costs here are probably higher, insofar as this requires a significant life-style change on the part of customers. Putting the three forces together, one would have to conclude that the fast-food restaurant industry is highly competitive, possibly even approaching the textbook definition of perfect competition.

The final two forces in Porter's framework relate to a company's relative bargaining position with its suppliers and customers. In particular, both suppliers and customers can alter input and output prices in order to extract a firm's profits if they have a bargaining advantage. Consider the desperate situation of a small firm in the automotive parts industry, one which manufactures plastic parts. A few large corporations control the market for the raw plastic pellets that are used as inputs, leaving little room to negotiate a better price on the input side. And on the output side the situation is even worse. The automotive firms have many alternative sources for plastic parts. They enjoy so much power over their suppliers that they occasionally give themselves price concessions on existing contracts. Without even consulting the supplier, they simply pay less than the full amount on their accounts payable, expecting that the supplier will either acquiesce or lose all business in the future.

As you analyze the industry, remember that less competition means that abnormal levels of industry profitability are easier to sustain. Of course, we should also remember that various regulatory bodies are charged with preventing business practices that restrain competition. In the United States, the Federal Trade Commission's Bureau of Competition and the U.S. Department of Justice's Antitrust Division are the pertinent regulatory bodies.

3.4 THE FIRM'S STRATEGY

Firm profitability is not solely a function of industry profitability. For example, McDonald's was able to generate consistently high profits while operating in the highly competitive restaurant industry for many years. What explains this anomaly? Strategists would say that McDonald's developed a strategy for creating and sustaining a competitive advantage. Strategy textbooks attempt to identify and categorize such winning strategies. Three common categories are "cost leadership," "product differentiation," and "focus." A cost leadership strategy aims for low production costs and thin margins, with profits coming from a high volume as customers are attracted by the low price. Product differentiation is achieved by producing a product with unique attributes that are valued by buyers who will pay a premium price, resulting in higher profits. Finally, the idea behind focus is to develop a niche strategy that supplies one segment of the market with exactly what they want, be it low cost or a differentiated product.

The most important point to keep in mind is that it is extremely difficult to sustain a competitive advantage. Each of the generic strategies above will be difficult to sustain in the long run. A cost leadership strategy is vulnerable to imitation and to shifts in technology that lead to new, lower cost production methods. A differentiation strategy is also subject to imitation. Moreover, differentiation strategies are often short-lived fads. For example, the specialty retail and apparel industries are characterized by many differentiated brands that go in and out of style over time—Levi's are out and Silver's are in, at least as of this writing. Finally, a focus strategy is also subject to imitation and the risk that changes in market conditions make the targeted segment non-viable.

The best source for information concerning a firm's strategy for achieving competitive advantage is the first section of a firm's Form 10-K filing with the Securities and Exchange Commission. This section must provide a description of the registrant's business. The applicable securities laws require the description of business to include:

> Competitive conditions in the business involved including, where material, the identity of the particular markets in which the registrant competes, an estimate of the number of competitors and the registrant's competitive position, if known or reasonably available to the registrant. Separate consideration shall be given to the principal products or services or classes of products or services of the segment, if any. Generally, the names of competitors need not be disclosed. The registrant may include such names, unless in the particular case the effect of including the names would be misleading. Where, however, the registrant knows or has reason to know that one or a small number of competitors is dominant in the industry it shall be identified. The principal methods of competition (e.g., price, service, warranty or product performance) shall be identified, and positive and negative factors pertaining to the competitive position of the registrant, to the extent that they exist, shall be explained if known or reasonably available to the registrant. [extracted from SEC Regulation S-K]

Thus, management is required to give its best shot at describing both the degree of industry competition and the firm's own perceived source of competitive advantage. However, you should always take management's ravings about their own wonderful sources of competitive advantage with a grain of salt. Simply admitting that the firm doesn't really have any competitive advantage would probably not sit well with investors, so management will typically spin some sort of yarn. Your job is to check that the alleged source of competitive advantage is real and delivers superior financial performance.

Synergy Analysis

Not all firms operate a single business in a single industry. Corporate synergy analysis focuses on how firms can generate abnormal profits by bringing two or more businesses under the same corporate umbrella. Theories abound in this area. Synergies are created by leveraging proprietary assets, eliminating transaction costs, eliminating redundant overhead, increasing market power, or any number of other activities. The important point to remember here is that the free market is a very good disciplining mechanism that is eliminated when too many activities are brought inside a single firm. For instance, it could be that synergy is created when a sawmill company acquires a timber company, or it could be that the timber segment no longer harvests trees efficiently because it no longer has to sell logs on the open market—the sawmill segment simply takes their timber as an input. Without the discipline of competing in an open market, the timber segment gets lazy. Empire-building managers are often quick to identify the benefits of mergers, but fail to appreciate the costs that can result from coordination and control issues that surface once market discipline is removed.

3.5 CONCLUSION

When you purchased eVal, you were probably hoping that it would take all the hard work out of equity analysis and valuation. If so, then you should now realize that you were sorely wrong. There is no substitute for a thorough understanding of the business underlying the equity security. Anyone who tries to convince you that you can accurately value a business by extrapolating past trends or applying fixed multiples to key historical financial statement variables is wrong. But the good news is that there are many investors out there who use such simple rules to value equity securities. If enough of these investors trade using these simple rules, then they will have an impact on the price. Armed with a thorough understanding of the underlying business, you will be in a position to determine when such simple rules are causing a security to be mispriced.

There is still more work to do before you are ready to value a firm's equity. We still need to talk about how to quantify your knowledge of the underlying business and how to develop good projections of the future financial statements based on this knowledge. These projections are the ultimate drivers of your value estimate. We turn to these tasks in the following chapters.

3.6 REFERENCES

Understanding Boston Chicken's Business Model

This is the first of a three-part case on Boston Chicken. This part analyzes Boston Chicken's business strategy in the competitive fast food segment of the restaurant industry. We find that Boston Chicken not only operates fast food restaurants, but also franchises restaurants and operates a lending operation to finance its franchisees. A complete analysis of Boston Chicken's corporate strategy across these three interdependent lines of business provides key insights into its business model. This case is available on the eVal website.

Further Readings on Macroeconomics

Macroeconomics by Andrew Abel and Ben Bernanke (1998) is a good standard text on macroeconomics. The main focus is the domestic macroeconomy, but the latest edition provides new coverage of the global macroeconomy.

Further Readings on Strategy

Economics of Strategy by David Besanko, David Shanhove, and Mark Shanley (1999) brings a structured microeconomics-based approach to the analysis of corporate strategy.

Competitive Strategy by Michael Porter (1998), a landmark book in the strategy literature, lays out Porter's five forces for industry analysis and his three generic strategies for achieving competitive advantage.

Stategic Management by Garth Saloner, Andrea Shepard, and Joel Podolny (2001) weaves economics and organizational theory together in the search for a sustainable competitive advantage.

Harvard Business Review on Corporate Strategy (1999) provides a summary of current thinking in this fast-developing field.

CHAPTER FOUR

Accounting Analysis

4.1 INTRODUCTION

Traditional valuation texts are usually very good at telling you how to value an equity security assuming that you already know the security's future cash distributions. But in practice, forecasting these cash distributions is the most important and difficult task in valuation. Moreover, past cash flows are rarely a good indicator of either past performance or future cash flows. For example, successful growth firms often generate negative cash flows as they invest to expand their future operating activities. The problem with cash flows is that they measure the distribution of value rather than the creation of value. For this reason financial statements, prepared in accordance with generally accepted accounting principles (GAAP), have evolved to provide more useful information about value creation in a company. These statements provide a "language" for evaluating a firm's past performance and forecasting its future performance. It is the language that is spoken by the financial community, and it is the language that we will use throughout the valuation exercise.

At this point, you may ask yourself, If accountants already measure value creation, what is left for the rest of us to do? It turns out that financial statements are not designed to value a company. Instead, the financial statements are intended to provide information that is useful in helping others conduct a valuation. Since we are the "others" who actually get to do the valuation, there are three key questions we need to answer about accounting information:

1. What information do financial statements provide?
2. How does this information help in valuation?
3. What are the key limitations of this information?

The purpose of this chapter is to address these questions.

We begin by reviewing the conceptual underpinnings of accounting. Our objective is not to teach you basic accounting. We assume that you already have a working knowledge of basic accounting principles. Instead, our objective is to discuss the nature of the information provided in the financial statements and how this information relates to firm value. We also discuss the limitations of financial statement information, including how management can manipulate reported earnings.

4.2 THE UNDERPINNINGS OF ACCOUNTING

Although we assume you already know basic accounting principles, we fear that you may have lost the forest among the trees. So let's review the basics. The building blocks of accounting are assets and liabilities. Assets represent future benefits and liabilities represent future obligations. Accountants periodically identify and assign dollar values to a firm's assets and liabilities. The difference between the value of the assets and the value of the liabilities represents the equity in the firm that belongs to the owners. The owners' equity is also referred to as the "net assets" or "book value" of the firm. This relation, rearranged and given as an equation, is:

$$\text{Assets} = \text{Liabilities} + \text{Equity}$$

Because this accounting equation must always hold, the balance sheet must always balance (hence its clever name!). At the end of each accounting period, accountants prepare a *Balance Sheet* or *Statement of Financial Position* listing and valuing the firm's assets and liabilities. The balance sheet and its relation to the other financial statements are illustrated in Figure 4.1.

If accountants recorded each item on the balance sheet at its fair market value, taking into account all the interactions between assets and properly measuring all

FIGURE 4.1
Overview of Basic Building Blocks of Accounting

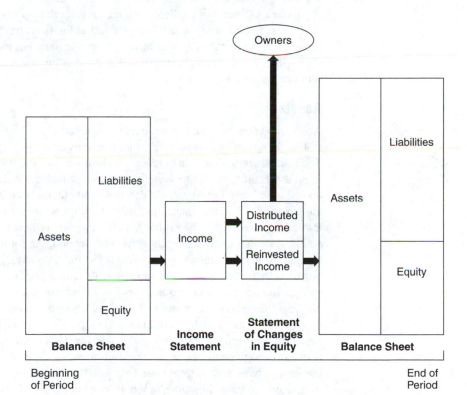

Beginning of Period — End of Period

The equity

the associated future benefits and obligations, then the equity on the balance sheet would also be market value of the firm. But accountants are adamant about the fact that they are not measuring the fair market value of every asset and liability and that the resulting equity is not a measure of the equity's market value. Accountants ignore many future benefits and obligations altogether and value others at amounts having little connection with their fair market value. Why do accountants employ rules that result in incorrect valuations? It turns out that once we move away from simple examples like bank accounts or lemonade stands, it would be impossible to measure the fair market value of many assets and liabilities. The accountant may know the value of some equipment immediately after the company purchases it, but what about halfway through its useful life? And how should our poor accountant deal with the fact that the equipment will produce goods whose value is partially determined by the success of the company's advertising campaign? In deciding what information to provide, accountants trade off relevance with reliability. We may all want to know the present value of the cash flows associated with a firm's operating activities, because it would be very relevant information, but any attempt to measure this would be highly subjective, and therefore quite unreliable. The historical costs of operating assets, on the other hand, can be measured reliably. Accountants view their role as providing the capital markets with reliable information, while leaving the more subjective forecasting of the unreliable but highly relevant stuff to us.

Given the limitations inherent in accounting, the primary role of accounting analysis is to determine which benefits and obligations have been ignored in the financial statements and which have been recognized but incorrectly valued. We start with the accounting rules governing the recognition and measurement of assets and liabilities.

Assets

probable & transaction/event

Accountants define assets as probable future economic benefits obtained or controlled by a firm as a result of past transactions or events. This rather dry definition imposes two important hurdles for a future economic benefit to be recognized as an asset. First, the future benefit must be "probable." Accountants have developed a long list in GAAP to help determine whether a benefit is sufficiently probable to make it into the financial statements. Important examples of future benefits that are *not* deemed to be probable include those associated with most research and development and marketing activities. Second, the future benefits must have resulted from past transactions or events. The most important manifestation of this hurdle is that future benefits associated with selling goods and services cannot be recognized until the sale has actually been consummated (the realization principle). So future benefits associated with anticipated future sales revenues are not recognized. It is virtually certain that General Electric will generate more than zero dollars' worth of sales during the next few years, but that accounting system does not recognize the value of these future transactions. And many start-up drug companies have zero current sales (because they have not yet marketed their first drug), but are valued by the stock market as being worth millions of dollars. All because of anticipated future sales. Accountants ignore all these future benefits.

So what future benefits are the accountants willing to recognize? There are three broad types of assets. First, there are cash and cash equivalents, which are valued quite simply at their face value. Second, there are amounts of cash owed to the firm as a result of past transactions or events (for instance, trade receivables and loans). These monetary receivables are generally valued using the net present value of the expected future payments. Third, there are future benefits acquired by the firm as part of a past transaction or event (marketable securities, inventory, property, acquired intangibles). If the acquired future benefits are financial assets, such as marketable securities, they are generally valued using the observed market value. If the acquired future benefits are non-financial assets, such as a truck or a building, they are generally valued at historical cost, adjusted downward to the extent that the anticipated future benefits have either been used up or impaired.

Overall, accountants do a good job at recognizing and valuing future benefits associated with financial resources, but do a poor job at recognizing and valuing future benefits associated with operating resources. Accountants recognize only a subset of the future benefits associated with operating resources and they usually value these benefits based on what they cost rather than on the value of the cash flow streams they are expected to generate.

Liabilities

Accountants define liabilities as the opposite of assets; liabilities are probable future sacrifices of economic benefits arising from present obligations as a result of past transactions or events. The recognition hurdles imposed on liabilities correspond to those imposed on assets. The future sacrifices must be "probable." Important examples of future sacrifices that are *not* deemed probable include the expected costs associated with unsettled litigation and third party loan guarantees. The future sacrifices must also arise from present obligations as a result of past transactions or events. For example, we may have contracted with employees to purchase their services in the future. But we are not obliged to recognize a liability for the promised future payments until such time as we receive the promised services. Most liabilities are monetary in nature and are valued based on the present value of the promised payments.

Changes in Equity

There are two broad reasons why a firm's equity changes over time. The first is obvious—the firm engages in transactions with its equity holders, either paying distributions to them or receiving additional amounts from them. These transactions are recorded in the *Statement of Changes in Equity*. But the main reason equity changes is that the firm, typically through its operations, manages to collect more net assets than it consumes over the period. This is the miracle of value creation (although if it is negative then it represents the disappointment of value destruction). Therefore, assets and liabilities not only provide the building blocks for the balance sheet, but also for the *Income Statement*. While the balance sheet lists the resources and obligations of a firm at a point in time, the income statement measures the performance of a firm over a period of time. Recalling that equity equals assets less liabilities, periodic income is the "plug" in the following equation:

$$\text{Ending Equity} = \text{Beginning Equity} + \text{Income} -$$
$$\text{Net Distributions to Equity Holders}$$

and rearranging gives

$$\text{Income} = \text{Change in Equity} + \text{Net Distributions to Equity}$$

This is known as the *clean surplus relation*—all changes in equity that are not a consequence of transactions with the owners must be income. Intuitively, the income statement measures the net economic benefits generated by a firm for its owners over a period of time. And it does this using the same restrictive definitions of future benefits (that is, assets) and future obligations (liabilities) as the balance sheet. Figure 4.1 illustrates the relation between the balance sheet, the income statement, and the statement of changes in equity.

Armed with a balance sheet from the beginning of the period and another from the end of the period and the amount of distributions that were made to or received from owners during the period, it is a simple matter to compute income. So what is the incremental role of the income statement? The real information in the income statement isn't the bottom line; rather, it is in the classification of the various changes in assets and liabilities into different components of income. The income statement explains why the assets and liabilities changed over the course of the period. The key components of the income statement are illustrated in Figure 4.2. Each of these components has a different meaning when trying to understand past performance and forecast future performance. Each component is described below.

Revenues

Revenues are defined as increases in assets or reductions in liabilities that arise from the provision of the goods and services through the firm's operating activities. For the most part, revenues are simply the proceeds received for providing goods and services. Note that the goods and services sold must be part of the firm's intended operating activities. If a firm in the restaurant industry sells some cooking equipment, the proceeds of the sale will not be recorded as part of revenue, because the firm's intended operating activity is not the selling of cooking equipment.

A central question in accounting for revenue is deciding when it has occurred. In what period did the assets increase in value? The general revenue recognition rule in accounting is that revenue is recognized when the earnings process is substantially complete and collection is reasonably assured. While this sounds very reasonable, it clearly leaves room for interpretation. Consider a company that purchases land, does some minor improvements, subdivides it, and then sells plots to customers who sign a 10-year mortgage. Is wealth created when the firm purchases the land, when it finishes its minor improvements, when a customer signs the mortgage, or only as the customer makes the payments over the next 10 years? For most manufacturing firms the accounting rule is easy; revenue is recognized when the goods are shipped. But even this seemingly simple rule has received its share of abuse, as we discuss later.

FIGURE 4.2
Classification of Components of Income

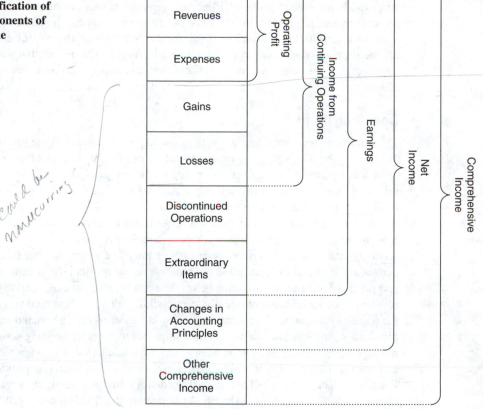

(handwritten note: "could be nonrecurring")

Revenues are the key driver of most other activities in the firm. Once revenue is recognized, the accounting rules attempt to measure the associated consumption of assets that was necessary to produce the revenue. Revenue recognition is the kick-off event for the measurement of income and, because of this, plays a central role in our analysis and forecasting.

Expenses

Expenses are defined as the opposite of revenues; they are decreases in assets or increases in liabilities that arise from the provision of the goods and services as part of a firm's operating activities. As with revenues, the costs must be associated with the firm's intended operating activities. For example, the cost of the cooking equipment sold in the restaurant example above would not be an expense.

Expense recognition rules attempt to match the consumption of specific assets to the production of specific revenues whenever possible, but they frequently have to resort to an arbitrary allocation of costs over the useful life of the asset. For example, we might all agree that the cost of the raw materials used to produce the finished goods should be matched against the revenue from the sale of the goods. But exactly how much property, plant, and equipment was consumed to convert the raw materials into the finished goods? How much of the corporate Learjet was consumed in the production of the goods? What about the cost of deferred compensation to the sales force? What about interest on the money that was borrowed to purchase the equipment that was used to convert the raw materials into finished goods?

Operating Profit

The difference between a firm's revenues and expenses represents the profit associated with the firm's ongoing operating activities. This amount is often referred to as the "operating income" or "operating profit" of the firm and is the primary driver of firm value. If a firm can't generate a respectable operating profit then it probably won't be around for very long.

An important role of the income statement is to distinguish between the profit from the ongoing operations of the company and the myriad of other, largely non-recurring transactions and events that cause equity to change. Revenues and expenses are intended to capture the ongoing operating profits. The remaining bits and pieces of income are discussed below. But just because an item is classified as revenue or expense does not rule out the possibility that it is non-recurring. Even the ongoing operations of a company are subject to non-recurring demand and supply shocks. And it is not uncommon for companies to generate ongoing sources of non-operating income from investments they have made in other companies. Recall from Chapter 2 that the Management Discussion and Analysis provided in Form 10-K and Form 10-Q is required to identify any potentially non-recurring components of revenue and expense. As you study the firm's income statements think carefully about the extent to which each item is likely to recur.

Gains

Gains are increases in the net assets of a firm that occur in the normal course of business and contribute to the earnings of a firm, but are incidental or peripheral to the firm's operating activities. Returning to our previous example of the restaurant firm that sells some cooking equipment, if the proceeds from the sale exceed the book value of the equipment sold, then we would report gain. Since we are not in the business of selling cooking equipment, the proceeds and costs associated with the sale of the cooking equipment are not classified as revenues and expenses. Instead, they are netted and recorded as a gain in the income statement. By separating gains from revenues and expenses, we can discriminate between profitability that is directly associated with the provision of goods and services and profitability from incidental transactions and events. This distinction is very useful from a forecasting perspective, because these incidental transactions and events are less likely to recur. Common examples of gains include proceeds from the sale of assets, winning a lawsuit, and certain increases in the value of marketable securities.

Losses

Losses are decreases in the net assets of a firm that occur in the normal course of business and reduce the earnings of a firm, but are incidental or peripheral to the firm's operating activities. If our restaurant firm sells some cooking equipment and the proceeds from the sale are less than the book value of the equipment sold, then we would report a loss. As with gains, losses are likely to be one-time occurrences, so it is useful to distinguish them from revenues and expenses. Common examples of losses include legal settlements, asset impairments, and restructuring charges.

As shown in Figure 4.2, revenues, expenses, gains, and losses combine to produce a firm's "income from continuing operations."

Other Items

There are a few other oddities on the income statement that are zero for most firms most of the time, but still arise occasionally. Most of these items are typically non-recurring. If a firm sells a major division or segment of its business, any operating income, gains, or losses related to that segment must be reported separately on the income statement as Discontinued Operations. There is also a separate line item reserved for extraordinary gains and losses. To be extraordinary, gains and losses must be both unusual and infrequent. However, GAAP defines these terms so narrowly that even business losses associated with the September 11, 2001, terrorist attacks were not deemed to be extraordinary. So what can be put here? Gains and losses associated with the early extinguishment of debt are allowed, as are certain losses associated with natural catastrophes and confiscation of assets by foreign governments. As shown in Figure 4.2, revenues, expenses, gains, losses, discontinued operations, and extraordinary items combine to produce a firm's earnings. Earnings measure the performance of the firm for the period and include all components of periodic performance, regardless of whether they are expected to recur.

If the accounting rule-makers change the rules, the cumulative effect on retained earnings from the change in accounting principle must be reported separately following extraordinary items in the income statement. The reason that this component of income is not included in earnings is that it is unrelated to current period performance. Instead, it is a "catch-up" adjustment that measures the cumulative effect of the change in earlier periods. Deducting the effect of changes in accounting principles from earnings gives a firm's net income. Net income is the traditional "bottom line." However, if the company has preferred stock then preferred stock dividends are deducted from net income to arrive at net income available to common stock. This is the real bottom line for common equity holders.

The final component of the income statement is other comprehensive income. This component consists of a variety of other changes in equity that accountants could not bring themselves to include in earnings. Remember that accounting is a political process, and corporations lobbied to keep most of the items in this section out of earnings. But because they involve changes in assets and liabilities that cause equity to change, they had to be put somewhere—hence this component. Examples include unrealized gains and losses on marketable securities, foreign currency translation adjustments, and minimum pension liability adjustments. These final adjustments make sure that we preserve the clean surplus relation, written carefully as

$$\text{Comprehensive Income Available to Common Equity} =$$
$$\text{Change in Common Equity} + \text{Net Distributions to Common Equity Holders}$$

On the bottom of the Financial Statements sheet in eVal you will notice a line item titled "Clean Surplus Plug (Ignore)." We use this item to clean up the company's prior financial statements by putting all the other comprehensive income here. But because these items are not expected to recur, we force it to be zero in the forecasted financial statements. That's why we keep saying to "Ignore" the clean surplus plug. In addition, we use the shorthand "Net Income" for "Comprehensive Income Available to Common Equity"; typically, they are the same thing.

4.3 ACCOUNTING INFORMATION AND VALUATION

By now, we should have driven home the point that the financial statements were never intended to yield a final measure of firm value. Instead, they provide information that is useful when trying to value a company, but more work needs to be done. In this section, we explain why and how accounting information is useful. We'll be kind to accounting in this section, concentrating on the positive ways in which it provides information that facilitates valuation decisions. But accounting information also has many shortcomings that we discuss in the next section.

In most businesses, the accounting system can be thought of as classifying the business into a series of current and expected future *sales transactions*. The balance sheet measures the cumulative amount that has been invested in the past to generate future sales transactions. The income statement measures the current and expected future cash flow consequences associated with sales transactions consummated during the period. The sales transaction is the critical event that leads to the recognition of value creation in the financial statements. A sale triggers the recognition of revenue, which measures the net assets created by the sales transaction, and expenses, which measures the net assets used to generate the sales transaction. The net effect is recognized as operating profit in the income statement.

It is important to note that the net assets resulting from sales transactions during a period rarely coincide with the actual net cash receipts during the period. Consequently, net income and net cash receipts will typically be different within an accounting period. The accounting rules that measure changes in net assets as income, regardless of the actual cash receipts, are collectively known as *accrual accounting,* and the differences between accounting income and cash receipts are referred to as *accruals.* It is the difference between the net income and the net cash receipts that creates all the non-cash assets and liabilities on the balance sheet (a completely cash-based accounting system would have no non-cash assets or liabilities). But over the long run, net income and cash flows will be the same. All accrual accounting rules do is change the timing of the recognition of cash receipts and payments.

Accountants go to great lengths to make sure that the net assets resulting from a particular sales transaction include all the past and expected future cash consequences of that sales transaction but do not include the cash consequences of future sales transactions. Some examples should make this clear:

- The expected future cash collections associated with credit sales are usually recognized in revenues in the period that the sales transaction occurs.
- The cash outflows associated with inventory purchases are usually not recognized as expenses until the inventory is sold.
- The cash outflows associated with the purchase of a machine are usually recognized as expenses gradually over the periods in which the machine is expected to generate sales.
- The expected future cash outflows associated with post-retirement benefits earned by workers producing sales in the current period are usually recognized as expenses in the current period.

Although the financial statements do not attempt to measure the expected future cash consequences of future sales transactions, they nevertheless provide a rich source of information. Most firms stay in the same lines of business for many accounting periods and the competitive environment facing those businesses usually changes only slowly over time. Hence, by measuring the cumulative cash consequences of current sales transactions, the financial statements provide useful forecasting information. Specifically, the historical financial statements help in forecasting the amount and profitability of future sales transactions in three ways.

1. Historical balance sheets provide a detailed breakdown of the types of investments that were necessary to generate historical sales.
2. Historical income statements provide a detailed breakdown of the cash consequences associated with the firm's historical sales transactions.
3. The most recent balance sheet lists past investments that are expected to generate future sales.

Accounting Information and Value

To develop the link between accounting information and firm value, recall the basic valuation model we introduced in Chapter 1 (and will discuss in more detail in Chapter 10). Equity value, V_0, is equal to the net present value of the future cash distributions made by the firm to its stockholders:

$$\text{Value}_0 = \sum_{t=1}^{\infty} \frac{\text{Distributions to Equity}_t}{(1 + r)^t}$$

where r is the cost of equity capital. Distributions to equity can be derived from the financial statements using the clean surplus relation. Recall from the clean surplus equation in the previous section that net income measures all changes in equity over a period except for Net Distributions to Owners. This gives us

$$\text{Net Distributions to Equity} = \text{Net Income} - \text{Change in Equity}$$

One important implication of this relation is that we cannot value a firm by simply discounting its income. We first need to adjust for changes in equity. The intuition for this adjustment is clear. Net income is the result of accrual accounting and so may consist of cash receipts and disbursements relating to past or future periods. But whenever we record net income without an associated distribution to equity, we must have also added assets or removed liabilities from on the balance sheet. By adjusting net income for changes in equity, we work back to cash distributions to equity for the period. The increase in equity is also what we refer to in Figure 4.1 as *reinvested income*. This relation tells us that if we can forecast an income statement, and forecast beginning and ending balance sheets, we can easily solve for the implied distributions to equity during the period.

By directing us to the forecasting of future income statements and balance sheets, accounting organizes the forecasting process into three distinct tasks. First, we forecast future sales revenues. The sales transaction is the basic level at which accountants recognize value, and so sales forecasts are the starting point for forecasting income statements and balance sheets. Second, we forecast the income statement components associated with the forecasted sales revenues. Third, we forecast the balance sheets associated with the forecasted sales revenues and income statement components. Each of these tasks is discussed in much greater detail in the chapters that follow. For now, all we want you to see is that past financial statements tell us a lot about expected future financial statements, and future financial statements can be used to value the firm.

4.4 LIMITATIONS OF ACCOUNTING INFORMATION

Unfortunately, our love fest with accounting lasts only a short while. It's time to look at accounting's dark side. In order to think about the limitations of accounting, it is useful to introduce a benchmark. This benchmark should reflect how we would interpret accounting information in the absence of any limitations. Consider a bank savings account. In a bank savings account, an initial amount is invested in order to generate a future stream of interest. Over a period of time, interest is earned on the account and additional contributions or withdrawals can be made from the account. The ending balance in a savings account is equal to the beginning balance plus interest earned less any withdrawals:

$$\text{Ending Balance} = \text{Beginning Balance} + \text{Interest} - \text{Withdrawals}$$

The key measure of investment performance for a savings account is the interest rate earned, computed as

$$\text{Interest Rate} = \text{Interest/Beginning Balance} = (\text{Withdrawals} + \text{Increase in Balance})/\text{Beginning Balance}$$

The equality between the two prior expressions is important. The first expression tells us that we can compute the interest rate by dividing interest by the beginning balance. The second expression says that we can compute the interest rate without direct reference to interest. This is because any interest that is not withdrawn from the account is reinvested. So we can always impute interest by summing withdrawals and the increase in the savings account balance.

The accounting for a savings account is simple enough. The reason accounting works so well in this case is because, over any period of time, we know exactly how much interest has accrued. Equivalently, we always know exactly what the account is worth. Now extend the same logic to an equity investment. Simply replace the savings account balance with the book value of equity and the savings account withdrawals with the distributions to equity. The clean surplus relation given earlier is then written as

$$\text{Ending Equity} = \text{Beginning Equity} + \text{Net Income} - \text{Net Distributions to Equity}$$

Following the same procedure as we did for the savings account to compute the rate of return on the equity investment gives

$$\text{Rate of Return} = \text{Net Income/Beginning Equity} = (\text{Net Distributions to Equity} + \text{Increase in Equity})/\text{Beginning Equity} = \text{Return on Equity}$$

The return on equity (ROE) perfectly measures the rate of return on the equity investment only if the accounting rules can perfectly measure the income earned over a period or, equivalently, if the accounting rules can perfectly measure the value of the equity claim at a point in time. But while such measurements are easy with a savings account, they are almost impossible for an equity claim. To illustrate how ROE is affected by imperfections in accounting measurements, we will introduce some new notation. Suppose that, as a result of divine intervention, we could create the perfect accounting system. Let "Economic Income" denote the true wealth creation over the period and let "Investment" denote the true value of the equity claim. (We really need only one of these measures; with one, we can compute the other.) The clean surplus relation for this perfect accounting system would be

$$\text{Ending Investment} = \text{Beginning Investment} + \text{Economic Income} - \text{Distributions to Equity}$$

The underlying economic rate of return is given by

$$\text{Economic Rate of Return} = \text{Economic Income/Beginning Investment} = (\text{Distributions to Equity} + \text{Increase in Investment})/\text{Beginning Investment}$$

Now define ϵ as the *measurement error* in equity. It is the difference between the book value of equity, as computed by the imperfect accounting system, and the true value of the investment, computed with our divinely perfect accounting system:

$$\epsilon = \text{Equity} - \text{Investment}$$

Solving for the relation between accounting net income and economic income gives

Net Income = Distributions to Equity + Increase in Equity

= Distributions to Equity + Increase in Investment + Increase in ϵ

= Economic Income + Increase in ϵ

ROE can be expressed as

$$ROE = (\text{Economic Income} + \text{Increase in } \epsilon)/$$
$$(\text{Beginning Investment} + \text{Beginning } \epsilon)$$

Measurement error in equity has a two-pronged effect in distorting ROE relative to the economic rate of return. First, changes in the measurement error between two dates are reflected in the numerator. This is because accounting net income picks up the effects of any changes in the book value of equity between two periods. Second, the level of error at the beginning of the period is reflected in the denominator. The overall distortion in ROE relative to the Economic Rate of Return (ERR) depends on the relative size of the numerator and denominator effects. Possible alternatives are listed in Table 4.1.

A positive beginning ϵ causes a negative bias in ROE, because the denominator in the ROE calculation is overstated (and vice versa for a negative beginning ϵ). A positive change in ϵ induces a positive bias in ROE, because the numerator in the ROE calculation is overstated (and vice versa for a negative change in ϵ). If the sign of the beginning ϵ and the change in ϵ are the same, the two biases work in the opposite direction, and the overall bias in ROE is ambiguous. In this case, we need to quantify the errors in order to determine the exact nature of the bias.

We don't want to leave you with the vague impression that "it all depends," so here is a general rule of thumb to use when thinking about how accounting mea-

TABLE 4.1

The Effect of Measurement Error on ROE

	Change in $\epsilon < 0$ (Net Income Understated)	Change in $\epsilon = 0$ (Net Income Correct)	Change in $\epsilon > 0$ (Net Income Overstated)
Beginning $\epsilon < 0$ (Equity Understated)	Effect on ROE versus ERR is ambiguous	ROE > ERR	ROE > ERR
Beginning $\epsilon = 0$ (Equity Correct)	ROE < ERR	ROE = ERR	ROE > ERR
Beginning $\epsilon > 0$ (Equity Overstated)	ROE < ERR	ROE < ERR	Effect on ROE versus ERR is ambiguous

ROE is return on equity, ERR is the true economic rate of return, and ϵ is the measurement error in accounting, defined as the book value of Equity minus the true value of Net Capital Investment.

(1) book equity = true investment + ϵ

(2) Net Income = Economic Income + $\Delta \epsilon$

surement error influences ROE: the denominator effect is usually dominant. In steady state there is no change in the measurement error, so the only effect is in the denominator. The change in measurement error in the numerator may work with this effect or against it when the firm is not in steady state, but it is only one year's worth of measurement error, whereas the denominator effect is the cumulative effect of many years of measurement error.

4.5 EXAMPLES OF ACCOUNTING MEASUREMENT ERRORS

So far, we've talked a lot about accounting theory and enjoyed some algebra. Now it is time to get practical and talk about what actually causes the book value of equity to measure the true value of the investment with error. Recall from the accounting equation that equity is the difference between assets and liabilities. So measurement error in equity must arise from measurement error in the underlying assets and liabilities. We can divide the sources of measurement error into three broad categories:

1. Measurement error caused by GAAP accounting rules.
2. Measurement errors caused by lack of perfect foresight in the use of accounting estimates.
3. Measurement error caused by management's intentional manipulation of the financial statements.

We discuss each of these sources of error in more detail below.

Measurement Error Caused by GAAP Accounting Rules

The major sources of measurement error introduced by GAAP accounting rules relate to the recognition and valuation of non-financial assets. The problem arises because investments made in non-financial assets are typically expected to generate benefits over multiple accounting periods. Because the timing and amount of these benefits is not known early in the life of the asset, measurement error is unavoidable. But worse still, the accounting rules for many types of investments often result in systematic and predictable measurement errors. Recall that GAAP accounting rules trade off relevance and reliability, and reliability usually wins. Because they can be reliably computed and easily verified, accounting rules often use simple procedures for setting asset values. Examples include the immediate expensing of certain investment expenditures and the use of mechanical depreciation and amortization techniques to assign periodic asset values to investment expenditures. We discuss the biases created by these simple procedures next.

Immediate Expensing of Internally Generated Intangibles

This is an example of an asset that GAAP misses. Under GAAP, expenditures made on internally developed intangible assets are required to be expensed immediately. In other words, it is assumed that these expenditures produce no benefits beyond the accounting period in which they are incurred. Examples include most research and development expenditures, advertising expenditures, and administrative expenditures. Many of these expenditures clearly generate benefits that extend well beyond the period in which they are incurred but, rather than attempt to estimate the value of these investments, GAAP uses the safe and reliable value of zero. So a firm gets to capitalize the cost of constructing a new building, but not the cost of developing a new drug. Immediate expensing of internally developed intangibles means that no asset is recognized on the balance sheet, causing the value of equity to understate the actual investment. This results in systematically negative measurement error in equity (because assets are understated) in all periods during which the expenditures generate future benefits.

The impact of this accounting distortion on net income relative to economic income is somewhat more involved. If the firm is increasing its investments in internally developed intangibles, then immediately expensing the investment lowers net income relative to economic income. When the firm's investment in these intangibles starts to decline, however, the expense recognition also declines but the benefits of previous investments continue to flow, so net income is overstated relative to economic income. Which effect dominates depends on the amount of the investment in the current and previous periods, and on the rate that previous investments benefit future periods.

The overall effect on ROE is also ambiguous. The systematic understatement of equity inflates ROE because of the denominator effect (it puts us in the first row of Table 4.1). If we are in a period when expenditures on internally generated intangibles are high relative to prior periods, income is most likely understated and the numerator and denominator effects move ROE in different directions, so the overall nature of the bias is ambiguous (we are in the first cell in the first row of Table 4.1). But if we are in a period when current expenditures are less than prior expenditures, income is most likely overstated, and ROE is biased upward (we are in the third cell in the first row of Table 4.1). Finally, if we have to guess quickly, the rule of thumb is that the denominator effect dominates, so in steady state ROE will be overstated.

Depreciation and Amortization of Capitalized Nonfinancial Assets

While GAAP ignores internally developed intangible assets, GAAP generally recognizes tangible assets (e.g., property, plant and equipment) and purchased intangibles (e.g., patents). The accounting for such expenditures at their inception is straightforward. Since these expenditures are investments that are expected to generate future benefits, the full amount of the expenditures is initially placed on the balance sheet as an asset. This process is often referred to as "capitalizing" the expenditure. The difficult part is deciding how to subsequently reduce the value of the asset over the future periods in which it generates benefits. This process is known as *depreciation* for tangible assets and *amortization* for purchased intangible assets. Ideally, the depreciation/amortization method should reflect the flow of expected future benefits generated by the initial investment expenditure. However, implementing such a method would entail subjective forecasts of the future benefits. So once again the accountants sacrifice relevance for reliability by requiring the firm to follow a predetermined depreciation schedule, with the most common method being straight-line whereby the initial value of the asset is reduced in equal increments over the expected life of the asset.

The general effect of these measurement errors is to understate asset values by depreciating them too quickly, leading to exactly the same sorts of biases that we discussed in the case of the immediate expensing of expenditures on internally developed intangibles. The degree of bias is not as great, however, because we simply depreciate the asset too quickly rather than expensing the entire asset immediately. One consequence of this is the so-called "old plant trap." Firms with old plant that has been almost completely depreciated will have low book values that result in high accounting rates of return. But once this old plant is replaced, book values will increase, causing accounting rates of return to fall. The old plant trap is sprung when investors mistake the high accounting rates of return for firms with old plant for high economic rates of return.

A Numerical Example

If you found the preceding discussion a bit too abstract, perhaps the following numerical example will illustrate how distortions in the accounting rules distort equity, net income, and ROE. The example is based on a real accounting issue that arose at America Online.

In the mid 1990s America Online blanketed the country with disks promoting their online service and offering 10 hours of free connection time. In 1995 alone AOL spent more the $110 million on this advertising campaign to attract more subscribers, more than 30 percent of their total revenue for the year. AOL accounted for the cost as if it was an asset. But later, under pressure from the SEC, AOL switched to expensing this cost immediately. Is this $110 million really an asset that benefits future periods or is it an expense in the current period? Which accounting treatment best reflects economic reality depends on how many years a typical customer hangs around after they initially sign up. In truth, nobody knew what would happen. Most of AOL's existing customers were very new and, with the Internet changing so rapidly, it was anybody's guess as to how long a customer would stay with any one service.

Let's use the AOL example to illustrate the life cycle of an accounting distortion. Suppose that AOL has revenues and advertising expenditures that are increasing in years 1 and 2, constant in year 3, and decreasing in years 4 and 5. The advertising expenditures combine with the assets on the balance sheet to produce the revenue stream shown in Table 4.2. If the advertising costs are expensed then the accounting is very simple, as shown in panel A of Table 4.2. But this example was constructed so that, for every dollar AOL invests in advertising, they get $3 of revenue in the current period and $3 in the next period. That is, the economic reality is that the investment creates an asset that has a two-period life. Consequently, a perfect accounting system would capitalize the advertising costs, amortizing half in the year of the expenditure and the other half the following year. Panel B of Table 4.2 shows the accounting in this case. In year 1, for example, 50 percent of the advertising costs are amortized and show up on the income statement, with the remaining 50 percent staying on the balance sheet as an asset. In year 2 the remaining 50 percent are expensed, along with half of the 200 spent in year 2,

TABLE 4.2

Anatomy of an Accounting Distortion

Panel A Expense Advertising Costs Immediately						
Year	0	1	2	3	4	5
Income Statement						
Revenue		300	900	1200	900	300
Advertising Expense		100	200	200	100	0
Profit		200	700	1000	800	300
Profit Margin		66.7%	77.8%	83.3%	88.9%	100%
Balance Sheet						
Assets	1250	3700	4900	3650	1200	0
Equity	1250	3700	4900	3650	1200	0
ROE (on beginning equity)		16.0%	18.9%	20.4%	21.9%	25.0%

Panel B Capitalize Advertising Costs and Expense Equally over Two Years						
Year	0	1	2	3	4	5
Income Statement						
Revenue		300	900	1200	900	300
Amortized Cost		50	150	200	150	50
Profit		250	750	1000	750	250
Profit Margin		83.3%	83.3%	83.3%	83.3%	83.3%
Balance Sheet						
Assets:						
Other Assets	1250	3700	4900	3650	1200	0
Advertising	0	50	100	100	50	0
Equity	1250	3750	5000	3750	1250	0
ROE (on beginning equity)		20.0%	20.0%	20.0%	20.0%	20.0%

Each dollar of advertising (shown in panel A as the line item Advertising Expense) generates three dollars of revenue in the current period and three dollars in the next period. The example is constructed to yield a constant 20 percent ROE using the perfect accounting policy in Panel B.

resulting in a recognized expense of 150. As expected, the example shows that expensing the advertising cost decreases reported profit in years 1 and 2, when AOL is growing, relative to profits when the costs are capitalized as an asset. But in years 4 and 5, when the expenditures on advertising slow down, the benefits from previous investments continue to pay off. By capitalizing and then amortizing these expenses, the accounting in panel B continues to match the investment to the revenue it generates (note that the profit margin is 83 percent each period). However, panel A shows that, if the advertising costs were expensed when incurred, then in years 4 and 5 the firm enjoys the revenue from the previous investments without the associated expense, so profits are higher than in panel B (note that the profit margin has increased to 100 percent in year 5). Finally, the sum of reported profits over the five years is 3000, regardless of the accounting method. Distortions in accounting cause income to be reported in the wrong periods, but do not ultimately change the total amount of income recorded. Eventually accrual accounting always gets it right.

We have constructed our example to yield a constant ROE of 20% in the case of perfect accounting shown in Panel B. In Panel A the effect of immediately expensing the advertising costs unambiguously lowers ROE in year 1—income is lower and the beginning balance of equity is unaffected. In year 2, however, the effect could go either way, as discussed earlier. In this particular example, the effect of understanding income is greater than the effect of understanding equity in year 2 and so ROE is less than 20% in Panel A. However, if we change the example to have an Other Assets balance of 700 at the end of year 1, then the ROE in both Panel A and Panel B is 100%. In this case the income effect and the balance sheet effect perfectly offset each other. When the investment flow hits steady state or declines, as is the case for years 3, 4 and 5, the effect of immediately expensing advertising costs on ROE is unambiguously positive. In this case equity is understated and income is either correct or overstated.

Asset Impairments

As we have discussed above, GAAP generally requires non-financial assets be carried at their (amortized) historical cost. This means that the carrying value of the asset represents an estimate of the amount that has been invested in order to generate future benefits rather than a forecast of the value of the expected future benefits. However, GAAP also contains an important exception to that rule. If it is determined that an asset has been impaired—that is, its carrying value is greater than the undiscounted sum of the cash flows it is expected to generate—GAAP requires the asset to be restated to fair value. This rule introduces a nasty asymmetry into asset valuations. If the asset's value falls below its carrying value, it gets revalued based on the estimated future benefits, but if the asset's value exceeds the current carrying value, no revaluation is allowed. Hence, we cannot interpret aggregate asset values as either estimates of past amounts that have been invested or as estimates of expected future benefits. Rather, they represent a mixture of the lower of these two amounts.

From a practical perspective, we need to remember that firms with asset impairments have potentially flawed business models. Corporate managers often encourage investors to focus on net income before asset impairment charges. They reason that these charges are non-recurring and are not indicative of future performance. But remember that an asset impairment is basically an admission by management that they are invested in unprofitable assets. Moreover, by taking an asset impairment today, net income and ROE will both be overstated in future periods. If an asset impairment is recorded every time management makes a bad investment, it stands to reason that net income before impairments will always look good, since it excludes the income effects of all the bad investments. However, we should not draw the conclusion that management is doing a good job. We need to look at the aggregate performance of both the good and bad investments to draw overall conclusions about firm performance.

Omission of Contingent Liabilities

We have already discussed the fact that the accounting rules do not allow for the recognition of investments in internally generated intangibles as assets. The reason for this is that the future benefits are deemed to be so uncertain that they cannot be reliably measured. For the same reason, liabilities are not recognized for contingent liabilities where the amount of the loss is not sufficiently probable or not reasonably estimable. Two common examples of contingent liabilities are pending litigation against a firm and environmental cleanup costs. Because liabilities are not recognized for most contingent liabilities, net assets and equity are overstated (we are in the bottom row of Table 4.1). In the periods that a contingent liability arises, measurement error increases so net income is overstated and the impact on ROE is ambiguous (we are in the third column of the bottom row in Table 4.1). In subsequent periods, as long as the contingent liability remains contingent, equity will be overstated and there is no effect on net income, so ROE will be understated (we are in the first column of the bottom row of Table 4.1).

Measurement Error Caused by Imperfect Foresight

The measurement of many assets and liabilities requires the estimation of future amounts. GAAP requires that these future amounts be measurable with some minimum level of reliability before they qualify for recognition in the financial statements. Just because accountants found the nerve to recognize them, however, certainly doesn't mean that the assets and liabilities in the financial statements have little estimation error. Quite the opposite is often true. For example, the employee post-retirement benefit liability requires a forecast of healthcare costs decades into the future. Even if management has made a good faith estimate, we should recognize that the amount recorded on the balance sheet might differ greatly from the actual future obligations it represents.

If management has done a thorough job at estimating inherently subjective future amounts, then there is probably little that you can do to improve upon their estimates. It is very important, however, that you understand the amount of potential estimation error in the various assets and liabilities presented on a company's balance sheets. Understanding estimation error is important for at least two reasons. First, the precision of forecasts based on financial statement data is directly related to the precision of the financial statement data itself. Second, the inherent risk of a business is a direct function of the risk of its underlying assets and liabilities.

Unfortunately, there are only a few broad-brush rules we can give you for establishing the amount of potential measurement error that is typically associated with particular classes of assets and liabilities. We can safely tell you that cash and short-term investments have little measurement error. For accounts receivable, however, the amount of potential measurement error can be very small or incredibly large. A bank that lends only to highly creditworthy customers will generally be able to measure its receivables with much less potential error than a firm that makes sub-prime loans. A detailed understanding of the nature of the assets and liabilities being measured and the techniques used to measure them is required to make a good assessment of the amount of potential measurement error. This can be accomplished only through a careful analysis of Form 10-K, particularly the notes to the financial statements.

Measurement Error Caused by Managerial Manipulation

The final source of error in the financial statements is error introduced through intentional managerial manipulation. Given the many estimates that the accounting rules require, it is inevitable that some managers will use this discretion to achieve their own short-term objectives. The most common goal of managers when manipulating the financial statements is to inflate reported earnings in a particular period, either by recognizing revenue that has not yet been earned or by failing to recognize an expense that has really been incurred. But accounting income always adds up to the right answer given enough time, so this type of "earnings management" is really about shifting income from one period to another; it simply isn't possible to inflate income forever.

The key to detecting "earnings management" is to zero in on the assets and liabilities for which management exercises the most discretion, which usually are not going to be cash, short-term investments, debt, most payables, and others for which the accounting rules are fairly rigid and also there isn't much that requires a managerial estimate. Just as we advised in the previous section, you should devote extra attention to those assets and liabilities that require the most *estimation*. This is where it is most likely that management will succumb to temptation.

We can categorize earnings management opportunities based on how they impact the income statement. Below, we briefly discuss each such category, identifying the assets and liabilities that are most likely to be so "managed."

Revenue Manipulation

Revenue manipulation is the most common type of earnings management. The sales transaction is the trigger for the recognition of value creation under GAAP, so there is no better place to start looking for some additional income. The asset most commonly involved in revenue manipulation is accounts receivable. A cash payment from a customer is a good indication that the customer is committed to the transaction (although the revenue may still not have been earned—more on this below). When the customer has not yet paid, however, the balance lives in the accounts receivable, and there is greater uncertainty about whether the customer is committed to the transaction, or even knows about the transaction, or has the ability to make the contracted payment.

A common form of revenue manipulation is "trade loading" or "channel stuffing," shipping product to a customer before the customer really needs it, an activity most prevalent at the end of a reporting period whereby management is effectively stealing from next period's sales in order to inflate this period's sales. Another form of revenue manipulation overstates the value of the net receivables by understating the allowance for uncollectible accounts. It is easy to increase the volume of sales transactions by granting more generous credit terms or by selling on credit to customers with lower credit quality, but the cost of increasing sales in this way is the increased amount of expected uncollectible accounts. If accounts receivable is not adjusted downward to reflect the increased expected uncollectibles, then accounts receivable, revenue, and earnings will all be overstated.

A variety of ratio analysis techniques can be used to identify firms that are potentially overstating revenue and accounts receivable, and these are discussed in Chapters 5 and 6. It is important to analyze these ratios in the context of the firm's business strategy and accounting policies. There have been examples of firms that have made strategic choices to loosen their credit terms that have paid off nicely. While unusually high receivables are an important "red flag," they are not a definitive indicator of revenue manipulation.

Accounts receivable is not the only account that can be used for revenue manipulation. Suppose a customer pays in advance for a product or service, such as a subscription or a product that includes a servicing agreement. In such cases, GAAP requires that revenue recognition should be delayed until the good or service is delivered to the customer. This creates a liability account representing the future obligation of the firm to provide the promised goods or services. Common titles for this account are "Unearned Revenue" and "Advances from Customers." Unfortunately, the total sales price is allocated to different periods based on very subjective proration schedules. Unlike receivables, the collection of cash is already assured in the case of such sales. It is simply the timing of the revenue recognition that is at issue. Nevertheless, understatement of the liability to provide future goods or services can be a powerful tool for revenue manipulation. For example, a firm can boost current period sales transactions by promising to provide enhanced future service or additional future products at discounted prices. If the cost of these future obligations is not recorded as a liability, then current period equity and earnings will be overstated.

Expense Manipulation

Whenever an asset is used up or a liability is created in the process of providing goods and services to customers, GAAP requires an expense to be recognized. The theory is straightforward. Like revenue recognition, however, there are many gray areas that open the door to earnings management.

Perhaps the biggest gray area is the "capitalize versus expense" decision. Whenever an asset is used up in a firm's operating activities, an expense must be recognized *unless* a new asset is created. In other words, there must be a future benefit that satisfies the criteria for recognition as an asset. Therefore, earnings can be manipulated by capitalizing costs that should really be expensed. A good example is the costs incurred to develop and produce software. GAAP requires that costs incurred beyond the point of technological feasibility to be capitalized. But the determination of "technological feasibility" is subjective and lends itself to manipulation. In order to lower expenses, management can simply claim technological feasibility has been achieved. The auditor, not being an expert in software development, is in a poor position to question such a judgment. In an interesting twist on earnings management, Microsoft has been accused of understating income by expensing all software development costs, regardless of technological feasibility. Following the logic illustrated in the numerical example of Table 4.2, we should expect that when Microsoft slows its investment in new software, its profit margin will predictably increase. A good check for expense manipulation of this kind is to compare the total proportion of costs that are capitalized by a firm with its industry counterparts. If a firm is capitalizing a greater proportion of its costs than other firms in the industry, it is more likely to be manipulating earnings. But it is always possible that the firm really is better at producing future benefits than its competitors.[1]

Inventory accounting also lends itself to expense manipulation. In times of changing prices, the cost flow assumption used to account for inventory (FIFO, LIFO, etc.) can be very important in determining the amount of inventory that has been used up and therefore recognized as cost of goods sold. Management can time inventory purchases and change cost flow assumptions in order to manipulate earnings. They can also manipulate the allocation of joint costs. In a slaughterhouse that produces pork products, how should we allocate the cost of the pig between bacon and sausage? If we sell bacon more quickly than we sell sausage, we can boost earnings by assigning more costs to sausage, hence leaving these costs in inventory longer.

Yet another technique for manipulating earnings using inventory accounting is to purchase a diverse range of inventory and offer it for sale at a high mark-up. The firm makes big profits on the product that sells, and leaves the product that doesn't sell in inventory. The problem here, of course, is inventory obsolescence. This type of earnings management is particularly prevalent in the specialty retail industry, where seasonal fashions are difficult to predict. By failing to write down the obsolete inventory on a timely basis, the firm can manipulate expenses.

Another avenue for expense manipulation involves non-current assets that are used up gradually over many periods, such as property, plant, and equipment. GAAP calls for these assets to be depreciated, amortized, or impaired over time using a variety of rules. All of these rules provide management with considerable latitude in determining the periodic expenses recorded, however. An interesting example here is Blockbuster, a video rental chain. In the early years of video, Blockbuster depreciated its rental videos over a longer time period than its competitors. At the time, there was considerable uncertainty about the useful life of rental videos, particularly because the demographics of video renters was changing rapidly as video players became more affordable. As a result, Blockbuster looked more profitable than its competitors and so attracted more capital and cemented its position as the leading player in the industry.

[1]The numerical example in Table 4.2 is a case in which capitalization is appropriate. You can easily change the situation to make expensing appropriate by assuming that every dollar of advertising results in three dollars of revenue in the current period, and nothing in the subsequent period. Recompute the revenue amounts in panels A and B of Table 4.2 and you have an example of manipulation through overcapitalization.

Expense manipulation is not restricted to assets. Expenses can also be manipulated by understating liabilities. Consider the accounting for warranty liabilities. When a firm sells a product with a warranty, the expected future costs of the warranty should be recognized as an obligation of the company at the same time that the sales transaction is recognized, resulting in an increase in liabilities and a decrease in equity and earnings. By understating or ignoring the warranty liability, management can overstate earnings. One spectacular example of expense manipulation in this vein involved Regina Company. Regina manufactured vacuum cleaners that were reputably so durable they would last a lifetime. In fact, Regina offered a lifetime warranty on its products, but the high quality of its products meant that few warranty costs were ever incurred. Then, a new CEO boosted Regina's earnings and stock price by using cheaper components in the vacuum cleaners. The lower costs meant higher profits in the short run. But, as you would expect, costs associated with the lifetime warranty skyrocketed in the long run, and Regina subsequently went broke. The higher expected warranty costs should have been recorded as a liability and an expense recognized when the cheaper components were introduced. If they were, Regina would never have shown higher profits in the first place. But we doubt that the new CEO would have liked that accounting treatment very much.

A final important area for expense manipulation is employee pensions and other retirement benefits. GAAP requires these amounts be estimated, recognized as a liability, and charged off as an expense in the same period that the employees provide the services that earn the benefits. There is huge subjectivity involved in determining these amounts. What will be the ultimate amount of the benefits? What rate of return will be earned on benefit plan assets? What discount rate should be used to value the benefits? Small changes in these assumptions can have huge impacts on the financial statements and so management has considerable leeway to manipulate earnings. Again, you should conduct an industry comparison of the accounting assumptions to determine whether a particular company is likely to be managing earnings.

In summary, every cash flow that is not recognized as revenue or expense in the same period necessarily creates an asset or liability. Consequently, the key to detecting accounting manipulations on the income statement is careful examination of the associated balance sheet items. So far, we have focused exclusively on traditional revenue and expense manipulation. There are other more subtle forms of financial statement manipulation. Following is a brief discussion of four of them.

Related Party Transactions

A key occurrence for the recognition of many assets and liabilities on the balance sheet is a transaction with another party. The maintained assumption under GAAP is that these transactions represent arm's-length business dealings. For example, if inventory is purchased, the underlying assumption is that the purchase price represents the fair market value at the date of purchase. Also, if a sale is made, the assumption is that the sale will not be reversed at a later date.

Given the heavy reliance of GAAP on transactions with other parties, one possible technique for manipulating the financial statements is to engage in transactions with related parties. For example, a firm with an earnings shortfall could sell product to a director with a verbal agreement that the sale will be reversed or the director reimbursed in some other manner (a stock option grant, for example). Such practices are technical violations of GAAP, but they can be difficult to prove. Further, related party transactions are not confined to earnings management. A director may make a "long-term loan" to a company just before the end of a reporting period in order to create the impression of improved short-term liquidity on the balance sheet and then reverse the loan shortly thereafter.

Fortunately, U.S. accounting rules require that all material related party transactions must be disclosed in the financial statements of the reporting entity. The nature of the relationship and the amount and nature of the transactions must be reported in the notes to the financial statements. Unfortunately, if management really wants to deceive you with related party transactions, it is unlikely that they will say so in plain English in the financial statement footnotes.

Off-Balance-Sheet Entities

Off-balance-sheet entities have many similarities with related party transactions. With off-balance-sheet entities, the firm creates a separate legal entity that is not required to be consolidated in the firm's financial statements. The firm nevertheless exercises influence over this new entity and uses the entity to manipulate the financial statements. The firm usually exercises influence over the off-balance-sheet entity by appointing related parties to the management of the entity or by being a key financier, supplier, customer, or guarantor of the entity. Once established, there are several ways in which the off-balance-sheet entity can then be used to manipulate the financial statements of the firm. For example, the off-balance-sheet entity may purchase goods and services from the firm at inflated prices, directly boosting equity and earnings. In many past cases, these purchases have been funded by loans from the firm itself and simply represent sham transactions designed with the sole intent of boosting earnings. Off-balance-sheet entities can also be used to hide financial leverage and other sources of risk from investors. For example, a firm could boost revenue by using an off-balance-sheet entity to provide customers with loans for making purchases from the firm. If the firm itself guarantees these loans, then the risk associated with the loans is ultimately borne by the firm, but is hidden from investors because the loans themselves are in the off-balance-sheet entity.

The analysis of off-balance-sheet entities can be extremely difficult. Firms that create such structures in order to manage the financial statements will go to great lengths to make it as difficult as possible for investors to figure out what is going on. Moreover, because we typically don't have financial statements for these off-balance-sheet entities, we really don't have much to work with. The well-known rise and sudden fall of Enron was primarily attributable to the aggressive use of off-balance-sheet entities to boost earnings and hide risks from investors. The best advice we can give you here is that if you see any sign that off-balance-sheet entities are being used, you should make sure that you understand how they are being used. If you don't feel that you have enough information to make a meaningful assessment, you should assume the worst.

How do you know if any off-balance-sheet entities are out there? There are three potential disclosures in the notes to the financial statements that you should look for. First, there is the related party note. This note must report any unconsolidated transactions with entities in which the firm has ownership, control, or significant influence. Second, there is the note relating to equity investments and other unconsolidated investments. You should ascertain whether any of these investments give the firm influence over the operating policies of the investee. Finally, there is the contingent liabilities footnote. If the firm has guaranteed the debt of any unconsolidated entities, then these guarantees should be identified in the contingent liabilities note.

Off-Balance-Sheet Financing

Off-balance-sheet financing is used to finance the acquisition of resources without showing the associated assets and liabilities on the balance sheet. By doing so, the firm usually hopes to create the impression that it has less financial risk than it really does. The most common technique for implementing off-balance-sheet financing is the operating lease. A firm enters into a contract in which it acquires the right to use an asset in return for periodic payments to the owner of the asset. If the contract covers a substantial portion of the useful life of the asset, then the economic substance of the transaction is identical to one in which the firm borrows money and then buys the asset. But because the legal form of the transaction is a lease contract, no assets and liabilities are recognized.

GAAP has developed a complex set of rules to determine whether leases can be kept off the books as operating leases or must be put on the books as capital leases, where the accounting pretends that the money was borrowed and the asset purchased. While we won't drag you through all these rules here, suffice it to say that creative accounting consultants have found ways to help management get whatever accounting treatment they want, regardless of the economic substance of the transaction. As a result, most leases remain off the balance sheet.

Fortunately, figuring out the impact of operating leases is straightforward. Firms are required to disclose future payments on most long-term operating leases in the notes to the financial statements. By taking the present value of these payments, you can immediately get a good idea of how much off-balance-sheet financing is attributable to operating leases.

Operating leases are not the only way off-balance-sheet financing can be achieved. Any contract in which a firm acquires the right to use a resource in return for financial commitments constitutes off-balance-sheet financing. Other common forms of off-balance-sheet financing include take-or-pay contracts, sale of receivables with recourse, unconsolidated finance subsidiaries, joint ventures, and other equity investments. You should be able to discover the existence of these and other off-balance-sheet financing techniques by studying the notes to the financial statements, particularly the investments and contingent liabilities notes.

Non-Recurring Charges and Pro Forma Earnings

A final form of financial statement manipulation that has become popular of late is the strategic use of non-recurring charges, such as asset impairments, losses on the sale of long-lived assets, and restructuring charges. Because these charges are non-recurring, it has become usual for management, analysts, and investors to focus on the recurring component of earnings that excludes such charges. This non-GAAP definition of earnings is often referred to as "pro forma" earnings in analyst reports and firms' press releases.

In recent years, the magnitude and frequency of non-recurring charges have exploded. Moreover, firms have starting to exclude recurring charges from pro forma earnings with the lamest of excuses. The idea is to reclassify as many recurring charges as possible into a non-recurring charge and hence report higher "recurring" or "pro forma" earnings. For example, if a firm writes down its fixed assets today in a non-recurring impairment charge, recurring earnings will be higher moving forward, because the carrying value of these assets is lower and hence future expenses will also be lower when these assets are depreciated or amortized. As a result, many firms are consistently reporting large non-recurring charges year after year. Management wins twice with this manipulation. First they convince you to ignore the non-recurring charge in the period they take it, arguing that it is old news that is irrelevant to the future. Second, expenses in the future are lower because of the writedown of assets in the current period. Ignoring expenses that management labels as non-recurring is like evaluating a fund manager after she throws out the bottom 10 percent of performers in the portfolio. The key to dealing with non-recurring charges is to determine what is really included in them and make a careful assessment about what they imply about the abilities of management and the strategies of the firm. A bad management team may well blunder from one bad business decision to the next. Are the losses associated with each of these bad decisions non-recurring simply because they relate to different business decisions? The answer is no.

4.6 CONCLUSION

You should take away three lessons from this chapter. First, the GAAP-based financial statements provide the universal language for evaluating past performance and forecasting future performance. Second, the financial statements provide timely information on just a sub-set of value-relevant events. The financial statements are not the accountants' attempt to value the firm. Rather, their goal is to provide information that is useful to others in conducting a valuation. Third, despite the fact that accountants limit themselves to reporting on reasonably reliable information, lots of subjectivity and discretion is still allowed in the production of the financial statements. This opens the financial statements to potential errors and managerial manipulation.

To build a good valuation model you must be intimately familiar with a firm's financial statements and the accounting policies underlying those financial

statements. Are the accounting policies consistent with the firm's business operations and strategies? What important events are captured in the financial statements on a timely basis and what events are missing? Which assets, liabilities,
revenues, and expenses are measured with the least reliability? Is there any evidence suggesting management is manipulating the financial statements? You need
to answer all these questions before you attempt to forecast the firm's future
financial statements and value the company.

4.7 LINKS AND REFERENCES

Prepaid Legal Services

This case combines an innovative business strategy involving a unique product
and an aggressive marketing strategy with a significant accounting issue. The case
centers on the accounting for Prepaid's sales commissions, which Prepaid has
been capitalizing as an asset. Combining an analysis of Prepaid's business strategy with non-financial data on membership persistency rates provides key insights into Prepaid's financial health and earnings quality. This case is available
on the eVal website.

Turnaround at Bally Total Fitness?

A new management team turns around an ailing fitness club chain through the in-
troduction of a membership-financing scheme. Is the return to profitability real or
purely an accounting illusion? A careful analysis of Bally's business strategy and
key accounting policies answers this question. This case is available on the eVal
website.

EnCom Corporation

This case involves a fictitious company and illustrates how aggressive and conservative accounting can temporarily distort accounting rates of return. It also illustrates how the residual income valuation model is not affected by accounting
distortions as long as we correctly forecast their reversal. This case is available on
the eVal website.

- eVal website—www.mhhe.com/eval

CHAPTER FIVE

Financial Ratio Analysis

5.1 INTRODUCTION

Valuing an equity security requires you to interpret and forecast a huge quantity of financial data. Ratio analysis provides a framework for doing this in an organized and systematic manner. By converting the financial statement data into ratios, we standardize it in a way that identifies basic relationships. For instance, margin analysis reveals how much profit a firm keeps from each dollar of revenue it receives and turnover analysis reveals the amount of assets needed to generate each dollar of revenue. It is extremely important that you learn to identify a firm's performance in terms of the financial ratios presented here. This is the language that analysts and management use to discuss a company's performance, and we will use this language to construct forecasts of the future. Ratio analysis is traditionally applied to historical data to evaluate past performance, but we will also use it to evaluate the plausibility of our forecasted future financial statements.

5.2 TIME-SERIES AND CROSS-SECTIONS

Ratio analysis involves comparing individual ratios with their levels in prior years and their levels in other firms. Comparing a firm's ratios to their levels in prior years is called "time-series analysis." Time-series analysis identifies changes in financial performance and helps to detect the underlying cause. It also helps you to see whether the firm's most recent performance is unusual, in which case it shouldn't be expected to recur in the future, or whether it is just one in a series of very similar outcomes. If you have a flair for quantitative analysis, you might be tempted to estimate a complicated time-series model on a firm's past ratios in order to predict their future values. But we don't recommend this. As a general rule, financial ratios are not amenable to mechanical modeling techniques. Instead, it is more important that you evaluate changes in ratios in the context of changes in the underlying business operations and strategies of the underlying company. eVal provides you with five years of historical data, which is about as far back as you should ever need to go in your time-series analysis. In addition, the Ratio Analysis

Graphs worksheet displays time trends in all the major ratios computed on the Ratio Analysis worksheet.

Comparing a firm's ratios with their levels in other firms is called "cross-sectional analysis." If management has done a consistently bad job, then this will not be readily apparent in a time-series analysis, but it will be revealed by a cross-sectional ratio analysis with the firm's competitors. Does the company command a premium margin on its products? Is it the most efficient producer in its industry? Is it gaining market share from a rival firm? These are the types of questions that you can answer only by comparing a firm's financial ratios with those of another firm or an industry average. It isn't always easy, but you should try to triangulate a firm's ratios with its business strategy. If the firm is attempting to differentiate its product, it should enjoy a higher gross margin than its competitors. If a firm is attempting to be a cost leader, it should have lower margins but a higher asset turnover than its competitors.

You can conduct cross-sectional analysis in eVal by loading one or more competitor companies into eVal, and then comparing ratios across companies. You can also load in the industry or sector average. To see a list of competitors in the firm's industry, first sort the companies on the Data Center sheet by industry using the button at the top of the sheet, then scroll to the industry you are looking for. Double click on any industry code to load the industry averages into eVal, or double click on a specific ticker to load a competitor's financial statements into eVal.

If you don't have any idea who a firm's closest competitors are, and the list of firms in the industry on the Data Center sheet is too long to be useful, then you might get some help from Hoover's Online, which gives a short list of the firm's top competitors. Alternatively, in the proxy statement the firm is required to graph its stock's performance relative to its "peers." The firm gets to pick its peers, and there is evidence that management does this opportunistically to make themselves look better, but this still might help to identify some good comparison companies. Hit the link labeled All Filings on the Data Center sheet to find the proxy statement.

You may be forced to use an external source for industry averages if the data in eVal isn't sufficiently current. A good external source for industry or sector averages is Multex, but there are some disadvantages to using an external source of industry data. First, the external services are unlikely to use the same comprehensive framework that is used by eVal and they may define the ratios using different formulas (more on this below). Second, the firms grouped into an "industry" may not be particularly comparable, and it is sometimes difficult to determine which firms are included in the industry definition.

Ratios Tend to Mean-Revert

From a valuation perspective, the main reason we want to study the historical performance of a firm's financial ratios is to guide us in forecasting the future values of these ratios. To this end, you should remember a common theme in the evolution of financial ratios over time—they tend to mean-revert. This means that if they are unusually high they tend to come down and if they are unusually low they tend to come up. For example, firms that experience an extremely high or extremely low net profit margin (net income over sales) in a given year probably had something unusual happen—a windfall gain on the sale of an asset, a write-off of inventory, a surprisingly successful advertising campaign, or an embarrassing product recall, to list just a few possibilities. In these cases it is unlikely that the extremely high or extremely low profit margin will persist into the future because the unusual event that happened once is unlikely to happen again.

 We don't want to oversell the power of mean-reversion. It is an observable tendency for many different ratios in a large sample of firms, but there are many exceptions. And, as we discuss below, how quickly and how completely a ratio mean-reverts varies greatly by the ratio, and varies greatly across firms.

5.3 SOME CAVEATS

Despite their usefulness, ratios are also frequently misunderstood and abused, so we start with some important caveats regarding ratio analysis.

There Is No "Correct" Way to Compute Many Ratios

Many people assign the same name to ratios that are computed quite differently. Consider the Return on Assets (ROA) ratio. The numerator (income) is sometimes computed on a before-tax basis and sometimes computed on an after-tax basis. If it is computed on an after-tax basis, either net income or net income adjusted for the after-tax interest cost may be used. The numerator may or may not include any non-recurring and/or non-operating items for the period. The denominator (assets) usually represents total assets, but is sometimes measured as net operating assets (in which case the ratio is sometimes referred to as the Return on Net Operating Assets). The key point here is that there are no standards such as GAAP governing the computation of ratios. Thus, when interpreting a ratio, you should make sure you understand how it was computed.

Ratios Do Not Provide Answers, They Just Tell You Where to Look for Answers

It is common to hear of rules of thumb that attach certain interpretations to ratios falling in certain ranges. For example, a firm with an Interest Coverage ratio less than 2 is often alleged to be financially distressed, or a firm with an ROA less than the yield on U.S. treasuries is labeled a "dog." Unfortunately, financial analysis is not that simple. There are many reasons why ratios can have unusual values, from accounting distortions to subtle differences in the way a firm does business. Ratio analysis guides you in your search for answers, but ratios themselves rarely provide the answers.

Managers Know that Investors Use Ratios

Managers are well aware that investors rely on ratios to summarize their firm's financial performance. Hence, they can and do use their discretion over accounting, operating, investing, and financing decisions to make their key ratios look more appealing. A common example is the use of operating leases and other off-balance-sheet financing techniques to reduce leverage ratios. It is therefore important to anticipate and undo the effects of any managerial "window dressing" of your firm's key financial ratios.

5.4 A FRAMEWORK FOR RATIO ANALYSIS

With the previous caveats in mind, we will now describe how to conduct a comprehensive ratio analysis of a firm's financial performance. We encourage you to follow along by working through the ratio analysis of Kohl's, which is the default company in eVal. If you haven't heard of Kohl's before, they are a department store chain located primarily in the Midwest and Midatlantic. They target middle-income families with a low-cost strategy. Target Stores (ticker symbol TGT) is one of Kohl's chief competitors, so our ratio analysis will compare Kohl's with Target and with the Retail Department Stores industry as a whole (industry code MG731). Our analysis is based on financial statement data through fiscal 2001, which ended on February 2, 2002, for Kohl's. A pdf of Kohl's fiscal 2001 10-K filing is provided in the eVal2 Programs Folder.

The results from the ratio analysis are displayed on the Ratio Analysis worksheet. You will find it helpful to display Excel's formula bar so that you can see how the ratios in each cell have been computed. The formula bar can be displayed by selecting the Formula Bar menu item from the View menu in eVal. You may also want to load Target Stores into eVal and then print out the Ratio Analysis sheet to compare with Kohl's.

Ratio analysis begins with the two pillars of firm value: *growth* and *profitability*. Profitability measures the return that a firm is generating on its invested capital. Growth measures changes in the scale of operations on which the firm is able to generate the profitability. Ideally, we would like to invest in a firm that can simultaneously achieve high growth and high profitability. Our ratio analysis starts with summary measures of each. We then examine the components of each in increasing detail, attempting to isolate the key drivers for the business and identify the cause of any unusual performance.

5.5 GROWTH

The analysis of growth is relatively straightforward. Growth rates are commonly reported for a variety of performance metrics, including sales, earnings, and cash flows. As will be stressed in the discussion of forecasting sales, the *growth in sales* is the key long-term driver of growth in all other metrics. It is difficult to sustain growth rates above the average growth rate in the overall economy for long periods of time. Indeed, if a firm is able to grow faster than the world economy forever, it will eventually take over the world. Thus, one useful reality check on growth rate assumptions is to make sure that your assumed sales growth in the distant future—called your terminal growth rate—is no greater than the anticipated growth rate in the economy as a whole. Another useful way to evaluate the reasonableness of your growth assumptions is to evaluate the feasibility of the projected levels of sales toward the end of your forecast horizon. Are the forecasted sales consistent with plausible assumptions about overall market growth and relative market share? For example, Home Depot has been growing sales at about 25 percent per year for the past few years. But if you forecasted that this growth rate would continue for the next 20 years, Home Depot sales would eventually exceed $4 trillion, more than one-third of the U.S. Gross Domestic Product. That's a lot of do-it-yourself home improvements! Growth rate information is provided in the first part of the Ratio Analysis sheet.

Growth rates in assets, common equity, and earnings are closely related to the growth rates in sales. In fact, when sales growth and profitability reach a steady state, the growth rates in all key performance metrics quickly converge to the steady-state sales growth rate. During years when sales growth and profitability are fluctuating, however, the growth rates in the other performance metrics will generally differ from the growth rate in sales. The intuition behind these differences is quite straightforward, and we will work through the other growth metrics in the order that they appear in the Ratio Analysis worksheet. *Asset growth* will differ from sales growth when a firm's level of assets that is required to generate a given level of sales is also changing. *Common equity growth* will differ from sales growth because of changes in both the amount of assets and the amount of debt that is used to finance the assets that generate the sales. *Earnings growth* will differ from sales growth because of changes in the firm's profit margin. Finally, *free cash flow growth* will differ from sales growth because of changes in the profit margin, and the cash investment required to support the asset growth. Note that as we work our way down from asset growth to free cash flow growth, the number of complicating factors increases. Thus, in the short run, asset growth is usually the closest to sales growth, while free cash flow growth is usually the furthest from sales growth.

The final growth ratio that we report is the *sustainable growth rate*. This ratio is computed as

$$\text{Sustainable Growth Rate} = \text{Return on Equity} \times (1 - \text{Dividend Payout Ratio})$$

Given its current level of profitability and dividend policy, the sustainable growth rate is the maximum rate at which a firm can grow without additional external financing. If a firm's forecasted sales growth rate exceeds its sustainable growth rate, be sure you understand how the additional growth will be financed. One possibility is through increased future profitability. However, if the increased profitability is not achieved, then the growth plans may be curtailed. Alternatively, the additional growth may be financed externally through the issuance of debt and equity. This also introduces uncertainty, because advance planning is required to raise external financing, and capital markets must be receptive to the firm's growth plans. A final option is for the firm to cut its dividend payout ratio; however, given that the dividend payout ratio is usually close to zero in growth firms, this final option is often not available.

Analyzing Kohl's Growth

Turning to eVal, you will note that Kohl's growth in assets and common equity is much more volatile than its growth in sales, for the reasons we just discussed. Note also that growth in earnings exceeds sales growth in every period. This occurs because Kohl's has improved its margins in every period, as we will see more directly when we examine their profitability statistics. If a growth rate is shown as #NA, as is the case for Free Cash Flow to Investors for Kohl's, this means that the value of the underlying series is negative at the beginning of the period, so a growth rate is not defined.

If you load the industry average for Retail Department Stores (ticker = MG731) into eVal you will see that annual sales growth has been volatile the past few years. Most of this volatility, however, is due to changing the number of companies included in the average—total industry sales growth has been much more stable. Within this industry, Kohl's has grown very fast, with annual sales growth ranging between 20 percent and 35 percent. This rate of growth is considerably faster than Target Stores (TGT), which has experienced annual sales growth of between 8 percent and 10 percent over the past five years. However, Target is much bigger than Kohl's, with annual sales in fiscal 2001 of $39 billion, as compared to Kohl's annual sales of $7.5 billion. Kohl's is clearly in a phase of rapid expansion, increasing its number of stores by 19 percent in fiscal 2001 while Target is closer to a steady state, increasing its number of stores only 5 percent over the same period (numbers of stores can be found in the MD&A of each company's Form 10-K filing).

5.6 PROFITABILITY

While the analysis of growth is relatively straightforward, the analysis of profitability has an endless number of nuances. The starting point for the analysis of profitability, and the ultimate ending point, is the *return on equity,* computed as

$$\text{Return on Equity (ROE)} = \frac{\text{Net Income}}{\text{Average Common Equity}}$$

ROE is the accounting measure of the rate of return that the firm has provided to its common stockholders. It represents the amount of profit generated per dollar of book value of common equity. It is analogous to the interest rate that is generated by a fixed income investment. However, accounting rates of return are complicated by two factors. First, the income-generating process for a firm is much more complicated than for a fixed income security. Second, as discussed in Chapter 4, GAAP accounting does not recognize many economic assets and liabilities and so does not perfectly capture the creation or depletion of wealth. Consequently, common equity and net income are both distorted, causing ROE to provide a distorted measure of true economic performance.

Because ROE is the premier measure of a firm's performance, it will be the focus of our financial analysis of the past, and it will be one of the major diagnostics of our forecasts of the future. In the remainder of this chapter, we will discuss some of the general properties of ROE, we will decompose ROE into its more fundamental drivers, and we will discuss the meaning and interpretation of each of these more fundamental building blocks.

Benchmarking the Return on Equity

ROE is one of the few ratios in whose application it makes sense to make comparisons with a well-defined benchmark. If you were considering investing in a fixed income investment, you would compare its interest rate with similar fixed income investments. Similarly, to evaluate how well management generates a return on its invested capital, you can compare the firm's ROE with the ROE of similar firms. Other things equal, the higher a firm's ROE, the greater the return generated per dollar of equity invested in the firm. Moreover, to value a firm you are required to estimate the firm's cost of equity capital. Loosely speaking, the cost of equity capital represents the expected return that an equity investment must generate before it looks attractive relative to similar equity investments. Just as you would rather invest in a fixed income investment with an interest rate higher than the "market" rate, you would rather invest in a firm with an ROE that is higher than its cost of capital. Thus, the cost of equity capital is a natural benchmark for a firm's ROE. Indeed, this is the logic behind some much-hyped performance measurement systems, such as Stern Stewart's EVA. Historically, the cost of equity capital has been about 10–12 percent for the average firm in the U.S. economy, so this is a crude benchmark you can use to assess a firm's ROE. Unfortunately, there are two key drawbacks with such comparisons. First, it is difficult to say with any certainty what a particular firm's cost of equity capital really is. Second, as we have mentioned before, the vagaries of GAAP accounting rarely result in measures of net income and common equity that correspond with their economic counterparts. So, to make these constructs more meaningful, we need to do more work.

Consider our working example, Kohl's. The Ratio Analysis sheet shows that their ROE has been 18–19 percent for the past few years. This compares favorably to the 12 percent average in the retail department store industry. Below we will explore how Kohl's has managed to beat the industry average by so much.

As shown above, ROE is computed by dividing net income for the period by the average book value of common equity that was used to generate the net income. Ideally, we would like to use a time-weighted average of the equity that was available during the year. But we generally get to see balance sheets only for the last day of each fiscal period, so we follow the common convention of dividing net income by the simple average of the beginning and ending balances of common equity. Because of this, the ratio can be distorted when there have been large changes in common equity near the beginning or the end of the year. For example, if a firm doubled its common equity on the second day of the fiscal year, the average common equity calculation would understate the true magnitude of the equity base that was available during the year, leading to an overstatement of ROE. This same concern arises any time we compute a ratio that compares flow variables (amounts generated over the course of the year) with stock variables (cumulative amounts present on the first or last day of the year).

Mean-Reversion in ROE

We stated earlier that many measures of financial performance tend to mean-revert, and ROE is no exception. Figure 5.1 shows the mean-reversion in return on equity for the entire sample of publicly traded firms between 1951 and 2001. We sort the firms into five groups in year 0 from lowest to highest ROE and then we plot the median ROE for each of these groups over the next 10 years. As the plot shows, the highest groups move down over time and the lowest groups move up over time, consistent with the notion of mean-reversion.

There are a few other observations to take away from Figure 5.1. First, the drastic improvement in the lowest ROE group in year 1 is a bit misleading (note that the actual values in years 0 and 1 are technically off the chart at −.50 and −.44, respectively). If the firm goes bankrupt it drops out of the sample, leaving only those firms that improved their performance enough to stay alive, and hence, remain on the graph. Even with this selection bias, it takes this bottom group six years to get back to zero ROE. So they mean-revert, but very slowly. Second, while the top two ROE groups decline and the bottom two groups improve, at no time do the lines completely converge. Even after 10 years the highest group has an ROE of almost 13 percent and the lowest group has an ROE of just over 4 percent. While mean-reversion has definitely brought the two groups closer together, it has not completely eliminated the disparity in ROE.

Why does ROE tend to mean-revert? The short answer is competition. If a firm enjoys a high return on equity, this catches the attention of other firms. Existing rivals undercut the firm's prices and new firms enter the market. As the firm responds to these competitive threats with a price cut of its own, its profitability suffers, driving down the ROE. Why is the mean-reversion in ROE less than complete? For reasons we discussed in Chapter 3, many firms enjoy imperfect competition and are therefore partially shielded from competitive forces. In addition, accounting distortions can generate long-term disparity in ROE across firms. Firms in the pharmaceutical industry report among the economy's highest ROEs, but this is partly because their most prominent economic asset—the intangibles created by their recent past R&D expenditures—is expensed immediately. Because an asset is not recorded as part of common equity, in steady state the ROE is biased upward.

It is reasonable to expect that some of the amounts on the income statement are more persistent than others. For this reason we also compute *return on equity before non-recurring items*. The idea is to exclude from the numerator items that are likely to completely disappear in subsequent years, thus providing a better indication of a firm's long-run sustainable ROE. We expect that ROE before non-recurring items will mean-revert more slowly than the regular ROE. Non-recurring items are most commonly found in the extraordinary items and discontinued operations, other income, and non-operating income line items on the income statement. Thus, eVal excludes these line items from the definition of net income used to compute ROE before non-recurring items. Non-operating income is a pre-tax item

FIGURE 5.1

Mean-Reversion in Return on Equity

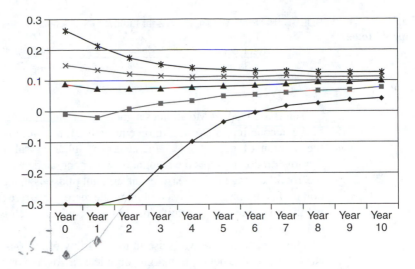

on the income statement, so it must be tax-adjusted before adding it back to net income. eVal does this by using the effective tax rate for the year. The resulting measure is as follows:

$$\text{Return on Equity before Non-Recurring Items} =$$

$$\frac{\text{Net Income} - \text{Non-Recurring Items (After Tax)}}{\text{Average Common Equity}}$$

where Non-recurring items (after tax) = Ext. items & disc. ops. + Other income (loss) + $(1 - \text{tx}) \times$ [Non-operating income (loss)], and tx = Effective tax rate.

You should remember that while eVal mechanically spits out this measure of ROE before non-recurring items, it is only a general guide, and you should engage in more detailed analysis in order to classify items as recurring or non-recurring. For example, the "other income" line item sometimes includes equity earnings, which may well be recurring. And in the case of Kohl's, examining the actual financial statements in their Form 10-K reveals that the "other income" line item is interest income, which will recur as long as Kohl's keeps the associated investments, so you probably shouldn't exclude it. Also, non-recurring items may be buried in other line items on the income statement, such as the effects of a LIFO inventory liquidation, which will be hidden in cost of goods sold (but can be recovered from the financial statement footnotes).

We will have much to say about how to use ROE as a performance measure in the remainder of this chapter. In the following sections we will decompose ROE into a few major drivers and discuss the insights that each component offers. We will also discuss each component's tendency to mean-revert.

Decomposing ROE—The Basic Dupont Model

It is very useful to decompose ROE into a few fundamental drivers of profitability. The Basic Dupont Model, pioneered by management at a predecessor of the Dupont Chemical Company, factors ROE into three components, as shown in Figure 5.2.

FIGURE 5.2
Basic Dupont Model

$$\text{ROE} = \text{Net Profit Margin} \times \text{Asset Turnover} \times \text{Total Leverage}$$

$$= \frac{\text{Net Income}}{\text{Sales}} \times \frac{\text{Sales}}{\text{Average Total Assets}} \times \frac{\text{Average Total Assets}}{\text{Average Common Equity}}$$

The Basic Dupont Model does a good job at highlighting the three key drivers of the accounting rate of return on equity. First, the Net Profit Margin measures the amount of net income generated per dollar of sales. Second, the Asset Turnover ratio measures the amount of sales generated per dollar of assets. Third, the Total Leverage ratio measures the amount of assets that can be supported by a dollar of common equity. By combining the three, we arrive back at the amount of net income generated per dollar of common equity, which is just our accounting rate of return on equity.

The Dupont breakdown is useful for a variety of reasons. First, if a firm can't earn a respectable net profit margin, or at least a positive one, then it doesn't matter how efficiently it operates its assets or how much leverage it applies. The first order of business at any hotdog stand is to sell the hotdogs for more than the cost of the meat and buns. The net profit margin extends this intuition all the way to the bottom line of the income statement—how much of each sales dollar remains after *all* expenses are deducted. Second, assuming the firm is making a net profit, the trick is to do so with the minimum investment in assets. If selling hotdogs requires an elaborate kiosk, or a fleet of home-delivery trucks, then the profit made might not be sufficient to justify the investment. Fortunately for the hotdog business, most stands run a large volume past a relatively inexpensive investment in assets; hence, the asset turnover is great.

The first two components of the Basic Dupont Model capture the operations of the business. How does the firm use its assets to make sales, and how profitably can it convert the sales into net income? These two components tend to trade off against one another; if you multiply them together, you get Net Income/Average Total Assets, labeled the *return on assets* (but beware of this term; it gets applied to many different ratios). We can characterize different firms and industries by the different trade-offs that are required between the margin and turnover. Capital-intensive industries, such as construction and heavy equipment manufacturing, have low turnovers and must therefore charge higher margins to get a competitive return on assets. On the other end of the spectrum, discount retailers and fast food chains generally have high turnover and therefore competition can drive their competitive margins relatively low. Within industries, we can also characterize firms based on the different margin and turnover trade-offs that they make. Firms that choose a cost leadership strategy, producing at the lowest possible cost and selling in large quantities, tend to have low margins and high turnover. On the other hand, firms that choose a product differentiation strategy, producing a premium product and selling in smaller quantities, tend to have higher margins and lower turnover.

As an example, consider the net profit margin and asset turnover of Wal-Mart and May Department Stores, as shown in Figure 5.3. For the year ending in January 2002, both Wal-Mart and May had a return on assets of about 8 percent, but

FIGURE 5.3
Trade-Off between Margin and Turnover

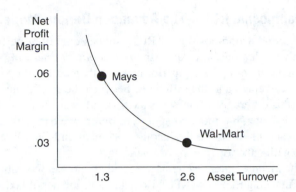

the route that they got there was very different. In retailing, Wal-Mart would be classified as a cost leader, with low margins and high turnover, while May Department Stores would be classified as a product differentiator, with relatively higher margins and lower turnovers. While both firms would like to have a high margin *and* a high turnover, in practice this is very hard to do. If Wal-Mart were to raise its prices in order to improve its margin, its sales volume would probably suffer, driving down its asset turnover. And if May were to carry lower quantities of less expensive inventory in an effort in improve its asset turnover, its customers would probably be unwilling to pay its higher margins. The very nature of each firm's strategy dictates where they will be on the margin versus turnover trade-off.

The trade-off between margins and turnovers plays out in a number of different business decisions. Putting inventory on sale lowers the profit margin but improves the asset turnover (assuming, of course, that the sale causes a buying frenzy among customers). Renting equipment rather than buying it improves the asset turnover but lowers the profit margin. Aging wine longer improves the quality and allows the winemaker to charge a greater margin, but necessarily lowers the asset turnover.

The first two terms in the Basic Dupont Model determine the firm's return on total assets. The return on equity can be made larger than the return on assets by leveraging the assets. This effect is captured by the third factor in the Basic Dupont Model, Total Leverage. Imagine a firm whose assets are financed by a small amount of equity and a large amount of liabilities. The small equity base claims the entire return on assets and will therefore enjoy a very high return on equity.

Management has lots of control over the firm's leverage, so why don't all firms increase their ROE simply by borrowing more money? Ignoring for a moment the added risk that additional leverage brings, the more basic answer is that the additional debt comes with additional interest, and the interest expense lowers net income and therefore lowers the Net Profit Margin. Thus, as Total Leverage increases, the Net Profit Margin decreases. Which effect dominates depends on whether the interest rate on the borrowed money is less than the pre-interest return that the firm earns with the borrowed money. This last effect is a weakness of the Basic Dupont Model; it doesn't cleanly separate operating decisions from financing decisions. The next decomposition of ROE does a better job of distinguishing between the two decisions.

Decomposing ROE—The Advanced Dupont Model

The second decomposition of ROE isolates operating performance much more cleanly, with a measure called the *return on net operating assets (RNOA)*. This core measure of operating performance is then adjusted up or down based on the firm's Leverage and the difference between the RNOA and the after-tax cost of debt (this difference is known as the Spread) to arrive at the ROE. This decomposition is better, but more complicated. Before we can present it, we need to associate each line item on the income statement and each line item on the balance sheet with either operations or financing.

The income statement items are divided into Net Operating Income (NOI) and Net Financing Expense (NFE). Both amounts are net of tax, so that Net Income = NOI − NFE. The tax rate used is not arbitrary; it is the effective tax rate for the period, defined as Income Taxes/Earnings before Taxes. The balance sheet items are divided into Net Operating Assets (NOA) and Net Financial Obligations (NFO), so that Common Equity = NOA − NFO. Obviously there are many different ways we can sort line items into either operations or financing, and there will be some ambiguous items, but the general goal is to isolate the effects of operating decisions from financing decisions. The most important thing is to be consistent between the classifications on the income statement and classifications on the balance sheet. It would be wrong, for instance, to classify the interest on capital leases as part of Net Financing Expense but then classify the capital lease obligation as part of Net Operating Assets. Similarly, it would be wrong to classify the minority interest in earnings as part of Net Operating Income but then classify the minority interest on the balance sheet as part of Net Financial Obligations. Figure 5.4 illustrates how eVal has made these classifications.

Having divided the income statement and balance sheet between operating activities and financing activities, we can now conduct ratio analysis on each piece separately, and then examine how they come together to determine the ROE. The two key ratios are shown at the bottom of Figure 5.4. They are

$$\textbf{Return on Net Operating Assets (RNOA)} =$$
$$\frac{\text{Net Operating Income (NOI)}}{\text{Average Net Operating Assets (NOA)}}$$

and

$$\textbf{Net Borrowing Costs (NBC)} =$$
$$\frac{\text{Net Financing Expense (NFE)}}{\text{Average Net Financial Obligations (NFO)}}$$

where

Net Financing Expense (NFE) = Interest Expense ×
(1 − tx) + Preferred Dividends

Net Operating Income (NOI) = Net Income + Net Financing Expense

Net Financial Obligations (NFO) = Current Debt + Long-Term Debt + Preferred Stock

Net Operating Assets (NOA) = Common Equity + Net Financial Obligations

Effective Tax Rate (tx) = Income Taxes/Earnings before Taxes (EBT)

Each ratio associates the income statement flows with the balance sheet items that caused them. Consider the RNOA. In the numerator, NOI represents the after-tax income earned by the operating assets; equivalently, it is net income with the after-tax financing charges added back. In the denominator, NOA represents the operating assets used to generate the NOI; equivalently, it is common equity with the net financial obligations added back. The result is a measure of the firm's operating performance that abstracts from the manner in which those operations are financed. RNOA is not affected by the firm's level of debt, the interest rate it

FIGURE 5.4

Decomposing the Financial Statements into Operating and Financing Activities

Income Statement

	Sales (Net)
−	Cost of Goods Sold
=	Gross Profit
−	R&D Expense
−	SG&A Expense
=	EBITDA
−	Depreciation & Amortization
=	EBIT
−	Interest Expense
+	Non-Operating Income (Loss)
=	EBT
−	Income Taxes
−	Minority Interest in Earnings
+	Other Income (Loss)
=	Net Income before Ext. Items
−	Ext. Items & Disc. Ops.
−	Preferred Dividends
=	Net Income (available to common)

Balance Sheet

	Operating Cash and Market. Sec.
+	Receivables
+	Inventories
+	Other Current Assets
=	Total Current Assets
+	PP&E (Net)
+	Investments
+	Intangibles
+	Other Assets
=	Total Assets
	Current Debt
+	Accounts Payable
+	Income Taxes Payable
+	Other Current Liabilities
=	Total Current Liabilities
+	Long-Term Debt
+	Other Liabilities
+	Deferred Taxes
+	Minority Interest
=	Total Liabilities
	Preferred Stock
	Paid in Common Capital (Net)
+	Retained Earnings
=	Total Common Equity

Net Operating Income (NOI) =

	(EBIT + Non-Operating Income)*(1− tx)
−	Minority Interest in Earnings
+	Other Income (Loss)
−	Ext. Items and Disc. Ops.

Net Financing Expense (NFE) =

	Interest Expense*(1− tx)
+	Preferred Dividends

where the effective tax rate (tx) = Income Taxes/EBT

Net Income = NOI − NFE

Net Operating Assets (NOA) =

	Total Assets
−	Accounts Payable
−	Income Taxes Payable
−	Other Current Liabilities
−	Other Liabilities
−	Deferred Taxes
−	Minority Interest

Net Financial Obligations (NFO) =

	Current Debt
+	Long-Term Debt
+	Preferred Stock

Common Equity = NOA − NFO

Return on Net Operating Assets (RNOA) = $\dfrac{\text{NOI}}{\text{NOA}}$

Net Borrowing Cost (NBC) = $\dfrac{\text{NFE}}{\text{NFO}}$

borrows at, or the tax shield that the interest creates. All these effects are isolated in the net borrowing cost (NBC), which associates the after-tax income statement flows that go to debt and preferred stock providers with the amount of capital they provided.

The absolute interpretation of the RNOA as a performance measure is similar to the interpretation of ROE. The key difference is that the long-term "hurdle rate" for RNOA is the after-tax weighted average cost of capital—a blend of the cost of equity capital and debt capital that we will discuss later in Chapter 9.

A final word of warning regarding RNOA. Many different variants for measuring the numerator and denominator are used in practice. For example, it is not uncommon to use total assets in the denominator, in which case the measure is usually referred to simply as return on assets (ROA). Another common variant measures the numerator before taxes, in which case the measure is usually referred to as the pre-tax ROA. Finally, the term Return on Invested Capital (ROIC) is also frequently used in place of the term RNOA. The bottom line is that when you see a return on "something like assets," you should make sure that you understand how it was computed before attempting to interpret it.

Putting all the pieces together, the Advanced Dupont Model decomposes ROE as

$$\textbf{ROE} = \textbf{RNOA} + \textbf{Leverage} \times \textbf{Spread}$$

where

$$\textbf{Leverage} = \frac{\text{Average NFO}}{\text{Average Common Equity}}$$

$$\textbf{Spread} = \text{RNOA} - \text{NBC}$$

and the other terms are as defined earlier.

Note that Leverage in this decomposition differs from the Total Leverage definition in the Basic Dupont Model, as it excludes operating liabilities. This model describes ROE as RNOA plus an adjustment for the amount of Leverage the firm employs times the "Spread" between RNOA and NBC.

To interpret this relation, first recall that RNOA measures a firm's operating performance. ROE, on the other hand, measures the return to the common equity holders after satisfying the claims of all the other capital providers that are funding the firm's operations. The common equity holders are the residual claimants on any operating earnings that remain after satisfying these other capital providers. Thus, if a firm's RNOA exceeds its net borrowing costs (NBC), then the ROE will exceed the RNOA because the common equity holders get more than a proportionate share in the net operating income. The extent to which ROE exceeds RNOA depends on the "Spread" between RNOA and the NBC, and the amount of Leverage the firm applies.

A simple illustration is a bank that borrows funds at one rate and lends at another (they hope higher) rate. The bank's RNOA is given by its lending rate. The ROE generated for the bank's owners depends on its borrowing rate relative to its lending rate (its spread) and the proportion of its lending that is funded by the bank's own debt. For example, if a bank lends at 10 percent and funds its lending with $9 of debt for each $1 of equity, and it borrows the debt at 8 percent, then the bank's ROE is given by

$$\text{ROE} = 10\% + \frac{9}{1}(10\% - 8\%) = 28\%$$

But leverage does not always increase ROE relative to RNOA. If a firm has a negative spread, then additional leverage reduces ROE relative to RNOA. For example, assume that the bank in our example can lend only at 6 percent. In this case we have

$$\text{ROE} = 6\% + \frac{9}{1}(6\% - 8\%) = -12\%$$

Thus, higher leverage increases ROE when RNOA is greater than the cost of non-equity financing and reduces ROE when RNOA is less than the cost of non-equity financing. In other words, additional leverage makes the good times really good and the bad times really bad. This is just another way of saying that additional leverage increases the risk of the returns to common equity holders.

To complete the Advanced Dupont Model, we can decompose RNOA into the net operating margin and the net operating asset turnover, much like we did in the Basic Dupont Model:

$$\text{RNOA} = \text{Net Operating Margin} \times \text{Net Operating Asset Turnover}$$

where

$$\textbf{Net Operating Margin} = \frac{\text{Net Operating Income}}{\text{Sales}}$$

$$\textbf{Net Operating Asset Turnover} = \frac{\text{Sales}}{\text{Average Net Operating Assets}}$$

Thus, RNOA is increasing in both the margin that a firm generates on a sale and the rate that the firm turns over the assets generating that sale, just as in the Basic Dupont Model. The difference between the two models is that the margin and turnover measures are based on "cleaner" measures of operating activities in the advanced model, and this has some important consequences. First, the net operating margin isn't polluted by interest expense or preferred dividends, as in the Basic Dupont Model. Second, the effect of operating liabilities is very different between the two models. In the basic model operating liabilities are part of the Total Leverage ratio, whereas in the advanced model they are netted against the total assets in the computation of net operating assets (that is, they reduce the net operating asset balance). If a firm can delay its payment of operating liabilities, this shows up in the basic model as increased Total Leverage, whereas it shows up in the advanced model as an increased net operating asset turnover. Insofar as delaying payment of operating liabilities is an operating decision, the advanced model treats the effect of this decision more appropriately. Further, recall that frequently there is interplay between the margin and the turnover. Extending our example, if the firm delays its payment of operating liabilities to improve its net

FIGURE 5.5
Advanced Dupont Model

Advanced Dupont Model

$$\text{ROE} = \text{RNOA} + \text{Leverage} \times (\text{RNOA} - \text{NBC})$$

$$\frac{\text{NOI}}{\text{NOA}} + \frac{\text{NFO}}{\text{Common Equity}} \times \left(\frac{\text{NOI}}{\text{NOA}} - \frac{\text{NFE}}{\text{NFO}} \right)$$

and $\quad$ RNOA = Net Operating Margin $\times$ Net Operating Asset Turnover

$$\frac{\text{NOI}}{\text{Sales}} \times \frac{\text{Sales}}{\text{NOA}}$$

where ROE is return on common equity, RNOA is return on net operating assets, NBC is net borrowing cost, NOI is net operating income, NOA is net operating assets, NFO is net financial obligations, and NFE is net financing expense, as defined in Figure 5.4.

operating asset turnover, its suppliers may demand slightly higher prices in the future, thus lowering the firm's net operating margin.

Figure 5.5 summarizes the Advanced Dupont Model in all its glory. As you can probably tell, we like this model a lot.

Financial Assets in the Advanced Dupont Model

eVal classifies all cash and marketable securities as part of net operating assets, yet in many cases these are really financial assets that are not directly tied to the operations. The firm needs to maintain some balance of cash for its operating needs but this is rarely more than a few percent of sales. To pick an extreme example, if you load Microsoft into eVal (ticker = MSFT) you will see that in recent years the operating cash and marketable securities line item exceeds 100 percent of sales. Microsoft doesn't need to maintain this much cash for normal operations; rather, they are accumulating financial assets (probably as part of some evil plan to take over the world). How should we deal with these financial assets in our Advanced Dupont Model? Ideally, we would net them against the Net Financial Obligations and we would net the investment income they produce against Net Financial Expense. They aren't really part of operations, so we should shuffle them into financing. eVal doesn't do this for a few reasons. First, we would be hard-pressed to specify for all firms at all times what the right amount of operating cash is, making it almost impossible to isolate the true financial assets. Second, without examining the as-reported financial statements and footnotes, it is impossible to know where the investment income has been included on the income statement, and hence impossible to know where the MediaGeneral standardization process has allocated this income in our data. It could be netted against Interest Expense and therefore included in that line item, it could be included in Non-Operating Income (Loss), or it could be netted against SG&A Expense. As we discussed in Chapter 2, you need to look at the as-reported financial statements and make sure the eVal income statement and balance sheet are in good order. Part of that exercise is making sure that the line item Interest Expense is only the interest outflow on the Current and Long-Term Debt; any interest income should be included in Non-Operating Income (Loss). An early indicator that your financial statements might have a problem in this regard is an extremely low, or even negative, Net Borrowing Cost. For example, if you load Best Buy Co. (ticker = BBY) into eVal you will see that their net Borrowing Cost is less than 1 percent. It isn't the case that Best Buy Co. can really borrow at such a low rate; rather, they have netted some interest revenue against their interest expense.

Decomposing Kohl's ROE

As a final illustration, consider how the Advanced Dupont Model decomposes the ROE of Kohl's. The first thing you notice about Kohl's ROE on the Ratio Analysis sheet in eVal is that it has been relatively constant in the 18–20 percent range in recent years. This stability is largely because of Kohl's RNOA, which has been even more constant, only varying between 14.7 percent and 15.3 percent. Combining the low variation in RNOA with low variation in the Net Borrowing Cost has caused the spread to remain almost constant. Consequently, the little variation in ROE that Kohl's has experienced in the past few years is caused almost exclusively by the minor variation in their leverage ratio; when this dipped in 1999 and 2000, the ROE dipped a bit as well.

Turning our attention to the details of the RNOA ratio, we see that, while the ratio as a whole has remained relatively constant, the net operating margin has been steadily improving and the net operating asset turnover has been steadily declining. Kohl's net operating margin has increased from 5.6 percent in fiscal 1998 to 7.1 percent by fiscal 2001, while at the same time the net operating asset turnover has decreased from 2.7 to 2.2. Each of these trends warrants further investigation.

A cross-sectional comparison between Kohl's and Target yields additional insights. Although Target's ROE is very close to Kohl's, ranging between 18 percent and 20 percent, the way they get there is very different. First of all, Target's RNOA of 11.1 percent in fiscal 2001 is considerably lower than Kohl's RNOA of 15.3 percent. While Target enjoys a slightly faster net operating asset turnover than Kohl's, its net operating margin is much lower, coming in at 4.2 percent in fiscal 2001, as compared to 7.1 percent for Kohl's. Both firms have similar net borrowing costs of 3.7 percent so, before even looking, we can conclude that Target must get back to the same ROE by carrying much more financial leverage than Kohl's. Indeed, Target's average financial leverage has been about 1.0 the past few years while Kohl's has been less than .40.

In the next few sections we drill down into the details of the margin, turnover, and leverage to gain further insight into the economics behind each ratio. By doing so, we hope to understand why Kohl's can generate a higher net operating margin than Target, why their turnover is lower, and why each of these ratios has been changing over time. We will also consider the costs and benefits to Target of employing more financial leverage than Kohl's.

5.7 PROFIT MARGINS

NOI/Sales

The net operating margin represents after-tax operating income divided by sales. In order to understand the drivers of the net margin, we must look at each line item and subtotal as a proportion of sales. Note that the Forecasting Assumptions sheet in eVal expresses many of the income statement line items as a proportion of sales. Rather than repeating this analysis, our ratio analysis focuses on just a few key margins. If the bottom line net operating margin is unusual, then work your way down this list of intermediate margins to identify the underlying line items that are driving this behavior.

The starting point is the *gross margin,* which measures the difference between sales and cost of goods sold as a proportion of sales:

$$\textbf{Gross Margin} = \frac{\text{Sales} - \text{Cost of Goods Sold}}{\text{Sales}}$$

This is the first level of profitability—the mark-up on the product. For each dollar of sales, how much more can the firm charge over the cost of making or buying the product. It is generally all downhill from here, so if a firm can't generate a positive gross margin, there is not much point in looking any further. This is also the ratio to watch if you are worried about increased competition. If the firm is lowering its prices to stay competitive, you will see it here.

The next key margin we report is the *EBITDA margin,* which gives earnings before interest, taxes depreciation, and amortization as a proportion of Sales. Another way to define the numerator is Sales less Cost of Goods Sold, R&D Expense, and SG&A Expense, as shown below:

$$\textbf{EBITDA Margin} =$$
$$\frac{\text{Sales} - \text{Cost of Goods Sold} - \text{R\&D Expense} - \text{SG\&A Expense}}{\text{Sales}}$$

The firm may enjoy a large mark-up on its product, but it could be that the key costs aren't the actual manufacturing and production of the goods. For instance, if you load Pfizer into eVal (ticker = PFE) you will note that their gross margin is more than 80 percent for the past few years. But the real cost to a pharmaceutical company is R&D and SG&A. The actual manufacturing of the drug is a relatively minor component. Consequently, Pfizer's EBITDA margin is between 30 and 40 percent. If you identify this ratio as unusual, you should then go back to the detailed income statement to identify the specific line items that are responsible. Note that this ratio abstracts from the effects of taxes and payments to providers of non-equity capital, which are not usually considered part of the operating activities of the firm.

The *EBIT margin* has subtracted from sales all the expenses except interest and taxes; hence the term "earnings before interest and taxes" describes the numerator. You will note that the only difference between this ratio and the EBITDA margin is the "DA"—depreciation and amortization.

$$\textbf{EBIT Margin} = \frac{\text{Earnings before Interest and Taxes}}{\text{Sales}}$$

As we move down the page from Gross margin to EBIT margin, the relation between sales and profits gets weaker. As sales increase, cost of goods sold will necessarily have to increase—the firm needs to make the goods that it is selling—so the gross margin ratio is relatively stable over time. But an increase in sales does not necessarily mean that R&D expense will increase in proportion to sales, as this is a much more discretionary expenditure. Similarly, depreciation and amortization bear no direct relation to sales. In the long run a firm needs these expenses to generate its sales, but in a given year, there is no reason why they should vary in direct proportion to sales.

The final margin that we report is the *net operating margin before non-recurring items*. This margin starts with net operating income but then adds back any non-recurring expenses, adjusted for their tax consequences (specifically, it adds back tax-adjusted Non-Operating Income, Other Income, and Extraordinary Items and Discontinued Operations). Unusual behavior in this margin that does not show up in the EBIT margin is attributable to taxes or costs of non-equity capital (specifically, tax-adjusted Interest Expense and Preferred Dividends).

$$\textbf{Net Operating Margin before Non-Recurring Items} =$$

$$\frac{\text{Net Operating Income} + \text{Non-Recurring Items (After Taxes)}}{\text{Sales}}$$

Finally, any unusual behavior in the bottom line net operating margin that does not show up in the above margin is due to non-recurring items. You should identify these items and make sure you are confident that they are indeed unusual and unlikely to recur.

Economies of Scale and Operating Risk

Many young and growing firms have negative net operating margins. They all claim that this is a temporary situation and that once they grow past some critical size, they will be hugely profitable. Of course, many of them never achieve this dream and fail, but the ones that succeed often do so because they experience some economies of scale. A typical situation might be a firm with a positive gross margin but a negative EBITDA margin, caused mainly by its SG&A expense. If the SG&A expense is composed of mostly fixed costs, then as sales grow, the SG&A expense does not increase proportionately, and eventually the EBITDA margin becomes positive. Be on the lookout for economies of scale as you study a company's margins. If sales are growing and the margins are steadily improving, this is a sign that the firm is exploiting economies of scale. Alternatively, if a firm claims that it will not be profitable until it grows to some larger size, but its past sales growth has not generated any significant improvement in its margin, then you should be suspicious. The company's claims of great margins in the future may be nothing more than wishful thinking.

While a cost structure with a large fixed cost component helps achieve economies of scale, it also imposes operating risk on the company. If the sales volume is highly variable then in periods of low volume the firm will be stuck with its fixed costs and insufficient revenue to cover them; in periods of high volume it will cover its fixed costs and then enjoy huge margins on all the remaining sales. In other words, the good times are really good and the bad times are really bad. The trade-off between asset turnover and profit margin we discussed earlier frequently has a direct impact on the operating risk of a company. As an example, compare a firm's decision to rent or own its equipment. Renting an asset tends to lower the profit margin but raise the asset turnover, relative to owning the asset. But renting the asset also makes the cost much easier to vary with revenue when compared to the fixed depreciation expense associated with asset ownership. So renting might be considered the lower operating risk decision. Managers often attempt to lower their operating risk by arranging their production to make all possible costs variable. However, they frequently find that there is little profit left over when they do this. No risk often means no reward.

Analyzing Kohl's Margins

In the previous section we noted that Kohl's net operating margin has increased steadily over the past few years. By examining the details we see that the gross margin has increased slightly each period, adding up to about 1 percent between fiscal 1997 and fiscal 2001. But this is only part of the story, because the EBITDA margin increased by about 3 percent over the same period. By toggling to the Forecasting Assumptions worksheet we see that the other main force behind this improvement is a decline in the ratio of SG&A to Sales. Kohl's has been growing rapidly in the past few years and it would appear that they are enjoying some economies of scale. Another minor contribution to the net operating margin comes from a declining effective tax rate (as seen on the Forecasting Assumptions sheet). If you get Kohl's 10-K for fiscal 2001 and find the tax footnote way in the back of the report, you will see that this is because of a decline in the state income tax rate in the states where Kohl's operates.

Comparing Kohl's with Target Stores, we see that Kohl's enjoys a higher gross margin and an even higher EBITDA margin than Target. This might reflect better cost management on the part of Kohl's, or it might reflect a subtle difference in the strategy between the two stores. Kohl's, while pursuing a low-cost strategy, also markets some high-margin brands such as Levi's and Nike that are not typically seen in Target and other discount retailers. Putting it all together, Kohl's has an enviable set of margins; they are better than their closest competitor and have been steadily increasing over time.

5.8 TURNOVER RATIOS

We now turn our attention to the amount of assets the firm requires to generate its sales, known as its turnover ratio. A net operating asset turnover ratio of 2 indicates that $.50 of net operating assets is required to generate $1.00 of sales. We use turnover analysis to examine how the underlying operating asset and liability line items on the balance sheet contribute to the overall net operating asset turnover ratio. The basic approach is to compute a turnover ratio for specific groups of operating assets and operating liabilities. A commonly sited turnover ratio is the *net working capital ratio,* computed as

$$\textbf{Net Working Capital Turnover} = \frac{\text{Sales}}{\text{Average Net Working Capital}}$$

where

Net Working Capital = Current Operating Assets −
Current Operating Liabilities

This ratio indicates how efficiently a firm is managing its working capital accounts. Ideally, a firm would like to generate sales with a minimum investment in working capital. Obviously this presents the firm with trade-offs. It is difficult to minimize the investment in inventory while still presenting the customers with a wide variety of choices and fast delivery. And all firms would like to collect on their sales immediately and pay their accounts payable very slowly, but such actions usually have other undesirable consequences.

It is common to compute individual turnover ratios for the three most important components of working capital—receivables, inventories, and payables—and there are a number of common modifications that are made to these ratios. First, they are often stated in the form of the average number of days that a dollar sits in the account. The relation between an annual turnover ratio and the average days outstanding metric is simply

$$\text{Average Days Outstanding} = 365/\text{Turnover Ratio}$$

For example, if we turn over our receivables 12 times per year, then the average receivable must have a life of approximately 365/12 = 30 days. Using this approach, the average days to collect receivables is given by

$$\textbf{Average Days to Collect Receivables} = 365 \times \frac{\text{Average Receivables}}{\text{Sales}}$$

Similarly, the average inventory holding period is given by

$$\textbf{Average Inventory Holding Period} = 365 \times \frac{\text{Average Inventory}}{\text{Cost of Goods Sold}}$$

Note that we made an additional modification in computing the average inventory holding period; we replaced sales with cost of goods sold. This is because inventories are carried at cost, and so we want a flow variable that measures the cost of inventories consumed during the period. Lastly, the average days to pay payables is computed as:

$$\textbf{Average Days to Pay Payables} = 365 \times \frac{\text{Average Payables}}{\text{Purchases}}$$

where

$$\text{Purchases} = \text{Cost of Goods Sold} + \text{Ending Inventory} - \text{Beginning Inventory}$$

Note here that the denominator is measured using purchases. This represents the amount of payables that were added during the period, measured on a cost basis, and so is directly comparable with the average balance in the payables account in the numerator.

The final turnover ratio that we report is property, plant, and equipment (PP&E) turnover, computed as

$$\textbf{PP\&E Turnover} = \frac{\text{Sales}}{\text{Average Net Property, Plant, and Equipment}}$$

PP&E isn't literally consumed in the sale the same way that inventory is. Nonetheless, it is an asset that is necessary in the production of the sale, albeit tangentially at times. In the short run, Kohl's corporate headquarters could probably blow up and sales in the department stores wouldn't be affected, but in the long run headquarters are probably necessary. We want to know if the firm is using its PP&E efficiently. Does it have idle capacity? Does it invest too heavily in non-producing assets, such as lavish headquarters and Learjets? Comparing the PP&E ratio of the firm with a few of its close competitors can frequently shed light on these questions.

Note that there are additional accounts, such as cash and intangibles, that may also drive unusual turnover. You should identify and understand these accounts. For example, if a firm has engaged in an acquisition involving significant goodwill, this will typically drive the net operating asset turnover down relative to the company's competitors. However, this is not necessarily a bad sign, and competitors may have similar amounts of internally generated goodwill that is not recognized on the balance sheet.

Analyzing Kohl's Turnover

As noted previously, Kohl's net operating asset turnover has been declining steadily over the past few years, almost perfectly off-setting the steady improvement in their net operating margin. A more detailed analysis of Kohl's turnover ratios shows that their working capital turnover ratio has gone from 8 to 6. While they lowered slightly the number of days that inventory is held, and they lengthened the time they take to pay their payables, these positives are overshadowed by the fact that they are taking almost twice as long to collect their receivables. Kohl's has a private label credit card, so one might conclude from this that they have extended the terms they grant to users of their card. While this might be partly true, the MD&A in their most recent 10-K reveals a very different cause for the increase. Prior to fiscal 1999 Kohl's factored their private-label receivables without recourse and, by so doing, could treat them as if they were collected, even though the customer hadn't actually paid the credit card bill. But starting in fiscal 2000 they began selling the receivables with recourse and so now the receivables remain on Kohl's books until collected. Thus, part of the decline in the net operating asset

turnover is a consequence of this change in the accounting for receivables. As we said at the start of the chapter, ratio analysis just tells you where to start looking for answers, it rarely provides the answers itself.

The other contributing factor to the decline in Kohl's net operating assets that our analysis reveals is a declining PP&E turnover ratio. But this too has an obvious answer that may well be wrong and an accounting-based answer that may well be the best explanation. You might be tempted to conclude from the declining PP&E turnover that Kohl's is operating its stores less efficiently. The 2001 annual report shows that the sales per square foot has steadily increased, however, from $261 per square foot in 1996 to $283 per square foot in fiscal 2001. So what gives? The disparity could be caused by an increase in non-store PP&E—fancy headquarters and corporate jets—or it could be something as benign as a change in the use of operating leases. In the Commitments footnote in the 10-K, Kohl's reveals that they use operating leases extensively, with approximately 1 billion dollars worth of present value already committed in non-cancelable operating leases. With such large amounts off the balance sheet, a small increase in the relative mix of company-owned stores versus leased stores could easily account for the decline in the PP&E turnover ratio.

We noted previously that Kohl's has a slightly lower net operating asset turnover than Target Stores (but that the difference was not large enough to offset Kohl's superior net operating margin). Examining the turnover rates of different accounts reveals some serious differences between the two companies. Target's net working capital turnover is almost three times better than Kohl's: They collect receivables faster, pay accounts payable slower, and hold their inventory for a shorter period of time. A likely explanation for Target's superior working capital management is that they are exploiting the bargaining position that comes with being five times bigger than Kohl's. Target can ask the suppliers to hold the inventory until just before it is needed, and they can negotiate more favorable payment terms than Kohl's. But if Kohl's continues to grow at the same breakneck speed, soon they too will be able to demand similar concessions from their suppliers.

5.9 LEVERAGE

In both the Basic and Advanced Dupont decompositions *financial leverage* makes the good times better and the bad times worse. As we analyze the firm's past, we can see how much leverage the firm employed, and whether it amplified superior or inferior operating performance. But leverage has a forward-looking feature that the previous ratios lacked. Leverage increases the riskiness of the expected future cash flows. Firms commit themselves to make fixed payments to creditors, and the common equity holders must ultimately surrender control of the firm to the creditors if these payments cannot be met. The more financial leverage a firm has, the greater the chance that unexpected poor performance will be amplified to the point that the firm cannot pay its creditors. The likelihood of defaulting on amounts owed to creditors is known as *credit risk*. Many of the ratios we discuss in this section form the basis for the debt covenants between the firm and the creditors.

In addition, a firm may have great long-term potential but if it runs into short-term liquidity problems, it may not live to see the long term. For this reason the analysis of credit risk also includes a detailed examination of the firm's ability to meet its obligations in the next year or two. Our Dupont decompositions examined how financial leverage contributes to the level and variability of ROE; now we want to assess the amount of credit risk that the leverage imposes on the claimants of the future cash flows.

In this section we first discuss some measures of a firm's capital structure and short-term liquidity that can be interpreted in isolation, or by comparison to a few similar firms. After examining credit risk variables individually, we will discuss how these and other variables can be combined to make an explicit prediction of the likelihood of default.

Long-Term Capital Structure

A firm's capital structure—its mix of debt and equity—is the primary long-term driver of credit risk. The most common way to represent a firm's capital structure is by its ratio of total debt to total common equity:

$$\textbf{Debt-to-Equity Ratio} = \frac{\text{Current Debt} + \text{Long-Term Debt}}{\text{Total Common Equity}}$$

Note that this is the definition of financial leverage used in the Advanced Dupont Model (with one minor difference: when decomposing the return on *average* equity we need to use the *average* debt to equity ratio but when analyzing the firm's capital structure we use the *ending* debt to equity ratio). In the context of credit analysis, this ratio provides an overall indication of the extent of a firm's long-term credit commitments. Other things equal, higher debt-to-equity implies a higher probability of financial distress. The weakness of this ratio is that it fails to take into account the firm's ability to pay off its creditors. For example, firms with very stable and predictable cash flows, such as utilities and commercial banks, frequently run very high debt-to-equity ratios. This is because they know there is very little risk that they won't be able to meet their debt payments, and so a high debt-to-equity ratio is not necessarily an indication of financial distress for these firms.

Our next ratio is funds from operations to total debt, computed as

$$\text{Funds from Operations to Total Debt} =$$
$$\frac{\text{Funds from Operations}}{\text{Average Current Debt} + \text{Average Long-Term Debt}}$$

Funds from operations represents the amount of working capital that the firm created or destroyed with its operations (funds from operations is computed on the Cash Flow Analysis worksheet in eVal). This measure directly compares the amount of debt with the flow of funds that will be used to service the debt. Thus, this measure overcomes the shortcoming described above for the debt-to-equity ratio. One benchmark for this ratio is that it should be comfortably above the interest rate that the company pays on its debt. Although this benchmark ignores any principal repayments that the firm may be required to make, it is a useful lower bound. A potential shortcoming of this ratio is that working capital can be tied up in illiquid current asset accounts, such as prepayments and inventories. In reality, it will be difficult to pay creditors with these assets. Thus, a common variant of this ratio is the cash from operations to debt ratio. This ratio backs the non-cash working capital accounts out of the numerator to get cash from operations (also computed on the Cash Flow Analysis worksheet in eVal):

$$\text{Cash from Operations to Total Debt} = \frac{\text{Cash from Operations}}{\text{Average Current Debt} + \text{Average Long-Term Debt}}$$

This ratio is a useful check, but you should not interpret it too literally. Growth firms frequently run negative cash from operations as they build working capital in response to sales growth. This growth is not necessarily a bad thing, but we need to make sure that the firm has the necessary plans in place to finance this growth.

Short-Term Liquidity

The above ratios focus on the firm's capital structure to assess the credit risk created by the firm's long-run capital structure decisions. Our final set of ratios focus on short-term liquidity. These ratios provide an indication of the firm's ability to meet its short-term cash commitments as they come due. The first ratio is the current ratio, measured as the ratio of current assets to current liabilities:

$$\textbf{Current Ratio} = \frac{\text{Total Current Assets}}{\text{Total Current Liabilities}}$$

Current assets represent the assets that the firm expects to convert to cash over the next 12 months. Current liabilities represent the obligations that the firm must pay with cash over the next 12 months. Thus a current ratio greater than 1 indicates that the company has enough current assets to meet the demands of the current liabilities. An obvious shortcoming of this measure is that, in the event of financial distress, some of the current assets may not be readily converted into cash at their carrying amounts. If no one is buying the company's inventory then it might not be worth its book value, and you can imagine the difficulty in converting prepaid rent back into cash. An alternative measure of the ability to meet current liabilities is the quick ratio:

$$\textbf{Quick Ratio} = \frac{\text{Cash and Marketable Securities} + \text{Receivables}}{\text{Total Current Liabilities}}$$

This ratio restricts the numerator to cash, marketable securities, and receivables, which are all likely to be converted into cash on short notice at close to their carrying amounts.

The next two ratios are called "interest coverage ratios." These ratios provide an indication of the ability of a firm to cover its interest charges based on its ongoing operating profits. The first ratio uses EBIT (earnings before interest and taxes) in the numerator and interest expense in the denominator, while the second ratio replaces the numerator with EBITDA (earnings before interest, taxes, depreciation, and amortization):

$$\textbf{EBIT Interest Coverage} = \frac{\text{EBIT}}{\text{Interest Expense}}$$

$$\textbf{EBITDA Interest Coverage} = \frac{\text{EBITDA}}{\text{Interest Expense}}$$

The key difference between the ratios is the exclusion of depreciation and amortization expense from the numerator of the second ratio. The rationale for excluding depreciation and amortization is that it represents a non-cash charge and therefore does not reduce the amount of cash available to meet interest payments. On the other hand, a firm must ultimately replace its depreciable assets in order to stay in business, and so it can also be argued that including these charges provides a more meaningful ratio.

Analyzing Kohl's Leverage

In the Advanced Dupont decomposition for Kohl's we noted that the average debt-to-equity ratio of about .4 is much lower than their peer, Target Stores, which has an average debt-to-equity ratio of about 1.0. Because Target has a positive spread between its RNOA and its net borrowing cost, the higher financial leverage increased the ROE. However, this increased ROE is not without cost. Note that Target's Funds from Operations (FFO) to Debt and Cash from Operations (CFO) to Debt are each less than half those of Kohl's. Similarly, Target's current ratio and quick ratio are less than half of Kohl's, as are their interest coverage ratios. In sum, Target is currently enjoying the benefits of financial leverage, but it is also exposed to more risk, having only about half the financial health that Kohl's enjoys. In the next section we will quantify each firm's financial health by estimating the likelihood that each will default on its debt.

5.10 MODELING CREDIT RISK

Predicting the likelihood that a company will default on a loan is one of the most common uses of financial statement analysis. Every junior loan officer at every local bank requires financial statements from a commercial loan applicant and, if the loan is granted, then requires that financial statements be submitted on a regular basis in order to monitor the financial health of the company. The loan contract contains covenants that limit subsequent borrowing or equity distributions by the company and sets up certain financial health tests. If the company fails a health test then the loan is declared to be in technical default and it becomes immediately due and payable in full. The idea is that, if the company starts to look sufficiently sick, the bank can rush back in and grab assets before they are all gone.

Being in technical default on a loan doesn't necessarily mean the firm will fail, or seek bankruptcy protection, but these events are highly correlated. In any case, defaulting on a loan has enormous consequences: legal fees skyrocket, vendors stop granting credit, and customers stop buying goods and services. Regardless of whether the firm can work out the default with its lenders or is forced into liquidation, default is a situation all parties wish to avoid.

Clearly, lenders and company management want to avoid default, but who beyond this cares about estimating the likelihood of default? Bond investors also estimate default probability as an important input into bond rating and bond pricing models. More surprisingly, in certain contexts the default probability is an important input when pricing a firm's equity. If the firm defaults, the value of the equity is approximately zero, so the expected value of the equity is really the probability that it won't default times the value of the equity given that it continues as a going concern. For most firms the probability of default is so low that we ignore this when valuing the equity, but for a firm in financial trouble, the probability of default is a key statistic. You can think of an equity investment in a troubled firm as purchasing an option—the default probability is the likelihood that the option ends up out of the money, in which case the equity holders can abandon their claim on the firm. We often refer to this option as the abandonment option, and we discuss it in more detail in Chapter 12.

Estimating the Likelihood of Default

Broadly speaking, you should approach default forecasting in the same way as any other financial statement analysis topic: Use the past financial statements to get a clear understanding of the company's past financial performance and current financial position, and then forecast how you believe the firm will evolve in the future. But there are a few twists. First, for the purposes of assessing the risk of default, we don't really care how successful a firm is beyond the point where we are confident that it will avoid default. The difference between good financial performance and great financial performance matters when forecasting the cash distributions to equity holders, but makes little difference to the cash distributions that flow to the debt providers. All the debt providers get is the agreed-upon interest and principal payments. Second, we have a very specific notion of what unsuccessful is—failure to make contractual interest and principle payments or a violation of debt covenants.

The long-term capital structure and short-term liquidity ratios discussed earlier give you a qualitative feel for the firm's credit risk. In this section we attempt to attach specific probabilities of default to different levels of these and other ratios. Specifically, at the bottom of eVal's Ratio Analysis worksheet, there are six ratios that have been shown to be predictive of future default. Under each ratio we report the historical frequency that firms with a ratio near this value defaulted on their debt during the subsequent five years. As a benchmark, over the past two decades the ex ante odds that an industrial firm will default during a five-year period is about 5 percent.

Before proceeding with our model of default probability, we want to issue a word of warning. The actual covenants found in a typical loan contract are extremely detailed. They spell out exactly how each ratio will be measured, what line items will be included and excluded over what time periods, and what the consequences are for violating different hurdle rates for each ratio. By comparison, the ratios below are very simplistic. This allows us to describe large-sample relations between different ratios and default probabilities. You should consider the ratios below as a general guide for the types of ratios found in actual debt covenants, knowing that in practice each ratio is custom-made for a particular firm.

Figure 5.6 graphs each of the six ratios we use to build our model of default probability. The distribution of each ratio is computed for the entire sample of public firms between 1980 and 1999, excluding banks, insurance companies, and real estate companies (because their financial characteristics are so different from the majority of firms). For each ratio we sort this data into 10 equal-sized groups, called deciles, and then plot the frequency that firms in each decile defaulted over the next five years.[1] Each figure also shows the cutoffs for each decile just above the axis; for instance, the line between decile 5 and 6 is the median value of the ratio for the entire sample.

Profitability

For the purposes of predicting default, we measure profitability as the return on total assets before extraordinary items: (net income − extraordinary items)/total assets. Regardless of the firm's other financial characteristics, if it is sufficiently profitable then it will generate enough cash each year to pay its creditors. But how much more likely is it for a firm to default on its debt when its profitability for the year is in the top 10 percent of all firms during the past two decades than if this ratio is in the bottom 10 percent? To get a feel for this, consider the top left graph in Figure 5.6. As expected, the graph slopes down—firms with higher levels of profitability are less likely to default on their debt. To quantify this, the graph shows that the median firm over the past two decades has a return on total assets of 2 percent, and an implied default probability of about 4 percent. However, the bottom decile of firms have return on total assets of less than −45 percent and the odds that they will default in the next five years jump to over 8 percent, while the top decile of firms have a return on total assets of 12 percent or more and a default probability of only 2 percent. In other words, it is over four times more likely that a firm in the bottom decile will default than a firm in the top decile.

Leverage

The greater a firm's financial leverage the less cushion available if profits fail to generate the necessary cash flow to pay its creditors. Because some firms have negative equity (and this would mess up our graph), Figure 5.6 plots total

---

[1]The default probabilities associated with different levels of each ratio are taken from Falkenstein, E., and A. Boral, and L. Carty. "Risk Calc™ for Private Companies: Moody's Default Model," Copyright 2000, Moody's Investors Service, Inc. 99 Church St., New York, NY 10007.

FIGURE 5.6
Implied 5-Year Default Probabilities for each Decile of the Ratio

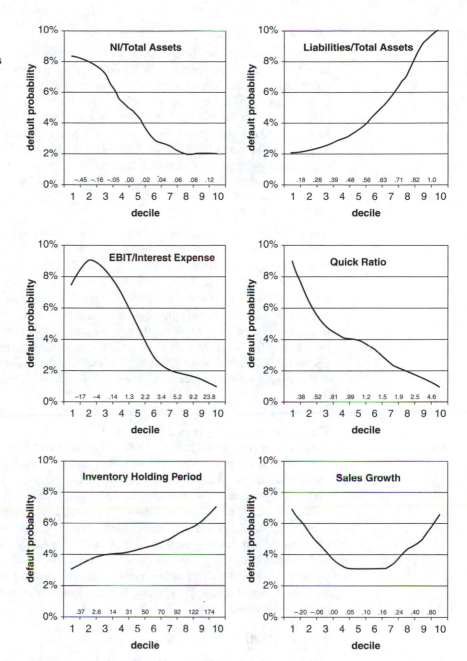

9 cutoffs
10 deciles

liabilities/total assets rather than debt/equity, which is the more traditional measure of leverage. As a firm's leverage increases, the default rate increases steadily, starting at 2 percent for the firms in the lowest decile and increasing to 10 percent for firms in the highest decile.

Liquidity

If you have enough cash, or assets that will soon become cash, you can surely pay your bills, hence the importance of liquidity ratios in credit analysis. As we discussed earlier, it is difficult to pay debt holders with inventory and certain other current assets, so the Quick Ratio (cash, marketable securities, and receivables divided by current liabilities) is the ratio we use to predict default. As Figure 5.6 shows, the Quick Ratio is predictive across the entire distribution, but the slope is steepest for the worst firms, those in the first two deciles. The default probability is 9 percent for firms with a Quick Ratio less than .38 but drops to 5 percent in the third decile, where firms have Quick Ratios between .52 and .81.

Interest Coverage

Interest coverage is typically computed in a very precise and complicated way in most debt covenants. But for our purpose, we simply graph EBIT/interest expense in Figure 5.6. Between the second and sixth decile, the slope of the interest coverage graph is very steep, showing that this ratio does a good job of discriminating winners from losers inside this region. The graph flattens out on the high end because it doesn't really make much difference if you are covering your interest 8 times or 10 times. On the low end the graph actually slopes up, which seems counterintuitive. But for firms with negative EBIT, an increase in interest expense lowers the EBIT/interest ratio, which probably explains the unusual shape of the curve in the low region. As a crude benchmark, the median EBIT/interest ratio is 2.2.

Inventory

The inventory holding period is less predictive than the previous measures, as seen by its modest slope in Figure 5.6. We include it nonetheless because it captures information that is very different from the previous default predictors. Previously we described the inventory holding period as a measure of how efficiently the company manages its inventory. All else equal, a shorter holding period is better. In the context of default prediction, if the holding period is very long then, besides suggesting inefficient inventory management, it may indicate an even more serious problem. It could be that the firm is having trouble selling its inventory and, consequently, may suffer financial distress in the future. Firms in the lowest decile of this ratio are probably service firms that have little or no inventory, so the ratio doesn't really apply to them; as a benchmark, the median inventory holding period is about 50 days.

Sales Growth

Unlike the previous graphs, sales growth has a U-shaped relation with default probability, as seen in the bottom right graph in Figure 5.6. While this makes it more difficult to interpret, we include it because it captures information that is very different from the more traditional ratios. In the lowest deciles, sales are declining (negative sales growth), which is clearly a bad sign. But more curiously, the odds of default are high for firms with the highest sales growth. The intuition is that the set of firms with the most rapidly growing sales includes a greater proportion of firms with unprofitable sales (think of Amazon's sales growth). Further, such rapid sales growth is more likely to be financed by additional borrowing and therefore indicate an increase in the risk of default. As a benchmark, the median annual sales growth for the sample is 10 percent, and this corresponds to the lowest default risk. Sales declines of more than 20 percent or sales growth of more than 80 percent imply twice as much default probability.

[handwritten margin note: much higher than GDP growth]

Final Thoughts on Credit Risk

As a summary statistic, the Ratio Analysis worksheet reports the simple average of the default probabilities from the six individual ratios. As seen at the bottom of this sheet, Kohl's faces very little risk of default. They are profitable and have a relatively low amount of financial leverage, their quick ratio is well above 1.0, and they cover their interest expense more than 14 times. It isn't surprising, therefore, that the model estimates only a 3.3 percent chance that they will default in the next five years, well below the 5 percent ex ante odds of default. Target Store's average default probability is slightly higher, at 3.6 percent in fiscal 2001, but it too is relatively small when compared to the population of default risk.

We stress once again that the ratios given here capture the spirit, but not the actual details, of the financial health tests specified in an actual debt contract. Further, if your forecasts imply that the firm will be wildly profitable in the near and distant future, then the implied default probabilities based on their historical performance don't really mean much.

5.11 LINKS AND REFERENCES

Comparative Financial Statement Analysis: Boston Chicken versus McDonald's

This is the third of a three-part case on Boston Chicken. This part of the case conducts a ratio analysis of Boston Chicken's financial statements using McDonald's financial ratios for comparative purposes. Comparing Boston Chicken's financial ratios with a seasoned competitor helps us to quickly identify some important financial issues at Boston Chicken. This case is available on the eVal website.

Ratio Analysis for Royal Caribbean Cruises

This is the first of a two-part case set in the cruise industry in 1998. This part of the case involves a comprehensive ratio and cash flow analysis of Royal Caribbean Cruises, comparing them to their closest rival, Carnival Cruises. Input files for eVal are provided. This case is available on the eVal website.

A Tale of Two Movie Theaters

This case uses financial health ratios plus lots of other detailed analysis to predict which of two movie theaters defaulted on their debt in the summer of 2000. The solution of the case reveals the companies' real identities and describes some of the costs of declaring bankruptcy. The case provides eVal input files and other statistical data that can be used to forecast bankruptcy. This case is available on the eVal website.

Falkenstein, E., A. Boral, and L. Carty. "Risk Calc™ for Private Companies: Moody's Default Model," Copyright 2000, Moody's Investors Service, Inc. 99 Church St., New York, NY 10007.

- Hoovers Online—http://www.hoovers.com/

The list of competitors is found under the company profile link.

- Multex—www.multexinvestor.com

Industry and Sector averages for financial ratios are found under the ratio comparison link.

- eVal website—www.mhhe.com/eval

CHAPTER SIX

Cash Flow Analysis

6.1 INTRODUCTION

One of the novel features of accrual accounting is that firms can report lots of accounting earnings in a period when they actually collect very little cash. As a simple example, when a firm sells its goods on credit it records Sales Revenue but doesn't actually receive any cash until the customer pays. And more complicated transactions can create even larger gaps between the accounting earnings for a period and the actual cash generated during the period. The fact that these two numbers are different isn't, by itself, a cause for concern. As we discussed in Chapter 4, the accrual accounting process was designed to generate a more timely measure of wealth creation than a simple cash system. Nonetheless, generating cash, not earnings, is the ultimate long-term goal of the corporation. Cash is what the firm needs to buy assets and pay creditors, and it is what investors ultimately want to receive as a return for their investment.

In this chapter we describe how eVal creates a Pro Forma Statement of Cash Flows based on your forecasted income statements and balance sheets. We then use the information in this statement to study the company's operating, investing, and financing activities. How are they funding their growth? Are they generating cash from their operations? Are they sending cash back to their capital providers? And what do the forecasted income statements and balance sheets imply about these activities going forward?

Besides studying the cash flows in their own right, we can learn many useful things by comparing a company's cash flow results with its accrual accounting results. If the analysis reveals suspicious gaps between cash flows and accounting earnings, we can raise a red flag and conduct further analysis. By comparing two different methods of measuring performance for the period, we gain a better understanding of the firm's wealth-generating process.

Finally, we develop the basic cash flow inputs that are used in the discounted cash flow valuation models. We defer the technical development of the models to Chapter 10; here we simply describe how to compute the main inputs and discuss how they can be interpreted as measures of wealth distribution. The machinery that we develop to compute free cash flows can also be used to construct measures of "accounting quality." At the end of the chapter we show how these measures can help identify suspicious accounting choices and how they flagged World-Com's trouble well before the SEC stepped in.

6.2 THE STATEMENT OF CASH FLOWS

We begin with a brief review of how to construct a Statement of Cash Flows. If this task is completely new to you, then we recommend you consult an intermediate accounting textbook.

The Statement of Cash Flows sets out to reconcile the beginning and ending balances in the Operating Cash and Marketable Securities line item given on the eVal Financial Statements sheet (this is our definition of "cash" and is one commonly used by companies).[1] You can intuitively think of it as a summary of the transactions that ran through the company's checking account during the year. To illustrate the logic behind the construction of this statement, we start with the basic accounting equation: Assets = Liabilities + Equity. We next divide Assets into Cash and NonCashAssets, take the change in each item over the year (denoted by Δ), and rearrange to get

$$\Delta\text{Cash} = -\ \Delta\text{NonCashAssets} + \Delta\text{Liabilities} + \Delta\text{Equity}$$

The Statement of Cash Flows explains the change in Cash on the left-hand side of the equation by decomposing the changes in NonCashAssets, Liabilities, and Equity on the right-hand side of the equation. The statement then organizes the reasons for changes in these accounts into three familiar categories: operating, investing, and financing. We have listed a few major reasons for changes in each of these categories in Figure 6.1. Operating Cash Flows increase with (i) decreases in Receivables (which is reflected as a decrease in NonCashAssets in the above equation); (ii) increases in Accounts Payable (which is reflected as an increase in Liabilities in the above equation); and (iii) Net Income (which is reflected as an increase in the retained earnings component of Equity in the above equation). For example, consider the collection of cash on a credit sale that was made in a prior period. The decrease in accounts receivable is accompanied by an operating cash inflow. Investing Cash Flows and Financing Cash Flows work similarly. Selling PP&E or issuing debt increases cash.

To see some of these computations in action, let's look at Kohl's Pro Forma Statement of Cash Flows, shown on the Cash Flow Analysis sheet in eVal and reproduced in Figure 6.2. Note that the Operating section starts with Net Income at the top and ends with Cash from Operations at the bottom. In between these two amounts are all the adjustments necessary to convert from the accrual measure of

[1]We note that Statement of Financial Accounting Standards 95 "Statement of Cash Flows" requires a more restrictive definition of cash than the one that we use in eVal. The standard requires that only marketable securities that represent short-term, highly liquid investments can be classified as cash equivalents. We use a more general definition of cash equivalents that includes all marketable securities held as current assets. We do this both because these assets are typically readily convertible into cash and because some standardized financial statement databases do not distinguish between cash and short-term marketable securities. As a practical matter, most companies with large "cash" balances put a sizeable portion in such marketable securities in order to generate more competitive returns than offered by checking accounts or T-bills. For example, Microsoft has accumulated balances of cash and short-term investments of over $40 billion, and parks about half this amount in short maturity corporate notes and bonds.

FIGURE 6.1 **Organization of the Statement of Cash Flows**

ΔCash	=	− ΔNonCashAssets	+ ΔLiabilities	+ ΔEquity
Operating Cash Flows	=	− ↓Receivables	+ ↑Payables	+ Net Income
Investing Cash Flows	=	− ↑PP&E		
Financing Cash Flows	=		+ ↑Debt	− Dividends

FIGURE 6.2
eVal Cash Flow
Statement for Kohl's

	A	B	C	D	E	F	G
1	**Cash Flow Analysis**	**($000)**					
2	Go To User's Guide	View Statement of Cash Flows					
3		View FCF Computations					
4	**Company Name**	Kohl's Corporation					
5							
6		Actual	Actual	Actual	Actual	Forecast	Forecas
7	**Fiscal Year End Date**	1/30/1999	1/29/2000	2/3/2001	2/2/2002	2/2/2003	2/2/200
8	**Pro Forma Statement of Cash Flows**						
9							
10	Operating:						
11	Net Income	192,266	258,142	372,148	495,676	590,761	70
12	+Depreciation & Amortization	70,049	88,523	126,986	157,165	193,540	23
13	+Increase in Deferred Taxes	8,683	12,685	17,774	29,972	23,082	2!
14	+Increase in Other Liabilities	5,108	4,896	8,609	6,680	9,813	1(
15	+Increase in Minority Interest	0	0	0	0	0	
16	+Preferred Dividends	0	0	0	0	0	
17	=Funds From Operations	276,106	364,246	525,517	689,493	817,195	96
18	-Increase in Receivables	(31,087)	(234,306)	(176,246)	(154,690)	(168,916)	(18)
19	-Increase in Inventory	(101,572)	(177,077)	(208,851)	(195,017)	(242,137)	(26
20	+Increase in Other Current Assets	(9,904)	(21,573)	(21,779)	(28,562)	(18,932)	(2
21	+Increase in Accounts Payable	62,247	123,506	63,507	78,931	96,763	107
22	+Increase in Taxes Payable	10,090	15,383	48,972	12,158	25,275	28
23	+Increase in Other Curr. Liabilities	22,015	36,621	35,042	70,735	52,456	5
24	=Cash From Operations	227,895	106,800	266,162	473,048	561,705	68
25							
26	Investing:						
27	-Capital Expenditures	(253,411)	(508,468)	(500,480)	(630,209)	(637,983)	(72!
28	-Increase in Investments	0	0	0	0	0	
29	-Purchases of Intangibles	5,200	5,200	5,200	5,200	(1,887)	(:
30	-Increase in Other Assets	(10,216)	(136,737)	(16,824)	(64,441)	(51,872)	(5
31	=Cash From Investing	(258,427)	(640,005)	(512,104)	(689,450)	(691,742)	(78<
32							
33	Financing:						
34	+Increase in Debt	234	279,137	233,067	287,189	224,664	24!
35	-Dividends Paid on Preferred	0	0	0	0	0	
36	+Increase in Pref. Stock	0	0	0	0	0	
37	-Dividends Paid on Common	0	0	0	0	0	
38	+/-Net Issuance of Common Stock	15,731	264,582	144,988	93,091	(26,714)	(7
39	+/-Clean Surplus Plug (Ignore)	0	0	0	0	0	
40	=Cash From Financing	15,965	543,719	378,055	380,280	197,951	176
41							
42	Net Change in Cash	(14,567)	10,514	132,113	163,878	67,914	7!
43	+ Beginning Cash Balance	44,161	29,594	40,108	172,221	336,099	40
44	= Ending Cash Balance	29,594	40,108	172,221	336,099	404,013	47!

performance, Net Income, to a cash flow measure of performance, Cash from Operations. The first adjustment, adding back Depreciation & Amortization, seems obvious because these are non-cash expenses. But note that our cash flow equation is still doing the work. Depreciation and Amortization reduced Net Income and NonCashAssets by the same amount, so the adjustment we see on the statement is to add back the reduction in NonCashAssets. Cash is consumed only when NonCashAssets are purchased, and these cash outflows are shown in the Investing section. After Depreciation & Amortization there are adjustments for a few other non-current operating accounts, leading to the subtotal Funds from Operations. This subtotal is the amount of working capital generated from operations; it makes no distinction between cash and other non-cash sources of working capital. The final adjustments are for changes in all the non-cash working capital accounts, leading to Cash from Operations of just over $473 million for Kohl's in the year ending 2/2/2002.

The Operating section of the cash flow statement is the only tricky one; the line items in the Cash from Investing and Cash from Financing sections are straight-forward. Note that in eVal a cash outflow is shown as a negative number. For example, in the most recent year Kohl's invested $689 million, mostly in capital expenditures on PP&E. They paid for these investments partly with the $473 million of internally generated Cash from Operations and partly by raising $380 million in debt and equity, as shown in the Cash from Financing section. The residual effect of the operating, investing, and financing cash flows is that the Cash balance increased approximately $164 million during the most recent year.

You may notice the Clean Surplus Plug sitting at the bottom of the Cash From Financing section on eVal's Pro Forma Statement of Cash Flows. As discussed in Chapter 4, this item is due to transactions that are not included in net income or dividends, but still affect retained earnings. This amount is actually correcting for a change in one of the other line items that didn't really create or consume the given amount of cash. If the plug is a large amount, and you are worried about exactly what it represents, then get the company's complete financial statements, go to their Statement of Shareholders' Equity, and see what items other than dividends or net income are causing the Retained Earnings balance to change. Going forward, this amount will always be zero in the forecasted financial statements (which is why we keep admonishing you to ignore it).

The Pro Forma Statements of Cash Flows shown in eVal are unlikely to exactly match the statements in the company's actual published financial statements. One reason is that our definition of "cash" may not match the company's definition (as is the case with Kohl's, which excludes the marketable securities from its cash definition in its published statements). Second, we construct the cash flow statements based only on the income statements and changes in balance sheets, which gives the correct net change in cash, but doesn't always classify the changes as operating, investing, and financing in exactly the same way as the company. Obviously the company's published Statement of Cash Flows is the best source of information about their past cash activity. We construct Pro Forma Statements for both the past and the forecasted future so that you can see a time-series of cash flow data computed on a consistent basis.

So what can we do with the information in the Statement of Cash Flows? First, we use it for evaluating the ability of the company to manage its cash flows, and second, we use it as a check on the quality of accrual accounting earnings. We then examine the forecasted future cash flow statements to assess the reasonableness of our forecasts of their future. Finally, we use the forecasted future statements to compute the company's cash flow inputs for the Discounted Cash Flow valuation models.

6.3 EVALUATING A FIRM'S PAST CASH FLOWS

Your first task is simply to figure out how much cash is coming and going as a result of the company's various activities. Is the Cash from Operations negative? If so, how has the company stayed afloat? Are they issuing debt, issuing equity, selling assets, or burning through a cash balance? If the Cash from Operations is positive, where is the money going? Are they reinvesting it, paying dividends, or paying off debt? If they are investing more cash than they are generating from operations, how are they financing it? In Chapter 4 we talked about why accrual accounting generally gives a better measure of the firm's performance in a period than a cash accounting system, but you can't beat the simplicity of the Statement of Cash Flows. It tells you how much cash the firm made during the year and where they spent it.

Using Cash Flows to Assess the Quality of Earnings—Part I

Next you should take a more detailed look at the Cash from Operations section of the Statement of Cash Flows. Compare the Net Income with the Cash from Operations for the past few years. The difference between these two amounts is caused by *Accruals*. This is the component of income that isn't backed up by cash; rather, it is based on accounting rules and managerial estimates. This is not to say that this portion of net income is worthless—a credit sale is probably still valuable even though the company hasn't yet collected the cash. But the accrual component of income is more subjective and less reliable than the cash flow component. So if your company has a high level of accruals (that is, Net Income far exceeds Cash from Operations) then you might be less inclined to forecast that this level of net income will be sustained in the future. You should also compare the rate of increase in Net Income with the rate of increase in Cash from Operations, assuming they are increasing. If income is rising at a faster pace than cash flows this means that accruals are getting larger and larger, which should make you a bit suspicious about the company's accounting decisions. Firms with this pattern are more likely, statistically speaking, to suffer large write-offs in the future when it turns out that their prior accounting was too aggressive.

An increasing gap between Net Income and Cash from Operations doesn't necessarily mean that the firm is engaging in fraudulent accounting manipulations. Imagine a firm that grants its customers 30 days' credit before their cash payment is due, and every customer pays, so there is no bad debt expense. If this firm increases sales by 10 percent each period then its accounts receivable balance will also increase 10 percent each period. The gap between reported sales and cash collections will widen, but this is simply because of the growth in sales, not any manipulative accounting activity. In summary, not all firms with large accruals are manipulating income, but just about all firms who manipulate income have large accruals.

Figure 6.3 offers some empirical evidence on how well the gap between earnings and cash from operations predicts accounting manipulations.[2] The figure

[2]Dechow, P., R. Sloan, and A. Sweeney, "Causes and Consequences of Earnings Manipulation: An Analysis of Firms Subject to Enforcement Actions by the SEC," *Contemporary Accounting Research,* Spring 1996, pp. 1–36.

FIGURE 6.3
Predicting Manipulation with Earnings and Cash Flows

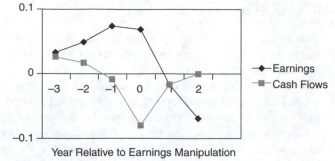

Year Relative to Earnings Manipulation

plots the earnings and cash flows for the five years surrounding a fraudulent accounting manipulation, as later identified by the SEC. Each variable is given as a percent of total assets, and year 0 is the year of the manipulation. Note from Figure 6.3 that three years prior to the manipulation, earnings and cash flows are very close. But the gap between the two increases steadily in the years prior to the manipulation and is almost 10 percent of total assets in the year of the manipulation.

After all this talk about accounting manipulation you may feel as if accrual accounting is out to get you, and seek refuge in the statement of cash flows. Surely cash from operations is safe from managerial manipulation and other accounting distortions. Or is it? Capitalizing a cash expenditure makes it an investing activity; expensing it makes it an operating activity. So by aggressively capitalizing cash expenditures a firm can make its cash from operations look healthier. And the large investing cash outflows make it look as if it is investing aggressively in a profitable enterprise. But isn't this also the exact picture we would hope to see from a successful and growing firm? So an unsuccessful growing firm can masquerade as a successful one by capitalizing some cash outflows that should rightfully be expensed. WorldCom, once the nation's second-largest long-distance phone company, used this basic manipulation to shift almost $4 billion from operation cash flows to investing cash flows. However, this type of manipulation will generate other indicators, so all is not lost. After we develop some additional cash flow measures in section 6.5, we will return to the issue of using cash flows as a way to assess the quality of the firm's reported earnings.

6.4 EVALUATING A FIRM'S FUTURE CASH FLOWS

After you forecast the company's future income statements and balance sheets, you get the future statements of cash flow for free. eVal constructs these pro forma statements using the cash flow formula described in section 6.2. We will use the forecasted future cash flow statements to evaluate the reasonableness of some of our forecasting assumptions, much the same way that we evaluated the firm's past cash flow activity.

Begin with the forecasted Cash from Operations. If it is significantly negative for some time into the future then you need to make sure you know where the firm is going to get all the necessary money to pay its bills. If the balance is positive, is it large enough to cover your forecasted Cash from Investing, which is typically a negative amount? If not, then you are effectively assuming the firm is going to finance its investments with Cash from Financing. If your forecasts imply a huge increase in borrowing, or a huge input of equity capital, then you might want to reassess the reasonableness of your forecasts. In particular, is the firm likely to be able to raise so much additional capital on the terms assumed in your model?

Besides comparing the Cash from Investing to the Cash from Operations, you should compare it to the firm's historical investment level. It is sometimes easy to get carried away forecasting sales growth and corresponding asset growth on a ratio basis without stopping to think about the level of investment this implies. Is it realistic to expect that the firm will suddenly start making much larger investments in assets than it has in the past? Analysts often ask management about their plans for future investment. If you can gather information on this item, usually from the capital resources section of the MD&A or from a company press release, then be sure to compare it with the implied investing cash outflows that you have forecast.

Finally, if there is any cash left after your forecasted Cash from Operations and Cash from Investing, what do your forecasts imply about where the money will go? Will the firm pay down debt, or will it increase dividends? How do the implied financing cash flows compare with the firm's historical activity and with any management communications about their plans for the future? It would be silly, for instance, to make forecasts that imply that the firm will pay large dividends in the near future when the firm has publicly stated that it has no intention of doing so. You should be particularly wary of firms with a record of wasting free cash flow on unsuccessful projects. Make sure that you don't inadvertently assume that such firms will stop this behavior and start graciously paying out all of their free cash flow as dividends.

6.5 CONSTRUCTING DCF VALUATION INPUTS

In Chapter 10 we present two different types of valuation models, each requiring a different type of input. The residual income models use net income and the book value of common equity as inputs and are therefore very easy to compute. The discounted cash flow (DCF) models require a bit more work because the appropriate cash flow input needs to be constructed from the forecasted income statements and balance sheet forecasts. Fortunately, we can use the results from the Pro Forma Statement of Cash Flows in eVal to make these calculations. Even if you don't plan to use the DCF valuation model you should probably read through these cash flow definitions. They are useful when searching for certain accounting manipulations.

Free Cash Flow to Common Equity

The Free Cash Flow to Common Equity is simply the net cash distributions to common equity holders. It can also be negative, meaning that the common equity holders provided more capital to the firm than they received during the year. This is the input to the most basic valuation model—the DCF to Common Equity—

FIGURE 6.4
Free Cash Flow to
Common Equity
for Kohl's

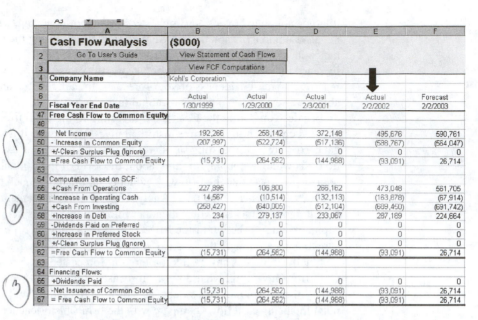

A	B	C	D	E	F
Cash Flow Analysis	**($000)**				
Go To User's Guide	View Statement of Cash Flows				
	View FCF Computations				
Company Name	Kohl's Corporation				
	Actual	Actual	Actual	Actual	Forecast
Fiscal Year End Date	1/30/1999	1/29/2000	2/3/2001	2/2/2002	2/2/2003
Free Cash Flow to Common Equity					
Net Income	192,266	258,142	372,148	495,676	590,761
- Increase in Common Equity	(207,997)	(522,724)	(517,136)	(588,767)	(564,047)
+/-Clean Surplus Plug (Ignore)	0	0	0	0	0
=Free Cash Flow to Common Equity	(15,731)	(264,582)	(144,968)	(93,091)	26,714
Computation based on SCF:					
+Cash From Operations	227,895	106,800	266,162	473,048	561,705
-Increase in Operating Cash	14,567	(10,514)	(132,113)	(163,878)	(67,914)
+Cash From Investing	(258,427)	(640,005)	(512,104)	(689,450)	(691,742)
+Increase in Debt	234	279,137	233,067	287,189	224,664
-Dividends Paid on Preferred	0	0	0	0	0
+Increase in Preferred Stock	0	0	0	0	0
+/-Clean Surplus Plug (Ignore)	0	0	0	0	0
=Free Cash Flow to Common Equity	(15,731)	(264,582)	(144,968)	(93,091)	26,714
Financing Flows:					
+Dividends Paid	0	0	0	0	0
-Net Issuance of Common Stock	(15,731)	(264,582)	(144,968)	(93,091)	26,714
= Free Cash Flow to Common Equity	(15,731)	(264,582)	(144,968)	(93,091)	26,714

alluded to in Chapters 1 and 4. We can compute this amount many different ways and, if we are careful, will always get the same answer. Figure 6.4 shows the Free Cash Flow to Common Equity in eVal for Kohl's.

The first method uses the clean surplus relation, as discussed in Chapter 4, and is illustrated using Kohl's results for year ending on 2/2/2002 (fiscal 2001):

$$\begin{matrix} \text{Free Cash Flow to} \\ \text{Common Equity} \end{matrix} = \begin{matrix} \text{Net} \\ \text{Income} \end{matrix} - \begin{matrix} \text{Increase in} \\ \text{Common Equity} \end{matrix}$$

$$-93,091 \quad = \quad 495,676 \; - \; (2,791,406 - 2,202,639)$$

Kohl's earned $495,676 in fiscal 2001 but common equity increased $588,767 over the same period, implying that common equity holders invested an additional $93,091 during the year.[3]

Now let's use the Statement of Cash Flows to arrive at the same answer. This method arrives at the free cash flow to common equity by following the flow of cash through the firm. We refer you again to Figure 6.4. Start with the Cash from Operations and then subtract any increase in the cash balance, since money placed in the firm's bank account is obviously money that wasn't paid out to equity holders. Now subtract the Investing Cash outflow (shown as adding a negative amount in Figure 6.4) and add the cash inflow from any increase in debt. What's left isn't in the firm's bank account, wasn't invested in assets, and wasn't used to retire

---

[3]If you are industrious enough to track down Kohl's 10-K (a pdf file is in the eVal2 Program Files folder), you will find that the statement of cash flows actually lists only $36,128 of proceeds from the issuance of common shares. Further investigation of the 10-K reveals that these proceeds come from the exercise of employee stock options, and the difference of $56,963 represents the tax benefit on the exercise of the options. If we corrected net income to include this $56,963 then the Free Cash Flow to Common Equity would equal negative $36,128.

debt, so it must have been paid out to common equity holders. You will note that the answer on the Cash Flow Analysis sheet is exactly the negative $93,091 we computed above.

③ The final computation is the most obvious. Simply look in the Financing section of the Statement of Cash Flows and pick out the two items that are cash transactions with the common equity holders—Dividends Paid and Net Issuance of Common Stock. Once again we see that common equity holders invested $93,091 in Kohl's during the year.

You shouldn't be too distressed that Kohl's free cash flow to common equity is negative; this is often the case for young and growing firms. Of course, you wouldn't want this number to stay negative forever. A quick rule that tells you whether the free cash flow to common equity will be negative or positive can be constructed from the equation above. Rewrite it as

$$D_t = CE_{t-1} \left(\frac{NI_t}{CE_{t-1}} - \frac{CE_t - CE_{t-1}}{CE_{t-1}} \right) = CE_{t-1} \, (ROE_t - \% \text{ growth in } CE_t)$$

where

D_t = free cash flow to common equity in period t

CE_t = common shareholders' equity at end of the period t

ROE_t = return on beginning common shareholders' equity in period t

So, free cash flow to common equity holders will be positive if, and only if, the return on beginning equity is greater than the percentage growth in common equity.

We have already touched on the pluses and minuses of free cash flow to common equity as a measure of the changes in the fortunes of equity holders in Chapter 4. It is a measure of wealth distribution, not wealth creation. As such, in any given period it is probably a very poor performance measure. However, in the long run, this is what the common equity holders actually get as a return on their investment. In this sense, it is the final arbitrator of value.

Free Cash Flow to All Investors

The Free Cash Flow to All Investors is the net amount of cash the firm paid to all providers of capital financing: debt providers (net of the tax deduction for interest), preferred stockholders, and common equity holders. This is the primary input to the traditional discounted cash flow model. As with the free cash flow to common equity, we can compute this a number of different ways and always get the same answer. Figure 6.5 shows the Free Cash Flow to Investor computations in eVal for Kohl's.

The first computation of the Free Cash Flow to All Investors makes use of the relation between net operating income and changes in net operating assets and is analogous to the clean surplus relation that we used to determine the free cash flow distributions to common equity above. Recall from Chapter 5 how the Advanced Dupont decomposition constructed the return on net operating assets by isolating the income statement and balance sheet items that were associated with

RNOA

FIGURE 6.5
**Free Cash Flow
to All Investors
Computation
for Kohl's**

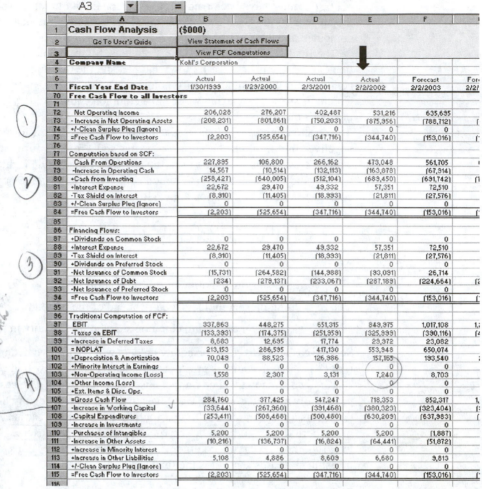

the firm's operating and investing activities. We can use the same approach to cal-culate the free cash flows generated by the firm's operating and investing activi-ties. Define net operating income and net operating assets as follows (and as given in Chapter 5):

Net Operating Income (NOI) = (EBIT + Non-Operating Income) ×
(1 − tx) − Minority Interest in Earnings + Other Income (Loss) −
Extraordinary Items and Discontinued Operations

where the effective tax rate (tx) = Income Taxes/EBT, and

Net Operating Assets (NOA) = Total Assets − Accounts Payable −
Income Taxes Payable − Other Current Liabilities − Other Liabilities −
Deferred Taxes − Minority Interest.

Using Kohl's for the year ending in 2/2/2002 as an illustration, we get

$$
\begin{array}{ccccc}
\textbf{Free Cash Flow} & = & \textbf{Net Operating} & - & \textbf{Increase in Net} \\
\textbf{to Investors} & & \textbf{Income} & & \textbf{Operating Assets} \\
-344{,}740 & = & 531{,}216 & - & (3{,}903{,}244 - 3{,}027{,}288)
\end{array}
$$

This calculation isolates net operating income, before consideration of any financing flows. Whatever amount of net operating income not invested in additional net operating assets (the increase in NOA) must have been paid out to providers of financing, either as interest or dividend flows, or as reductions in the balances of common equity, preferred equity, or debt. That is, they must have been Free Cash Flows to Investors.

The next two methods of computing Free Cash Flow to Investors make use of the Statement of Cash Flow data. The first one starts with the Cash from Operations. Next, we subtract any increase in the cash balance, and then we add any cash from investing. It would seem that the remaining amount of cash must have been paid out to capital providers, but we have one further adjustment. There is a minor flaw in the logic of the Statement of Cash Flows as defined by GAAP: It subtracts interest expense, and the tax consequences of interest, from the Cash from Operations rather than from the Cash from Financing. To correct for this, we must add the interest, net of its associated tax shield, back to get Free Cash Flow to Investors. The next approach to computing Free Cash Flow to Investors takes the most direct route—it simply picks the appropriate cash flows out of the financing section of the Statement of Cash Flows, again correcting for the misclassification of interest. Note that in all cases we get −$344,740 of Free Cash Flow to Investors for Kohl's most recent year.

Finally, there is one more method of computing the Free Cash Flow to Investors, labeled the "traditional" approach, because it is a recipe used for years in many finance textbooks. The logic behind this approach is that EBIT (earnings before interest and taxes) is "almost" on a cash basis. From this we subtract the cash taxes paid, which is computed applying the effective tax rate to EBIT and then adding the increase in deferred taxes (if you are an accounting guru, however, you will note that this still isn't the actual tax paid, because the balance of taxes payable might have changed). The subtotal labeled NOPLAT stands for "net operating profit less adjusted taxes." To this amount we add back depreciation/amortization because it is was deducted in the computation of EBIT but did not consume cash, and add other sources of non-financing income to get to the Gross Cash Flow. Finally, to account for investments, we subtract capital expenditures and any other increases in net operating assets, such as working capital or reductions in non-current operating liabilities. On the surface it may seem amazing that this recipe for Free Cash Flow to Investors gets to the same answer as the other methods, but look at it more carefully. It is actually recovering the first method— net operating income minus the increase in net operating assets. For example, by adding depreciation and subtracting capital expenditures, the recipe effectively computes the change in PP&E. And the other elements of EBIT that are not on a cash basis (for instance, credit sales) get picked up when the recipe subtracts the increase in working capital (in the credit sales example, this is the increase in accounts receivable). If you get out a large piece of paper, and pour a tall cup of coffee, you can reconcile the first method with the last method—all the pieces of the puzzle are present in each computation, they just get put together in a different order.

As with the free cash flow to common equity, we shouldn't be too concerned that Kohl's Free Cash Flows to Investors have been consistently negative. This is not uncommon for growing firms. It basically says that they are investing more rapidly than they are generating cash internally. We can also derive a quick rule to determine when the Free Cash Flow to Investors will be positive.

$$C_t = NOA_{t-1}\left(\frac{NOI_t}{NOA_{t-1}} - \frac{NOA_t - NOA_{t-1}}{NOA_{t-1}}\right)$$

$$= NOA_{t-1}\,(RNOA_t - \%\ \text{growth in } NOA_t)$$

where

C_t = free cash flow to all investors in period t

NOI_t = net operating income in period t

NOA_t = net operating assets at the end of the period t

$RNOA_t$ = return on beginning net operating assets in period t

The equation says the Free Cash Flow to All Investors will be positive if, and only if, the return on beginning net operating assets exceeds the percentage growth in net operating assets over the period.

6.6 ASSESSING THE QUALITY OF EARNINGS USING CASH FLOWS

In this section we develop some statistical measures of the "quality of earnings" by looking at the amount and composition of the firm's accruals. In section 6.3 we advised you to compare the company's Net Income with its Cash from Operations on the Statement of Cash Flows—this is one type of accrual measure. Now, armed with our definition of Free Cash Flow to All Investors from section 6.5, we can develop a more robust definition of accounting accruals and use it to flag suspicious accounting behavior. These flags for Earnings Quality are computed at the bottom of the Ratio Analysis sheet in eVal. But first we need to develop some new definitions.

At the most general level, an *accrual* is income that is recognized in a different period than the associated cash flow. If it wasn't for accruals, the firm would have a simple cash accounting system, and there would be no such thing as non-cash assets or liabilities. Non-cash assets and liabilities arise in the financial statements because the accounting rules recognize the economic benefits and obligations of transactions regardless of whether or not the actual cash exchange takes place during the same period. Consequently, when non-cash assets increase or liabilities decrease, it means that the accounting system has recorded net economic benefits ahead of the associated cash flow. In other words, it means that accruals have increased. The more accruals increase, the bigger the gap between accounting income and "cash income." As we discussed in Chapter 4, accruals generally help the accounting system to report a more timely measure of wealth creation. But when accruals get too extreme, or are concentrated in accounts that management has considerable discretion over, it can flag a potential quality problem with the accounting numbers.

Not all accruals are created equal. In particular, the accounting rules for debt do a reasonable job of capturing economic reality and are relatively difficult to manipulate. Consequently, changes in the long-term debt and the current debt accounts are unlikely to be the type of accruals that are associated with accounting shenanigans. On the other hand, non-cash net operating asset accounts are relatively easy to manipulate and the accounting rules frequently do a poor job of matching economic reality. For this reason our accounting quality flags focus on changes in the non-cash net operating assets. To make this precise, define

Total Operating Accruals = Increase in Non-Cash Net Operating Assets

where

Non-Cash Net Operating Assets = Net Operating Assets (NOA) − Operating Cash

For Kohl's in the year ended 2/2/2002, NOA increased by $875,956. Subtracting the increase of $163,878 in Operating Cash gives $712,078 of total operating accruals.

By using the definition of Free Cash Flow to all Investors from the previous section and substituting in the definition of total operating accruals, we can compute total operating accruals a different (but equivalent) way that illustrates the difference between cash and accrual accounting, again illustrated by Kohl's.

$$\begin{array}{ccccc}
\textbf{Total Operating} & & & \left(\textbf{Free Cash Flow} & \textbf{Increase in}\right) \\
\textbf{Accruals} & = & \textbf{NOI} & - \left(\textbf{to Investors} + \textbf{Operating Cash}\right) \\
712{,}078 & = & 531{,}216 & - (-344{,}740 \quad + \quad 163{,}878)
\end{array}$$

In words, Total Operating Accruals is the difference between the accounting system's measure of operating performance, as given by Net Operating Income, and what a cash-based accounting system would report, as given by Free Cash Flow to Investors plus the increase in Operating Cash. The idea is that if these two performance measures get too far apart, then something might be fishy with the accounting.

Figure 6.6 shows how eVal uses the Total Operating Accruals to flag questionable earnings quality. To get to this part of the Ratio Analysis sheet quickly, hit the Earnings Quality and Default button at the top of the page. Note from the figure that when we use accruals to identify earnings problems, we scale by the non-cash net operating assets at the beginning of the period to control for the size of the firm. This means that *scaled* total operating accruals is really just the percentage growth in non-cash net operating assets.

FIGURE 6.6
Earnings Quality Flags in eVal for Kohl's

Flags values beyond 90th percentile

	A	B	C	D	E	F	G
1	**Ratio Analysis**	Growth and Profitability		Margin, Turnover and Leverage			
2	Go To User's Guide	Dupont Models		Earnings Quality and Default			
3							
4	**Company Name**	Kohl's Corporation					
5							
6		Actual	Actual	Actual	Actual	Actual	Forecast	F
7	**Fiscal Year End Date**	1/31/1998	1/30/1999	1/29/2000	2/3/2001	2/2/2002	2/2/2003	2
67	**Analysis of Earnings Quality**						
68	(Red Shading = Quality Flag)						
69	Current Op. Accruals/NOA		0.039	0.178	0.118	0.076	0.072
70	+ NonCurrent Op. Accruals/NOA		0.143	0.369	0.160	0.174	0.130
71	= Total Op. Accruals/NOA		0.182	0.547	0.276	0.249	0.202
72							
73	Sales Growth		0.203	0.238	0.350	0.217	0.202
74	- increase in NOA Turnover		0.017	(0.250)	0.055	(0.026)	(0.000)
75	- Interaction		0.004	(0.059)	0.019	(0.006)	(0.000)
76	= NOA growth		0.182	0.547	0.276	0.249	0.202

We decompose total operating accruals two different ways. The first one is easy. We divide the total operating accruals into the current operating accruals and non-current operating accruals (Kohl's most recent year is shown below as an illustration):

Total Operating Accruals/Non-Cash NOA	=	Current Operating Accruals/Non-Cash NOA	+	Non-Current Operating Accruals/Non-Cash NOA
.249		.076		.174

where

Current Operating Accruals = Increase in Non-Cash Working Capital

Non-Current Operating Accruals = Increase in Non-Current Net Operating Assets

Each of these components has been shown to flag poor earnings quality independent of each other, so a firm that is extreme for both these categories of accruals is more likely to have poor earnings quality than one that is extreme on one dimension but not the other.

To understand the second decomposition shown in Figure 6.6, recall that, because we scale Total Operating Accruals by non-cash NOA, it is really just the percentage growth in non-cash NOA. This decomposition explains why non-cash NOA growth differs from sales growth. Using Kohl's for the year ending on 2/2/2002 as an illustration, this gives

Non-Cash NOA Growth	=	Sales Growth	−	Non-Cash NOA Turnover Growth	−	Interaction
.249	=	.217	−	(−.026)	−	(−.006)

where

Non-Cash NOA Growth = Total Operating Accruals$_t$/Non-Cash NOA$_{t-1}$

Sales Growth = (Increase in Sales$_t$)/Sales$_{t-1}$

TABLE 6.1   **Distribution of Accrual Components**

Accrual	50th Percentile	75th Percentile	90th Percentile
Current Operating Accruals/non-cash NOA	.01	.05	.11
Non-Current Operating Accruals/non-cash NOA	.02	.06	.14
Total Accruals/non-cash NOA	.08	.20	.38
% Sales Growth	.09	.21	.39
Increase in NOA turnover	.00	−.08	−.21

Source: Richardson, Sloan, Soliman, and Tuna (2003).

Non-Cash NOA Turnover Growth = [Increase in (Sales$_t$/Non-Cash Noa$_t$)]/
(Sales$_t$/Non-Cash Noa$_t$)

Interaction = Sales Growth × Non-Cash NOA Turnover Growth

This second decomposition highlights three important features of accruals. First, non-cash NOA growth is directly related to Sales growth. The second term shows that non-cash NOA may grow slower than sales if a firm increases its NOA turnover—that is, if it uses its operating assets more efficiently. Conversely, if a firm's non-cash NOA grows faster than sales, it is using its assets less efficiently. The third term captures the fact that Sales growth and non-cash NOA growth may be interactive. If the firm enjoys economies of scale, for instance, then as sales grow the firm becomes more efficient and its NOA turnover increases. This effect is shown in the interaction term. As with the first decomposition, extreme values for each of these three terms have been shown to identify poor accounting quality independent of the others. However, it is the NOA turnover growth that has been shown to be most informative. Other things equal, firms with slowing NOA turns are more likely to have low quality earnings.

Having extreme Total Operating Accruals, or extreme components of accruals, is a flag that there might be an accounting quality issue. Firms with extreme values of these variables have been shown to have lower persistence in earnings, have lower future stock returns, and be more likely to be the subject of an SEC enforcement action.[4] But what is the benchmark for "extreme"? Table 6.1 gives the 50th percentile (the median), the 75th percentile, and the 90th percentile for Total Operating Accruals and for each of its components computed for all publicly traded, non-financial companies between 1979 and 2000. Think of the 50th percentile as the "normal" level of accruals, and the 75th and 90th percentiles as being increasingly "extreme." Note that decreases in NOA turnover flag poor earnings quality, so the table shows extreme negative values. On the Ratio Analysis sheet, eVal computes each of these measures and flags values that are beyond the 90th percentile with pink shading. Anything with pink shading requires more accounting analysis.

[4] See S. Richardson, R. Sloan, M. Soliman, and I. Tuna, "Information in Accruals about Earnings Persistence and Future Stock Returns," University of Michigan Working Paper, 2003, for details.

Returning to Kohl's, what are we to think about all of the shaded cells that we see in Figure 6.6? The main observation is that Kohl's non-current operating assets have been growing very rapidly—more rapidly than 90 percent of the population of firms. Examining the financial statements reveals that this is due to the growth in PP&E and Other Assets. Is Kohl's inappropriately capitalizing expenses in the PP&E or Other Assets line items? We are particularly curious about what is in the rapidly growing Other Assets account. Unfortunately, Kohl's gives very few details about what is getting sorted into this account. Does this mean that Kohl's is pulling a fast one on us? Maybe, but all we really know is that they have one suspicious account. This, by itself, is hardly sufficient evidence to convict them, though until we know exactly what is going on with these accounts, we should maintain a healthy level of skepticism.

Applying the same accrual tests to WorldCom illustrates how extreme levels of operating accruals are typically present when accounting statements have been manipulated. In fiscal 2000 WorldCom's cash from operations was much greater than its net income so, by this measure, WorldCom would have appeared to have very high earnings quality. An examination of their non-current operating accruals reveals a very different story, however. WorldCom's non-current operating accruals had grown to more than 17% of non-cash NOA by the end of 2000. This is definitely beyond the 14% threshold for an extreme accrual. With hindsight, we know that WorldCom was inflating income and cash from operations by reclassifying normal operating expenditures into investing expenditures. The large increase in non-current NOA is the clue that something wasn't right with their accounting.

6.7 CONCLUSION

Every so often a writer in the financial press will get upset about some company's accounting methods and declare that "cash is king," implying that we should value this measure of performance above accrual-based measures. We take a more balanced view. Accrual accounting was designed to measure wealth creation in a timelier manner than simply waiting for the cash flows to materialize, and for most companies most of the time, these measures add information. Further, we don't have to choose between cash flows or earnings—we can have both. By using two different systems to examine a company's activities we learn much more about what really happened in the past, and we get a great check on the reasonableness of our forecasts of the future. The next few chapters present a systematic approach to forecasting the income statement and balance sheet, but you will need to cycle back to cash flow analysis repeatedly to be sure that the implied statement of cash flows makes sense.

6.8 LINKS AND REFERENCES

Evaluating Earnings Quality at Boston Chicken

This is the second of a three-part case on Boston Chicken. This part of the case analyzes the source of Boston Chicken's healthy and growing earnings in the competitive fast food segment of the restaurant industry. Combining the insights from the business analysis in the first part of this case with Boston Chicken's accounting policies reveals important insights into the source and quality of Boston Chicken's earnings. This case is available on the *eVal website*.

Dechow, P., R. Sloan, and A. Sweeney, "Causes and Consequences of Earnings Manipulation: An Analysis of Firms Subject to Enforcement Actions by the SEC," *Contemporary Accounting Research,* Spring 1996, pp. 1–36.

S. Richardson, R. Sloan, M. Soliman, and I. Tuna, "Information in Accruals about Earnings Persistence and Future Stock Returns," University of Michigan Working Paper, 2003.

CHAPTER SEVEN

Structured Forecasting

7.1 INTRODUCTION

Forecasting the future financial statements represents the ultimate goal of all the analysis we have discussed thus far. From a theoretical perspective, equity valuation requires forecasts of the future cash distributions to equity holders. From a practical perspective, however, most analysts focus on forecasting net income. We begin this chapter by reconciling these two perspectives. We lay out a forecasting framework that builds forecasts of the complete set of financial statements in a systematic manner. This framework highlights the joint role of income statement and balance sheet forecasts in generating forecasts of cash distributions to equity holders.

We next discuss broad issues that arise in constructing forecasts for the purpose of valuing equity securities. Should we forecast quarterly financial statements or annual statements? How many years into the future do we need to forecast? What are reasonable assumptions for forecasts that are in the distant future? What balance sheet item should we use as the "plug" that equates assets to liabilities and equity? We close the chapter by showing you how eVal guides you through the forecasting process. With these preliminaries covered, Chapter 8 provides more detailed advice about forecasting each of the line items in the financial statements.

7.2 A SYSTEMATIC FORECASTING FRAMEWORK

The cash distributions a firm pays to its equity holders are the result of a complex and interrelated set of operating, investing, and financing activities. The only sound way to proceed is to first forecast each of these underlying activities and then aggregate their financial implications into a forecast of the ultimate distributions to equity holders. We do this by building forecasts of both the income statement and the balance sheet. By forecasting both financial statements, we can take important interactions into consideration. A good example of the interplay between balance sheet forecasts and income statement forecasts is forecasted interest expense. Your forecast of interest expense on the income statement clearly depends on the amount of debt you forecast on the balance sheet. But the amount of debt will also depend on forecasts of the firm's net operating assets and capital structure. And your forecast of the net operating assets clearly depends on

FIGURE 7.1
Systematic
Forecasting
Framework

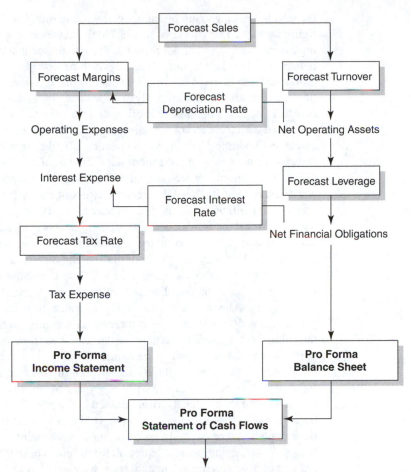

your forecast of sales growth. If we are going to keep track of all these interactions we clearly need to develop a systematic approach to forecasting.

Figure 7.1 illustrates our approach to this forecasting puzzle. The process begins with a forecast of sales. Sales is the primary input to the forecasting process for two reasons. First, recall that the sales transaction is the trigger for the recognition of value creation under GAAP. We forecast operating income by first forecasting sales and then forecasting all the operating expenses necessary to generate the sales. Second, the sales forecast is our basic statement about how rapidly the firm will grow. This in turn drives our forecasts of the required levels of net operating assets to generate the sales growth and the required amounts of capital to finance the operating assets.

The next two steps in the forecasting process are illustrated in Figure 7.1. On the left side of the figure we move from the sales forecast to the operating expense forecast by making assumptions about operating margins. On the right side of the figure we move from the sales forecast to the net operating asset forecast by making assumptions about turnover ratios. You should see that the forecasting process is like applying the Dupont ratio analysis in reverse. Instead of starting with the individual line items in the financial statements and then expressing them as ratios, we forecast the ratios directly and then back into what this implies for the individual line items in the forecast financial statements.

Armed with forecasts of operating expenses and net operating assets (operating assets less operating liabilities), the next task on the right side of Figure 7.1 is to forecast the net financial obligations. Our forecast of net operating assets indicates the total amount of invested capital that is required to support the future business activities. But we still need to forecast the mix of equity and non-equity financing that the firm will use to finance the forecasted level of invested capital. That is, we need to forecast the firm's future leverage. By applying leverage assumptions to the net operating assets, we obtain the required amount of non-equity forms of financing, such as short-term debt, long-term debt, and preferred stock. At this point you may be tempted to forecast common equity and thus complete the balance sheet. However, we have run out of degrees of freedom. We have forecast every item on the balance sheet except for common equity. Since the balance sheet must balance, we have already made an implicit forecast for common equity. Common equity is the "plug" that is found by subtracting the liabilities from the assets. This is an important point and one to which we return later in the chapter.

We have now forecast all the line items on the balance sheet. We refer to this forecasted balance sheet as a "pro forma" balance sheet to distinguish it from the actual balance sheets that the firm reported in the past. We still have more work to do on the left side of Figure 7.1 to derive the pro forma income statement. The three items we have omitted are depreciation expense, interest expense and tax expense. We could not forecast depreciation earlier because it clearly depends on the amount of assets on the balance sheet, so we needed to forecast the asset amounts first. Similarly, we couldn't forecast interest or taxes, because interest expense clearly depends on the amount of debt financing and tax expense clearly depends on the magnitude of the interest expense tax deduction. We needed the balance sheet forecast of debt before we could construct these income statement forecasts. By applying our forecast of the interest rate to the amount of forecasted debt financing, we generate an interest expense forecast. By deducting our interest expense from our forecast of operating earnings, we generate a forecast of earnings before taxes. Applying a tax rate forecast to earnings before taxes gives our tax expense forecast.

At this point, we are pretty much done forecasting the income statement. You may note that there are still a number of income statement components that we haven't mentioned: items such as gains and losses in other income, extraordinary items, and discontinued operations. Typically, by their very nature, these items are non-recurring and difficult to forecast. Therefore, ignoring them (that is, assuming that they are zero) is often the best that we can do. One final item to consider in your income statement forecasts is preferred dividends. If preferred stock is one of the non-common-equity sources of financing represented on the balance sheet, then there will typically be a stated dividend on this stock that should be incorporated in your income statement forecasts. Recall that we are trying to value the common equity, so we must deduct cash distributions to preferred equity holders in order to derive the net cash distributions to common equity holders.

We now have both our pro forma balance sheet and our pro forma income statement. Armed with these two statements, the preparation of our pro forma statement of cash flows is a mechanical task. You should remember from your introductory accounting class (and Chapter 4) that the statement of cash flows can be prepared using the information in the income statement and the beginning and ending balance sheets, so there is nothing left to forecast. And by referring to the financing section of the statement of cash flows, we can see how our pro forma income statements and balance sheets determine the cash distributions to common equity holders shown at the bottom of Figure 7.1. It is worth emphasizing that we need information from both the pro forma income statement and the pro forma balance sheet to extract our forecasts of distributions to common equity holders. We can see this by recalling the clean surplus relation that we first introduced in Chapter 4:

$$\text{Distributions to Equity} = \text{Net Income} - \text{Increase in Equity}$$

We get the net income forecast from the pro forma income statement, but this alone isn't sufficient for our valuation model. To solve for cash distributions to common equity holders, we also have to deduct the increase in common equity, which is extracted from the beginning and ending balance sheets. This latter adjustment takes account of additional capital that is required to fund the net operating assets of the business. Wall Street analysts often miss this subtlety, focusing almost exclusively on net income. But the clean surplus relation makes it clear that we should be concerned with both how much income is generated *and* how much additional capital has to be invested to generate this income.

7.3 FORECASTING QUARTERLY VERSUS YEARLY FINANCIALS

Exchange-listed firms in the United States are required to prepare financial statements on a quarterly basis. For the purpose of building financial forecasts for input into a valuation model, however, quarterly forecasting is overkill. The value of a firm is determined by its results over the next 10 or 20 years, not the next few quarters. And in addition to providing unnecessary detail, quarterly forecasting requires careful consideration of seasonal effects in financial data. For example, retailers' sales and profits are usually greatest in the fourth quarter, which covers the end-of-year holiday period. A quarterly forecasting interval requires us to build these seasonal patterns into our forecasts. But given that our value estimate will be determined by many years of forecasts, detailed knowledge of the quarterly numbers has little impact on the final answer. As a consequence, most valuation models, including eVal, use an annual interval for building financial statement forecasts. For simplicity, this annual interval typically corresponds with the fiscal year that the company uses for financial reporting purposes.

Despite the use of an annual measurement interval in most valuation models, the quarterly financial statements are still useful. The most recent quarterly financial statements provide the most current information on a firm's performance and financial position. If we are currently in a firm's fourth fiscal quarter and we are attempting to forecast the income statement for the full fiscal year, then we should obviously use the financial statements from the first three quarters as a starting point. But it is very important to be aware of any seasonal effects in the data before extrapolating financial statement data from earlier quarters to later quarters. There are two useful techniques for incorporating seasonal patterns in income statement forecasting. The first is to sum together the most recent four quarters of financial statements. By doing so, you will be sure that any seasonal patterns are present in your annual figure. The cumulative results for the four most recent fiscal quarters are often referred to as the "trailing twelve months" (TTM) or "latest twelve months" (LTM) results. The second technique is to perform "year-over-year" (YOY) comparisons for the most recent quarters. This involves comparing the most recent quarters in the current fiscal year to the corresponding quarters in the previous fiscal year. For example, we compare the third fiscal quarter of the current year to the third fiscal quarter for the previous year. By doing so, we control for any seasonal patterns in the firm's performance. Similar considerations apply to forecasting the balance sheet for the end of the current fiscal year. While the most recent quarterly balance sheet is the timeliest, it may also reflect seasonal patterns in net operating asset balances. For example, most retailers build up inventory during the third fiscal quarter and run it down during the fourth fiscal quarter. If you simply extrapolate the third quarter inventory balances into the future you will overstate the inventory necessary to sustain the annual sales. Year over year comparisons of quarterly inventory changes are the best technique for controlling for such seasonal patterns.

Another role for quarterly financial statements in valuation is in assessing the ongoing performance of the company relative to your previous forecasts. You may not want to wait until the end of the year to find out whether or not a company is meeting your forecasts. Indeed, quarterly earnings announcements are one of the most important catalysts for a stock price revision, suggesting that most market participants use information in the quarterly financial statements to update their forecasting models. For this reason, it is very useful to prepare explicit quarterly forecasts through the end of the current fiscal year.

7.4 FORECASTING HORIZON

Theoretically speaking, the valuation of an equity security requires us to estimate and discount all the future cash distributions for the infinite future. But, practically speaking, this would require way too many columns on our spreadsheet. Instead, we select a finite horizon over which to prepare explicit forecasts for each year and then we assume that after this point the financial statement line items settle down to a constant growth rate. In this way we describe an infinite series of future cash distributions without having to explicitly derive an infinite number of pro forma financial statements. Oddly enough, the period after the finite forecasting horizon is known as the "Terminal Period" even though, by definition, it never terminates. In later chapters we will discuss how the valuation formulas deal with the infinite series of future cash distributions. What we need to concern ourselves with in this chapter is the selection of an appropriate finite forecasting horizon.

The forecasting horizon should begin with the fiscal year that we are currently in and extend out to the point where we can no longer make a better forecast than to simply assume that all the financial statement line items will grow at the same rate as sales. To be more precise, the terminal period should begin when our forecasts meet the following four conditions. First, sales must settle down to a constant growth rate. Second, margins must remain constant. This condition, combined with the constant sales growth rate, ensures that the expenses on the income statement grow at the same constant rate as sales. Third, turnover ratios must remain constant. This condition, combined with the constant sales growth rate, ensures that the net operating assets on the balance sheet grow at the same constant rate as sales. Fourth, financial leverage ratios must remain constant. This condition, combined with the constant sales growth rate and constant turnover ratios, ensures that the financial obligations on the balance sheet grow at the same constant rate as sales. Together, these four conditions ensure that all the items in the income statement and balance sheet will grow at the same constant rates as sales. As a result, cash distributions to equity holders will also grow at this same constant rate.

It is important to note that we do not expect all these conditions to literally hold beyond the forecasting horizon. In reality, sales growth rates, margins, turnovers, and leverage ratios are all constantly changing and we expect them to continue to change beyond the forecasting horizon. But what is crucial is that we don't expect them to deviate from this constant growth rate in a systematic way. In other words, our forecasts in the terminal period should be unbiased estimates of where we expect these ratios to be in the long run.

How far out do we need to build explicit financial statement forecasts before it is reasonable to assume that things will settle down to this constant long-run equilibrium? It all depends on the nature of the business and the amount of information that is available to build the forecasts. At one extreme, we could be looking at a company in a mature industry with a well-established product, stable demand, a stable production technology, and stable input prices. Moreover, assume that the company offered no forward-looking information about expansion plans, there were no discernable industry trends, and you generally had every reason to believe that "more of the same" is the best description of the future. In such an extreme case it is reasonable to assume that the sales growth rate, margins, turnovers, and leverage ratios will remain constant at their recent levels. In this simple case, the finite forecasting period is non-existent and the first year in the forecast period is the terminal period. We generate the forecasted financial statements by naively extrapolating the past sales growth rate, margins, turnovers, and leverage ratios into the infinite future. This process is called "straight-lining" because, if sales growth, margins, turnovers, and leverage ratios will all stay constant at their current levels, they would plot against time as a straight line. Straight-lining is the default forecasting assumption that we generally use in eVal. We make this choice because, in the absence of additional information, it is the best that we can do. We'll take a closer look at eVal's default forecasting assumptions at the end of this chapter.

In most circumstances, however, straight-lining is a very naive forecasting technique. Instead, we should use what we have learned from our analysis of the past to build more sophisticated forecasts of the future. The length of the forecast horizon depends on how far into the future we can reasonably predict variation in the sales growth rate, margins, turnover, and leverage before they settle down to their long-run steady-state values. Consider each of these variables in turn. Sales growth won't settle to a steady growth rate until industrywide sales stabilize and the firm's market share in the industry stabilizes. Thus, firms in start-up industries or firms that are gaining market share from competitors are likely to require longer forecasting horizons.

Next up are margins. There are two key factors that affect the stability of margins. First, margins are a function of a firm's competitive advantage in the marketplace. Because it is very hard to sustain a competitive advantage for a long period of time, our forecast horizon should be long enough to capture the erosion of any competitive advantage, assuming this is what you believe will happen. Second, margins are subject to systematic accounting distortions. For example, a growing company in an R&D intensive industry will tend to have its margins temporarily depressed because of the immediate expensing of R&D. Your forecast horizon needs to be long enough to allow any temporary accounting distortions to play out.

Turnover ratios tend to be fairly stable over time, being dictated primarily by the production technology of the firm. Rapidly growing firms often enjoy economies of scale that lead to increasing turnover ratios as they grow, however, so you need to anticipate when these economies will be exhausted. Even if the sales growth rate is forecast to hit a steady-state level relatively soon, you might extend the forecast horizon a few years longer if you believe that the firm will continue to reap economies of scale as it grows.

Leverage ratios typically have little influence on the choice of the forecast horizon. A firm's target capital structure generally balances the cost of different types of capital, taking into account the tax benefits of debt and the risk of financial distress. Various factors can cause the actual capital structure to deviate from the target capital structure in the short run, but it is typically quite straightforward for a firm to get back to its target capital structure within a few years. The probability of financial distress is a function of level and variability of firm profitability. As firms mature and profitability settles down to a steady state growth rate, financial distress becomes less likely, and so firms typically add more debt to their capital structure in order to reap the tax benefits. Thus, if you are preparing forecasts for a young growth firm that is primarily equity financed, you will probably want to crank up the amount of debt financing as it reaches maturity.

The above analysis suggests that the two key determinants of the forecast horizon are sales growth and margins. First, the horizon must be long enough for sales

TABLE 7.1 Forecast Horizon Guidelines

		Industrywide Growth Prospects		
		Low (mature)	Medium (consolidating)	High (start-up)
Firm-Specific	None	5 years	10 years	20 years
Competitive	Yes, but only short run	5 years	10 years	20 years
Advantage	Yes, and for longer run	10 years	20 years	20 Years

growth to settle down to its steady-state level. Second, it must be long enough for the anticipated erosion of any abnormal profits resulting from competitive advantage in the marketplace. In other words, the forecast horizon must be long enough for any abnormal sales growth and abnormal profits to dissipate. For this reason, the forecast horizon is sometimes referred to as the "competitive advantage period." The selection of the forecast horizon should be based on a thorough analysis of industry growth prospects and the sustainability of any competitive advantage held by the firm in its industry. To get you started, we provide you with some broad-brush guidelines in Table 7.1.

While the table is intended only to provide you with general guidelines, it embodies three important lessons. First, even if you are valuing a firm in a mature industry with no competitive advantage, it is still wise to choose a forecast horizon of at least 5 years. Doing so will help you resist the temptation to simply straight-line the past. Even firms in mature and competitive industries are sensitive to the business cycle and are subject to demand and supply shocks that can take several years to work their way through the system. A good example here is the airline industry. While mature and competitive, this industry is characterized by large fixed costs and significant demand and supply shocks (business cycle, oil prices, consumer sentiment, terrorist threats, etc.). As a result, growth rates and profit margins can deviate from their long-run competitive equilibrium for several years at a time. (To see this, load the airline industry into eVal using the ticker M9770 and look at how volatile the past financial ratios are.)

The second lesson is that industrywide growth prospects are a very important determinant of the forecast horizon. The reason is that firms in growing industries also tend to be growing, and growth leads to accounting distortions in profit margins. We should therefore try to choose a forecast horizon that is long enough for the industry growth rate to slow down to the economywide growth rate. For a firm in a start-up industry that has significant research and development and/or marketing expenditures, it can take up to 20 years for the industry to mature. Good examples are the biotechnology industry today and the computer hardware industry in the 1970s.

The third lesson is that firm-specific competitive advantage is a relatively less important determinant of the forecast horizon than industrywide growth prospects. Why do we dare make such a sweeping generality? We have found that both students and practicing security analysts are biased toward overestimating how long firms can sustain their competitive advantage. Typically, when a firm has a new product or new service innovation that enables it to generate abnormally high profits, analysts get excited and extrapolate the abnormally high profits far into the future, not realizing that other firms will be quick to imitate the innovation and compete away the abnormal profits. There are some rare exceptions to this rule, such as Microsoft, Coca-Cola, and McDonald's, but these are very unusual cases. In these exceptional cases, the firm has usually created a key proprietary asset that gives it some degree of monopoly power. If this is truly the case, then it is reasonable to assume that the firm will sustain its abnormal profits indefinitely, and we can incorporate the abnormal profitability into the terminal value computation. We caution, however, that cases of indefinitely sustainable competitive advantage are rare.

7.5 TERMINAL PERIOD ASSUMPTIONS

Now that we are finished with the forecast horizon, we are ready to talk about the terminal period forecasting assumptions. Recall from the discussion above that the terminal period is the period in which we expect sales growth, margins, turnover ratios, and leverage ratios to settle down to their constant steady-state levels. The assumptions that we make about the levels of these variables will drive the terminal value computation and can have a great impact on our overall valuation results. It is therefore important that we choose plausible values for these terminal assumptions. This section provides some guidelines for plausible assumptions or, failing that, describes what assumptions might be considered ridiculous.

The first, most important, terminal value assumption is the terminal sales growth rate. We can offer you some tight guidelines for this one. If a company were to grow at a faster rate than the rest of the economy forever, then it would gradually become a larger and larger proportion of the total economy. Past some point, it would basically take over the whole economy—and then the world and then the universe! It therefore stands to reason that the terminal growth rate cannot be greater than the long-run expected economywide growth rate. Conversely, if a company were to grow more slowly than the economy forever, then it would gradually become a smaller and smaller proportion of the whole economy and eventually disappear. If your company produces a product that you think will eventually become obsolete, then such an assumption is reasonable. However, it is more usual to simply assume that the company will grow at the long-run expected economywide growth rate. This way, the company will maintain its size relative to the overall economy indefinitely. Historically, the annual growth rate in the U.S. economy, as measured by the nominal GDP growth rate, has averaged around 6 percent, composed of roughly 4 percent real growth and 2 percent price inflation. However, in the past decade it has been closer to 5 percent and the Congressional Budget Office estimates 5 percent nominal GDP growth through 2012 (3 percent real growth and 2 percent price inflation). So, in most cases, a terminal sales growth rate forecast of about 5 percent is reasonable, and should probably never exceed 7 percent. We use 5 percent as the default terminal value for Sales Growth in eVal. Finally, for reasons discussed in Chapter 9, your terminal Sales Growth assumption cannot exceed your cost of equity capital; if it does, you will get error messages.

Next, we must consider the terminal assumptions for margins, turnover ratios, and leverage ratios. Unfortunately, it is not possible to give tight guidelines for each of these assumptions. Recall from Chapter 5 that a company can trade off these performance drivers in an infinite number of ways. For example, more outsourcing will lead to higher turnover and lower margins, while greater product differentiation will lead to lower turnover and higher margins. This makes generalized guidelines impossible. Fortunately, however, we can offer more precise guidelines on the overall combination of assumptions that you choose. Margin, turnover, and leverage combine to give return on equity (ROE). ROE is an accounting measure of the rate of return on investment, and competition tends to force rates of return toward the cost of capital. In fact, if the following two conditions are satisfied, then the terminal ROE should be identical to the cost of equity capital:

1. The firm is operating in a long-run competitive equilibrium.
2. The accounting ROE provides a good measure of the economic rate of return on investment.

Under these conditions, the terminal margin, turnover, and leverage assumptions must combine to give an ROE that is equal to the cost of capital.

What are plausible levels for ROE when we relax these assumptions? Let's relax the first assumption and consider a firm that has a source of competitive advantage that is sustainable indefinitely. In this case, the terminal ROE will be greater than the cost of capital. How much greater depends on how much competitive advantage the company is able to sustain. Here again, we caution that it is very difficult to sustain competitive advantage indefinitely. Make sure that you have a very good case for such a scenario before incorporating it into your valuation model. Finally, you should remember that a terminal rate of return that is more than about 10 percent above the cost of equity capital is unrealistic. Even if competition fails to drive away the abnormal return, the Federal Trade Commission and Department of Justice will prevent the abnormal return from becoming too large (as Microsoft has recently been finding out).

Now let's relax the assumption that accounting ROE provides a good measure of the economic rate of return. As discussed in Chapter 4, there are many reasons accounting rates of return can provide distorted measures of the economic rate of return. Fortunately, most distortions to net income will "wash out" in a steady-state equilibrium. For example, the immediate expensing of R&D tends to downwardly (upwardly) bias income for firms that are spending more (less) on R&D today than they have in the past. But a firm in steady state will be spending a similar amount on R&D today as it did in the past, causing any distortions to "wash out." Unfortunately, distortions that are introduced into the denominator of the ROE calculation typically do not wash out. These distortions arise because GAAP accounting rules do not allow for the capitalization of certain investments. In order to compute an economic rate of return, we need to consider the amount and timing of all past investments that had to be made to generate a cash inflow. Unfortunately, GAAP requires many investments that generate cash inflows over multiple future periods to be expensed in the period that they are incurred. The most common examples of such expenditures are R&D, marketing, and administrative expenditures. Note that while the impact of immediate expensing "washes out" of the income number in steady state, it still causes shareholders' equity to understate invested capital.

In the face of such accounting distortions, the best way to figure out whether your terminal ROE is reasonable is to do a "pro-forma capitalization" of all expenditures that generate future benefits but are immediately expensed under GAAP. This requires you to identify all such expenditures, determine the period over which they are expected to generate future benefits, and then capitalize and amortize them over this period. Once you have done this, you should check that the resulting "pro-forma" ROE is within a plausible range of the cost of capital, given any sustainable competitive advantage. An example helps illustrate the importance of making the pro forma adjustments. Pharmaceutical companies have historically generated ROEs that average about 30 percent, whereas the cost of capital in this industry has only been in the range of 10–15 percent. Is this evidence of monopoly profits? Possibly, but first we need to consider that pharmaceutical companies' annual R&D expenditures have averaged around 25 percent of the book value of equity. Now let's assume that these R&D expenditures generate benefits evenly over the next 12 years, so at any given point there is an average of 6 years' worth of R&D investment missing from the book value of equity. This means we have omitted the capitalized value of R&D equal to about 150 percent of the reported equity value (25 percent per year times an average of 6 years). Hence, if ROE based on as-reported numbers is

$$ROE = \frac{NI}{CE} = 30\%$$

then pro forma ROE' is equal to

$$ROE' = \frac{NI}{CE(1 + 1.5)} = 12\%$$

which is in line with the cost of equity capital. No monopoly profits here!

Forecast Horizon and Terminal Value Assumptions for Kohl's

As we will discuss more in the next chapter, Kohl's is currently in a rapid growth phase. Based on their past growth and on their stated plans for the future, this phase should continue for approximately eight more years. Further, while Kohl's is currently experiencing unusually good performance for the Clothing and Accessories industry, we don't see anything so unique about their strategy that will yield a permanent competitive advantage and doubt that they can hold onto their current levels of profitability for much longer. Finally, there are no significant accounting distortions in Kohl's financial statements that will cause ROE to be systematically different from the cost of capital. Putting all this together, we set our forecast horizon for Kohl's at 10 years. In addition, we set the terminal period sales growth at 5 percent to match the forecast for the economy. As we fill out our detailed forecasts for Kohl's in the next chapter we will also be mindful to keep the terminal ROE below 15 percent, which represents a high estimate of the cost of capital in the Clothing and Accessory industry.

7.6 THE BALANCE SHEET "PLUG"

When we build a forecast of the balance sheet that contains 20 line items, we have only 19 degrees of freedom. In other words, since the balance sheet must balance, the forecasts for the first 19 line items determine the forecast for the 20th line item. More generally, regardless of the number of line items on the balance sheet, the forecast of one line item will always have to be set to make sure that the balance sheet balances. We call this line item the balance sheet "plug." But which line item should we select for the balance sheet plug? The net operating assets are determined by the level and nature of the firm's business activities and should therefore definitely be forecast, making them unsuitable as a plug. This leaves line items relating to financing activities. These line items are more suitable as a plug, because management can generally adapt them as circumstances require. In other words, management typically decides on their desired level of operating and investing activities and then picks a set of financing activities that provide sufficient capital to fund the operating and investing activities.

While most analysts would agree that the net operating assets should be forecast directly, there is less agreement on which particular financing line item should be used as a plug. Some analysts use cash as the plug (with a negative cash balance representing a bank overdraft). This approach has two shortcomings. First, it assumes that management will make no attempt to establish a financing policy that keeps their cash balance at the minimum level necessary to sustain their operating activities. This is a somewhat naive financing policy (but then again, it seems to be the one that Microsoft is using). Second, in the case of a bank overdraft, it presupposes that management would be able to secure an overdraft. In the case of a financially distressed firm, this may not be a reasonable supposition.

The other common choice is to plug to common equity. The appeal of this choice is that the common stockholders are the residual claimants of the firm and are thus the natural group to soak up any surpluses or deficits in the firm's financing activities. But this approach also has two shortcomings. First, in the case of a financing surplus, plugging to common equity assumes that management will pay a big dividend or make a big stock repurchase. But many managers instead choose either to keep surplus cash or to reinvest it in new projects. Second, in the case of a financing deficit, plugging to common equity assumes that the firm will issue new equity. As with a bank overdraft, this presupposes that management would be able to access capital markets on acceptable terms.

There is no perfect answer to this problem. eVal plugs to common equity, but we warn you not to take the results of this assumption blindly. You should look at

FIGURE 7.2
Forecasting Horizon in eVal

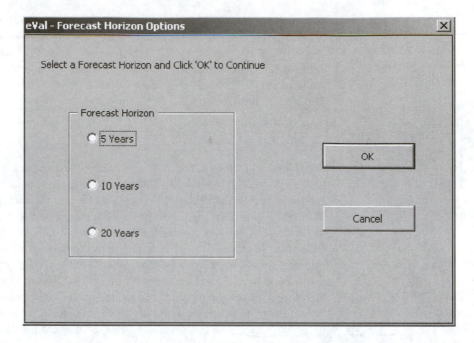

the plug amount and ask yourself whether the implied amount of stock issued or repurchased really represents what you think management will do. If not, then you need to iterate back through the other line items in your forecasting model until you get a complete set of forecasts that you are happy with. For instance, if you really believe that management will build a large cash balance rather than repurchase stock (as Microsoft has), then turn up the forecasted cash balance and the plug to common equity will automatically reduce the implied stock repurchase.

7.7 FORECASTING WITH EVAL

Now let's take a look at how eVal guides you through the forecasting process. Step 2 of the User's Guide sheet in eVal walks you through the forecasting process. You start by clicking the Input Forecasting Assumptions button. This will bring up the dialog box shown in Figure 7.2 prompting you to select a forecast horizon.

The horizon options are 5 years, 10 years, or 20 years. Use the guidelines provided in section 7.4 to select an appropriate forecast horizon. If you want to select a forecast horizon that is between the options provided, select the next longest forecast horizon and then straight-line your forecasts beyond your desired forecast horizon. For example, if you would like to use a forecast horizon of 14 years, then select a 20-year horizon and straight-line your forecasts for years 15 through 20.

FIGURE 7.3
Forecasting Assumptions Sheet in eVal

whAt date?

Volunteer date?

can't get back to Figure 7.2 once you select horizon

linearly interpolates between 1st & last yr

	A	B	C	D	E	F	G	H	I	
1	**Forecasting Assumptions**									
2	Go To User's Guide		Change Forecast Horizon							
3										
5	Company Name	Kohls Corporation								
6	Forecast Horizon	10 Years								
7	Estimated Price/Share=$41.77									
8		Actual	Actual	Actual	Actual	Actual	Forecast	Forecast	Forecast	Fo
9	Fiscal Year End Date	1/31/1998	1/30/1999	1/29/2000	2/3/2001	2/2/2002	2/2/2003	2/2/2004	2/2/2005	2/
10										
11	Implied Return on Equity		0.182	0.181	0.191	0.199	0.192	0.191	0.189	
12										
13	Income Statement Assumptions									
14	Sales Growth		20.3%	23.8%	35.0%	21.7%	20.2%	18.7%	17.2%	
15	Cost of Goods Sold/Sales	66.9%	66.5%	66.1%	65.9%	65.7%	65.7%	65.7%	65.7%	
16	R&D/Sales	0.0%	0.0%	0.0%	0.0%	0.0%	0.0%	0.0%	0.0%	
17	SG&A/Sales	22.8%	22.4%	22.1%	21.4%	20.8%	20.8%	20.8%	20.8%	
18	Dep&Amort/Avge PP&E and Intang.		8.1%	7.6%	8.2%	8.0%	8.0%	8.0%	8.0%	
19	Interest Expense/Avge Debt		7.3%	6.5%	7.0%	5.9%	5.9%	5.9%	5.9%	
20	Non-Operating Income/Sales	0.0%	0.0%	0.1%	0.1%	0.1%	0.1%	0.1%	0.1%	
21	Effective Tax Rate	39.9%	39.3%	30.7%	36.5%	38.0%	38.0%	38.0%	38.0%	
22	Minority Interest/After Tax Income	0.0%	0.0%	0.0%	0.0%	0.0%	0.0%	0.0%	0.0%	
23	Other Income/Sales	0.0%	0.0%	0.0%	0.0%	0.0%	0.0%	0.0%	0.0%	
24	Ext. Items & Disc. Ops./Sales	0.0%	0.0%	0.0%	0.0%	0.0%	0.0%	0.0%	0.0%	
25	Pref. Dividends/Avge Pref. Stock		0.0%	0.0%	0.0%	0.0%	0.0%	0.0%	0.0%	
26										
27	Balance Sheet Assumptions:									
28	Working Capital Assumptions									
29	Ending Operating Cash/Sales	1.4%	0.8%	0.9%	2.8%	4.5%	4.5%	4.5%	4.5%	
30	Ending Receivables/Sales	7.8%	7.4%	11.1%	11.1%	11.2%	11.2%	11.2%	11.2%	
31	Ending Inventories/COGS	25.2%	25.2%	26.4%	24.7%	24.3%	24.3%	24.3%	24.3%	
32	Ending Other Current Assets/Sales	0.4%	0.6%	1.0%	1.1%	1.3%	1.3%	1.3%	1.3%	
33	Ending Accounts Payable/COGS	7.4%	8.7%	11.2%	9.9%	9.7%	9.7%	9.7%	9.7%	
34	Ending Taxes Payable/Sales	1.3%	1.3%	1.4%	1.8%	1.7%	1.7%	1.7%	1.7%	
35	Ending Other Current Liabs/Sales	3.1%	3.2%	3.4%	3.1%	3.5%	3.5%	3.5%	3.5%	
36	Other Operating Asset Assumptions									
37	Ending Net PP&E/Sales	24.5%	25.3%	29.7%	28.1%	29.4%	29.4%	29.4%	29.4%	

Selecting a forecast horizon and clicking OK takes you to the Forecasting Assumptions worksheet shown in Figure 7.3. Reading across the columns of this worksheet you will see 5 years of historical data on each of the forecasting assumptions and 21 years of forecast data. The forecast data pertaining to the forecast horizon that you selected will be shaded yellow, indicating that you are free to edit the values listed in these cells.

We will give you lots of detailed advice on filling in the yellow cells in the next chapter; for now we just want you to become familiar with the overall way that eVal organizes your forecasting inputs. Reading down the rows of this worksheet, you will see each of the forecasting assumptions laid out following the forecasting framework outlined in Figure 7.1. For instance, we begin with the sales growth rate assumption. If you look at the default forecasting assumptions for sales growth, you will see that it makes a smooth progression over the forecast horizon from its value in the most recent historical year to a terminal year rate of 5 percent. If you change the sales growth forecast for the first year of the forecast period, eVal automatically smooths between this new growth rate and the terminal growth rate. The default eVal formula for most line items is similar, smoothing between the value in the first forecast period and value in the terminal forecast period. Therefore, one approach to quickly entering the forecasting assumptions is to forecast the first year and the terminal year and let the formulas smooth out everything in between. Or you can enter the first few years of forecasts and let the formulas smooth from the last year you entered to your terminal year forecast (play with it a bit—you'll soon get the hang of it!). Because eVal uses the most recent year for its default values, you should be particularly wary of unusual changes in this last year—go back and read that MD&A again!

The remaining income statement assumptions forecast the margins. The default assumption for most of the income statement items is to simply straight-line their values from the most recent historical year. The exceptions to this rule are Other Income/Sales and Extraordinary Items and Discontinued Operations/Sales. These line items typically contain non-recurring amounts, so a better default forecasting assumption is that they will be zero in all future periods. Of course, you should always take a close look at the exact nature of the items that have appeared here in the recent past and make your own assessment about the likelihood that they will recur in the future.

The balance sheet assumptions are listed further down the sheet and are presented in four groups. The working capital assumptions are basically forecasts of the associated turnover ratios, except that we put the balance sheet item in the numerator and divide by the corresponding flow variable (sales or cost of goods sold). This is basically the reciprocal of the turnover ratio. We have found that it is much more intuitive to put the balance sheet item in the numerator when we are

trying to forecast the balance sheet item. Note also that we are forecasting the ending balance of the item rather than an average over the period (unlike the turnover ratios in eVal's Ratio Analysis sheet which are based on average balance sheet amounts). While algebraically possible, forecasting the average balance and then backing into the implied ending balance causes the forecasted ratios to oscillate in very disconcerting ways. Consistent with the way in which we compute turnover ratios, we express inventory and payables as a percentage of cost of goods sold and all the other working capital accounts as a percentage of sales.

The next two groups of balance sheet forecasting assumptions are the other (noncurrent) operating asset and operating liability assumptions. As with the working capital assumptions, we forecast the ending balance of each of these line items as a percentage of sales. These assumptions fill out the asset side of the balance sheet and the operating portion of the liabilities (the net operating assets). All that is left on the balance sheet are the financial obligations and equity, which are determined by your financing assumptions. The debt, minority interest, and preferred stock assumptions are statements about the firm's leverage, expressed as a proportion of total assets. Having forecast the assets, the liabilities, and the preferred stock, the common equity balance is determined—it is the "plug" that we discussed earlier.

Notice that you are allowed to forecast the dividend payout ratio. You may wonder how the ending balance in common equity can be determined if you are free to forecast any dividend you like. Doesn't a dividend reduce the common equity balance? Technically, yes, but since the common equity balance is already determined by your other assumptions, eVal adjusts the implied stock issuances or repurchases to exactly offset any dividend that you forecast. That is, your forecasted dividends reduce retained earnings, but eVal increases the balance in paid in capital by exactly the same amount so as to leave common equity unaffected. Play with it a bit and you will see what we mean.

eVal provides you with a few diagnostics to help judge the plausibility of your forecasting assumptions. First, up at the top of the Forecasting Assumptions worksheet you will find the Implied Return on Equity. Recall from section 7.5 that while it is difficult to provide plausible bounds for each of the individual balance sheet and income statement assumptions, they should all combine to give a return on equity figure that is within a plausible distance from the cost of capital. Second, by returning to the User's Guide and hitting the buttons under step 2, you can see a complete ratio and cash flow analysis implied by your assumptions. Do these forecasted ratios jibe with your views about the firm's future? One particularly important item to look at in the cash flow analysis is Net Issuance of Common Stock. As we discussed earlier, this is the amount computed by eVal in order to make your balance sheet balance. A positive amount indicates the amount that will have to be raised through issuance of new stock; a negative amount indicates the amount that will be used to repurchase stock. You should ask yourself if the market conditions are conducive to raising new stock? Does management intend to use excess cash for stock repurchases? If not, then you need to iterate back through your forecasting assumptions until you have a more plausible scenario.

Suppose management told you they expected the balance in PP&E to be $100 million next year. To hit this amount on your forecasted balance sheet might be a bit tough—you would have to keep changing the PP&E/Sales forecast until you hit exactly $100 million on the financial statements. To make this a bit easier, eVal also lets you enter financial data directly into the financial statements. This is not the way that we recommend you build your forecasts in most cases, but it is sometimes helpful. To make this happen go to the Financial Statements sheet and click the Enter Raw Forecast Financial Data button at the top of the sheet. This will unprotect and shade in yellow all of the financial statement data relating to your currently selected forecast horizon. Upon leaving the Financial Statements worksheet, all amounts in the Forecasting Assumptions worksheet will be updated to reflect the raw forecast data that you entered. Note that using this option will override and remove all the smoothing algorithms from the Forecasting Assumptions worksheet. Please use this feature with care. Once you hit the Enter Raw Financial Forecast button, you have kissed goodbye to many of the internal consistency checks in eVal. If your balance sheet no longer balances, take a look in the mirror to see who is to blame.

7.8 FORECASTING EPS

The forecasts discussed so far are all at the firm level. However, investors in public corporations rarely buy the entire firm. Instead, they buy shares representing fractional interests in the firm. For this reason, it is common practice to express certain key forecasts on a "per-share" basis. This allows for direct comparisons with stock prices, which are also expressed on a per-share basis. Not surprisingly, the most common financial statement item to be expressed on a per-share basis is earnings. Earnings is the key accounting summary measure of firm performance, so it is useful to know just how much earnings a company is generating per share of outstanding common stock. Earnings-per-share, or EPS, is the most commonly published forecast by security analysts. Moreover, the extent to which reported quarterly EPS differs from the consensus analyst forecast of EPS is probably the single most important determinant of short-term movements in stock price.

In theory, the computation of EPS forecasts is quite simple. We simply divide forecast earnings by the forecast weighted-average number of shares outstanding for the period. In practice, however, the forecasting of the weighted average number of shares outstanding is troublesome. There are two distinct problems. The first is in forecasting the number of shares that will be issued and/or repurchased between now and the end of each future forecasting period. The second is in forecasting the number of common stock equivalents that will be outstanding at the end of future forecasting periods.

The first problem arises because we do not know the future prices at which any stock issuances and repurchases will take place. Our forecast financial statements tell us how many dollars of common equity we expect the firm to issue or repurchase in each future forecasting period. But in order to compute the associated number of shares, we need to know the prices at which these transactions will take place. This introduces a strange circularity into our computations. In order to forecast EPS, we first need to forecast the future price of a share of stock. But if we already knew the latter, we probably wouldn't be bothered about doing the former! Fortunately, there is a pragmatic and internally consistent solution to this circularity problem. We simply assume that our estimate of the stock's current value is correct, compound this amount by the cost of equity capital and then subtract any cash dividends that are forecast to arrive at the future stock price. Of course, all this is automated in eVal.

The aforementioned solution is fine if the current market price of the stock is close to the intrinsic price generated by your forecasting model. But what if the current market price of the stock is very different from the price implied by your model? In this case, either your forecasting model is wrong or the market price is wrong. If you conclude that the former is the case, then you should go back to the drawing board and build a better forecasting model. If you conclude that the latter is the case, then you have identified a mispriced stock. But before computing EPS forecasts, you need to consider the possibility that the firm could issue or repurchase shares of common stock in the future at a market price that differs from intrinsic value. Firms with mispriced stock can influence their own EPS (and intrinsic share price) by engaging in strategic transactions in their own stock. Firms with overpriced stock can increase EPS (and intrinsic share price) by issuing stock, while firms with underpriced stock can increase EPS (and intrinsic share price) by repurchasing stock. This is a complicated topic, and we will defer a more complete discussion to Chapter 12. At this point, you should simply be aware that the procedure used by eVal to compute EPS does not consider such complications; it simply assumes that future equity transactions will take place at the estimated price given in the model.

The second problem in computing EPS arises because analysts and investors most commonly forecast *diluted* earnings per share. If you are an accounting geek, you will remember that EPS comes in two varieties—basic and diluted. Basic EPS simply involves dividing earnings by shares outstanding. Diluted EPS involves dividing earnings by shares outstanding plus common stock equivalents related to potentially dilutive securities, such as employee stock options and convertible bonds. These potentially dilutive securities represent contingent claims on common equity, and incorporating them helps in figuring out what is likely to be left for the existing common stockholders. Unfortunately, the forecasting of future common stock equivalents is very complicated and difficult to do with much accuracy. We therefore focus on forecasting basic EPS. We can, however, offer you some simple practical advice if you want to forecast diluted EPS. Take a look at the firm's most recent financial statements. The income statement should report both basic and diluted EPS. If these two numbers are very similar, then potentially dilutive securities are probably not a big deal and so ignoring them is reasonable. If these two numbers differ by, say 10% or more, then common stock equivalents are important and should be considered. A good "base case" forecasting assumption is that the number of common stock equivalents related to potentially dilutive securities will remain constant in the future. But if you are looking at a firm that plans to restructure its employee stock option plan or refinance its convertible debt, you need to pull out your intermediate accounting text and burn some midnight oil.

To make the above discussion more concrete, let's take a look at the EPS forecasts for Kohl's using the default forecasting assumptions in eVal (and setting the valuation date to 9/3/2002). The EPS forecasts and associated computations are contained in the "EPS Forecaster" worksheet that can be accessed by clicking the "View EPS Forecasts" button on the User's Guide worksheet. This worksheet is reproduced in Figure 7.4. The key financial statement inputs to this sheet are the number of common shares outstanding at the most recent balance sheet date, the forecasted price of the company (based on eVal's current forecasting assumptions), the forecast of net income for each future year and the amount of common equity that is forecast to be issued (repurchased) in each future year. You can follow the formulas in the respective cells to trace each of these inputs back to their source worksheets.

The first computation in the EPS Forecaster worksheet is the forecast of the price at the end of each future year. The future price is computed by taking the estimated price at the end of the previous year (based on the eVal estimate), multiplying by one plus the cost of equity capital to reflect the expected return for the year, and then subtracting the forecast dividend-per-share for the year. Armed with the forecast price-per-share, the computation of EPS is straightforward. We first divide common equity issued (repurchased) for the year by forecast price for the year to obtain the number of new shares issued (repurchased) for the year. Next, we compute shares outstanding at the end of each year by adding (subtracting) shares issued (repurchased) for the year to the outstanding balance from the previous year. Finally, we divide net income by this average number of shares outstanding for the year to arrive at our basic EPS forecast.

FIGURE 7.4
EPS Forecaster
Sheet in eVal

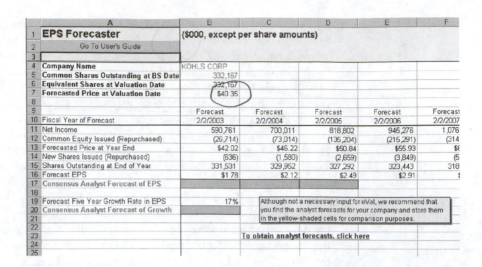

	A	B	C	D	E	F
1	**EPS Forecaster**	**($000, except per share amounts)**				
2	Go To User's Guide					
3						
4	Company Name	KOHLS CORP				
5	Common Shares Outstanding at BS Date	332,167				
6	Equivalent Shares at Valuation Date	332,167				
7	Forecasted Price at Valuation Date	$40.35				
8						
9		Forecast	Forecast	Forecast	Forecast	Forecast
10	Fiscal Year of Forecast	2/2/2003	2/2/2004	2/2/2005	2/2/2006	2/2/2007
11	Net Income	590,761	700,011	818,802	945,276	1,076
12	Common Equity Issued (Repurchased)	(26,714)	(73,014)	(135,204)	(215,291)	(314
13	Forecasted Price at Year End	$42.02	$46.22	$50.84	$55.93	$6
14	New Shares Issued (Repurchased)	(636)	(1,580)	(2,659)	(3,849)	(5
15	Shares Outstanding at End of Year	331,531	329,952	327,292	323,443	318
16	Forecast EPS	$1.78	$2.12	$2.49	$2.91	$
17	Consensus Analyst Forecast of EPS					
18						
19	Forecast Five Year Growth Rate in EPS	17%	Although not a necessary input for eVal, we recommend that			
20	Consensus Analyst Forecast of Growth		you find the analyst forecasts for your company and store them			
21			in the yellow-shaded cells for comparison purposes.			
22						
23			To obtain analyst forecasts, click here			
24						
25						

One of the most important functions of the "EPS Forecaster" worksheet is to allow you to compare your EPS forecasts with the consensus analyst forecast. We provide a link at the bottom of the "EPS Forecaster" worksheet that takes you directly to First Call's earnings estimates. Where possible, you should compare your forecasts to the consensus analyst EPS forecasts for each of the next two years. You will find these forecasts under the heading "Earnings Per Share" with the captions "This Year" and "Next Year" on the First Call earnings estimates web page. You should also compare your forecast of the five-year growth rate in EPS to the corresponding consensus analyst forecast. You will find this forecast under the heading "Earnings Growth" with the caption "Next 5 Years Est." on the First Call earnings estimates web page. Deviations between realized EPS and the consensus forecast of EPS are referred to as "earnings surprises" and are an important catalyst for stock price revisions.

7.9 CONCLUSION

Forecasting is where the rubber meets the road in equity valuation. A valuation is only as good as the forecasts that support it. And good forecasts come only from a careful synthesis of the findings from your business, accounting, and financial analyses. It is important that you forecast the complete financial statements and that you use a systematic forecasting framework that maintains internal consistency in the resulting statements. It is also important that your forecasting assumptions lead to economically plausible statements about the future.

So far we have talked about forecasting from the 30,000-foot level. The next chapter gets down to the nitty-gritty of forecasting the individual line items on the financial statements.

Forecasting Details

8.1 INTRODUCTION

The last chapter described our general framework for forecasting a firm's future financial statements. In this chapter we give more specific guidance about how to come up with a reasonable forecast for each financial statement line item. Obviously, we can't tell you what to forecast in every circumstance; rather, we try to give you a list of things to think about.

As you proceed through the income statement and balance sheet assumptions you may be plagued by the following two thoughts. The first is that there is always more you could do to develop a better forecast of each item. There is an endless amount of data available—maybe a little more hunting will produce the perfect indicator of the future for the particular variable you are trying to forecast. The second doubt is that, even after all your hard work, you still feel uncertain about the resulting forecast. Both of these feelings are valid but there is nothing we can do about them; the world is an uncertain place. We offer you a framework to guide you through the forecasting process, and we offer you some guidance about what reasonable forecasts might be, but we don't have the crystal ball that perfectly predicts the future.

This chapter will talk you through the individual income statement and balance sheet assumptions that eVal uses to construct the forecasted financial statements. For some of the forecasts it may help to build a more detailed model and then plug the results from the fancier model into the appropriate income statement or balance sheet assumption. For instance, you may want to forecast sales growth separately for each business segment and then add them up to arrive at the firm-wide forecasted sales growth rate. To give you a place to build such detailed models, eVal includes a User Worksheet. This is essentially a blank sheet that you can use for whatever purposes you want. Besides using this sheet to build more detailed models, you can use it to store links to useful news articles, clips from other electronic sources, or pictures of your dog.

8.2 FORECASTING SALES GROWTH

If God offers to fill in one row of your spreadsheet, this is the one to ask for. Sales growth, or the lack of it, is a huge driver of value. You should bring everything you can to bear on this forecast. eVal shows the firm's past history of sales growth but this is only a starting point. Extreme levels of sales growth mean-revert very quickly. Nissan and Penman (2001) report that in a large sample of firms between 1963 and 1999 the top decile of annual sales growth was about 80 percent. Firms in this decile had sales growth of only about 20 percent in the very next year, however, and only a bit over 10 percent in the year after that. So just because sales growth has been high in the past doesn't mean that sales growth will be high in the future.

Obviously we can't give you a recipe for forecasting sales that will apply to all companies in all situations. What follows is a basic approach along with a list of things that you should consider for most companies. We start by forecasting industry sales growth. With this as a benchmark you can then ask if the firm is likely to increase or decrease its share of industry sales. This exercise starts with macroeconomic data and works down to a firm-specific forecast. The next step is to consider all the firm-level data in more detail. Regardless of what is going on at the industry level, your firm may behave very differently. What information is there in the firm's own financial statements and other sources that can help you predict future sales growth?

Forecasting Industry Sales Growth

To build a forecast of industry sales growth, go back to Chapter 2 and look over the list of available macroeconomic data. What are the key drivers of sales in your industry? More important, what are the key indicators of *future* sales? For example, the aging of the baby boomers is a very predictable phenomenon that has huge implications for the health care sector. You could study past trends in personal expenditures on health care as a function of the median age of the population. As another example, suppose you are studying a house-building company in the South. The demand for houses is a function of many things, including age demographics, migration patterns across geographic regions, and interest rates. The U.S. government collects detailed statistics on all these variables. You could estimate the relation between these variables and past housing demand in the South and then extrapolate from this model the demand for future housing.

Building a model of industry sales that predicts the future is no easy task. And even if you find a set of variables that predicts industry sales very well, your particular firm may buck the trend. Nevertheless, we encourage you to spend some time on this task. Even if your work doesn't result in a great predictor of industry sales, the exercise will help you identify the key drivers of sales and this should help to keep your long-term sales forecasts reasonable. Also keep in mind that your goal is to predict future sales, not explain past sales. A macroeconomic variable that moves concurrently with industry sales will make for a beautiful graph, but unless you can generate decent forecasts of the variable, it won't be much help

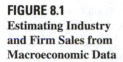

FIGURE 8.1
Estimating Industry and Firm Sales from Macroeconomic Data

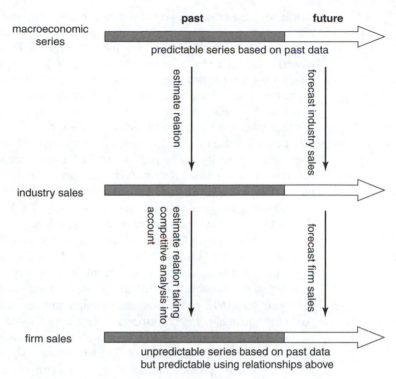

in forecasting future sales. For example, it turns out that the return on the S&P 500 is a great concurrent predictor of demand for cruise vacations; apparently, when the market is up the "cruising" segment of the population splurges on a great vacation. While this observation makes for a great graph, it is completely useless for predicting future demand for cruise vacations, unless you think you can predict future movements in the S&P 500. And if you can reliably predict future movements in the S&P 500, then you really don't need this book!

Figure 8.1 illustrates how you might think about linking macroeconomic data to industry sales and firm-specific sales. For this to be a useful exercise, you need two key relationships to be very strong. You need the macroeconomic data to be predictable in the future and you need the links between the macroeconomic data, the industry sales, and the firm sales to be strong. If both these conditions are true then you can build a sales forecast by first predicting the macroeconomic series, then forecasting industry sales from the macro prediction, and then forecasting firm sales from the industry prediction. Demographic trends, for example, are very predictable macroeconomic phenomena. It would be foolish to ignore these trends if your firm's customers come from a particular slice of the demographic pie. In addition, a number of macroeconomic trends are linked to GDP growth. While GDP growth isn't a simple series to predict, economists put so much effort into forecasting it that you can get decent forecasts from the web (check out the Congressional Budget Office or the Conference Board links at the end of the chapter). As an example, personal consumption expenditures on durable goods (for instance, washing machines) tend to grow rapidly as the economy comes out of a recession. If the GDP forecasts indicate a recession is ending, then this is a powerful indicator of a large increase in sales of durable goods in the immediate future. On the other hand, business investment in fixed goods takes much longer to start growing after a recession, so your prediction for an equipment supplier might be much more subdued.

Once you have a forecast of industry sales growth, the next task is to predict how this will relate to your particular firm's sales growth. At this step you need to consider the intensity of competition from alternative sources for the same products or services. Who are the firm's competitors and how intensely are they competing? The link between industry sales and firm sales is obviously stronger if the firm makes up a significant fraction of the industry. The link is weakest when the firm is small or when the industry is growing rapidly. As an example, the growth in grocery store sales in the United States has been remarkably stable over the past five years, ranging between 2 and 4 percent. No matter how much advertising stores place in the local newspapers, people can eat only so much. Sales growth, however, at the 50 publicly traded grocery store chains has been much more rapid, averaging almost 12 percent, as smaller mom-and-pop stores are swallowed up. And of the 50 publicly traded grocery store chains, Gristedes has enjoyed average annual sales growth of over 123 percent for the past five years, as it has grown from one store to six. So, while total sales by grocery stores is a very predictable amount, it doesn't provide much guidance for a firm such as Gristedes. Industry sales growth is a better benchmark for a large firm, such as Kroger, which makes up about 10 percent of all U.S. grocery store sales ($51 billion out of $470 billion nationwide). In fact, Kroger has grown at only 8 percent annually over the past five years, much closer to the industry average.

The firm-specific facts that we discuss in the next section are typically the main drivers of sales for small and growing firms. In addition, firms with winning strategies may generate unusually large sales growth in the short run by stealing market share from other firms. But in the long run even these companies can't escape the economic forces of the industry.

Firm-Specific Influences on Sales Growth

There are many useful predictors of future sales that come from the firm itself. One significant indicator of future sales is the firm's current and future investments, especially in new sales locations, recent promotional campaigns, or new products. Firms make investments to generate future income, so assuming the firm isn't making bad bets, these investments will be harbingers of future sales. As an example, you can divide retail sales growth into growth from opening new stores and growth from increased sales at existing outlets (known as same-store or comparable-store sales growth). California Pizza Kitchen can grow rapidly by opening up new restaurants all over the country but the very nature of a restaurant puts severe limits on the amount of sales growth that can be generated from the existing locations. Only so many people can squeeze into one booth. Retail companies frequently disclose their plans for new store openings over the next few years and you should use this information to estimate the contribution that new stores will make to total sales growth. You can then combine this with an estimate of the more modest contribution that same-store sales growth will make to arrive at the total sales growth rate.

This same logic extends well beyond forecasting in the retail sales business. Most investments are made to generate a sequence of future sales. When the newly invested capital goes online there is a big burst of new sales, followed by a reasonably steady stream of future sales from that investment. It is therefore useful to distinguish between the large bursts of sales growth that come from newly invested capital and the much lower growth in sales, if any, that comes from the more efficient use of previously invested capital.

You can frequently gain some useful information from the segment disclosure footnote in the financial statements, which describes sales, profits, and investments by major product lines and geographic regions. This information can help focus your attention on the largest sources of sales for the firm and show you where they are investing for the future. The firm's MD&A (capital resources section) is also a good source of information about the firm's future growth prospects.

Forecasting future sales is very important but very difficult. Take this part of the forecasting task seriously, but also be mindful that some fraction of future sales is inherently unknowable. Floods, pestilence, technological innovation, and the inherent fickleness of the American consumer all combine to make Sales a truly random variable. Use all of your collected wisdom to make educated guesses and to put reasonable bounds on your estimates but then move on.

Finally, we would like to repeat the warning from the previous chapter. Do NOT make the terminal year forecast of sales growth very large—7 percent might be a maximum. Think about what it would mean to forecast a large growth rate into perpetuity; as the company grows faster than the world economy it would slowly but surely take over the entire planet. So unless you mean to forecast this type of world domination, don't let your sales growth forecast get too big in the terminal period.

A Sales Forecast for Kohl's

We will illustrate our approach to forecasting sales using Kohl's. Recall that in the last chapter we decided to use a 10-year forecasting horizon for Kohl's. Since Kohl's is a small but rapidly growing firm, the macro approach to forecasting sales might not be very fruitful, at least for the next few years. In the short run we should forecast their sales based on estimates of their new store growth. In the long run, however, Kohl's will be subject to the undeniable fact that the Clothing and Accessory industry is a relatively stable and slowly growing industry. We will start by looking for the drivers of industry sales growth to guide our terminal period forecast but then develop our more immediate sales forecasts for Kohl's based primarily on company-specific data.

Figure 8.2 illustrates how sales growth in the Clothing and Accessories industry is related to growth in the gross domestic product and particularly to growth in

FIGURE 8.2 **Clothing and Accessories Industry Sales Growth Drivers**

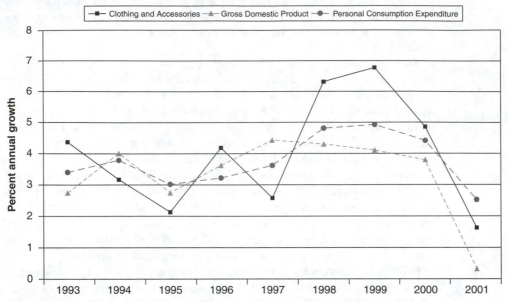

Source: Bureau of Census Retail Sales Survey and Bureau of Economic Analysis NIPA Tables.

personal consumption expenditures. While growth in Clothing and Accessories Sales is more volatile than growth in Personal Consumption Expenditures or GDP, all three series basically move together and average to about the same amounts over time. In addition, consumer expenditure survey data from the Bureau of Labor Statistics shows that the percent of personal consumption expenditures on apparel has remained almost constant over the past few years. Forecasted growth in GDP is therefore likely to be a good predictor of growth in the Clothing and Accessories Industry. The Congressional Budget office estimates that nominal GDP growth (real GDP growth plus price inflation) will be 3.4 percent in 2002, increase to 5.2 percent in 2004, and remain relatively constant thereafter. Given the correspondence between GDP growth and growth in the Clothing and Accessories Industry, we can use this as our industry forecast. Although Kohl's is likely to grow faster than the industry for some time, eventually it will be governed by these more modest growth forecasts.

Turning to company-specific information, we learn from Kohl's 10-K (available in the eVal2 program files folder) that they currently have 382 stores located primarily in the Midwest and the East. They also state that they expect to open 70 new stores in 2002 and 80 new stores in 2003, and plan to continue opening stores at this rate as they grow throughout the country. To estimate how many stores a fully built-out system would contain, we note that in Wisconsin and Michigan, two of Kohl's most developed states, they are averaging 3.5 stores per million

FIGURE 8.3

The Relation between Kohl's Number of Stores and Sales

people. Extrapolating to the U.S. population of 280 million, this suggests a mature system of about 980 stores (as a point of comparison, Target Stores has 1,053 stores). So we tentatively forecast that they will add about 80 stores per year for the next eight years in order to meet their growth objectives.

New stores certainly contribute to growth in sales, but in the retail environment an equally important statistic is the growth in sales from stores that have been open at least a year, known as comparable store sales. Kohl's notes with pride in their 2001 MD&A that they enjoyed 6.8 percent comparable store growth even though the general economy suffered (as a point of comparison, Target Stores had comparable store sales growth of 4.1 percent in 2001). Looking ahead, Kohl's MD&A notes that in the future they expect comparable store growth rates in the "mid single digits." We interpret this to mean 5 percent.

There are many wrinkles to weaving the new store growth estimate and the comparable store growth estimate together into a forecast of future sales. We will take only a quick look at it here. We begin by plotting Sales on the number of stores for each year since 1992, as shown in Figure 8.3. Obviously these two variables are closely related. The slope of the line indicates that each new store adds about $21 million in sales and the intercept is $-$533 million. If we extrapolate the line to 452 stores (382 old plus 70 new), we get a forecast for 2002 of $8,959 million. If we figure that 84 percent of those stores are old in 2002 and old stores will experience 5 percent comparable store growth, we can gross up the 2002 sales estimate to 8959[1 + (.84)(.05)] = 9335. This represents 24.7 percent growth in 2002. In similar fashion we can fill out the remaining forecasts, as illustrated in Figure 8.4.

Can Kohl's continue to outperform the industry sales growth forecast of 5 percent for the next 10 years? Based on their past it certainly seems possible, but remember that every dollar of sales growth Kohl's gets beyond 5 percent is being taken from someone else. As Kohl's continues to enter new markets it may face increasing competition. For this reason we drop the terminal year sales growth to 5 percent, matching the economywide GDP estimate.

FIGURE 8.4 **Sales History and Sales Forecasts for Kohl's**

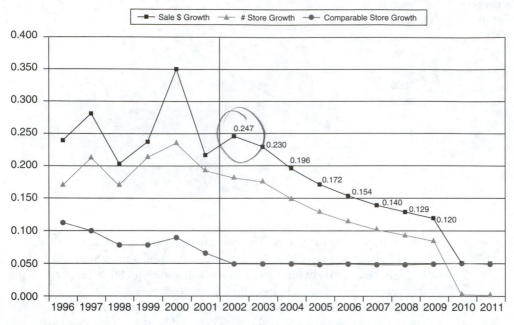

8.3 EXPENSE FORECASTS

As a roadmap to the expense forecasts, Figure 8.5 shows the Income Statement Assumptions section of eVal's Forecasting Assumptions sheet. Having completed the sales growth forecasts, now it is time to think about how expenses are going to eat away at those revenues. To follow along in eVal set the forecast horizon to 10 years and modify the forecasting assumptions as described. You need to use the financial data for Kohl's that is preloaded in eVal. If you load Kohl's from the Data Center sheet you will get more recent data than used in this example.

Many expenses move with sales, such as Cost of Goods Sold and Selling, General and Administrative Expenses, and so we forecast these expenses as a percentage of sales. However, just because the forecast input is a percentage of sales doesn't mean that you should forecast it as a *constant* percent of sales. Firms may enjoy economies of scale as they grow or they may implement cost management programs; both would lower these expense ratios. In addition, remember that a sales price increase has the same effect as lowering expenses when it comes to forecasting expenses as a percentage of sales.

In some cases the account balances rather than sales levels are the drivers of the income statement items. For example, there is a very strong relation between the Debt on the balance sheet and the Interest Expense on the income statement—the debt balance times the interest rate equals the interest expense. So for interest

FIGURE 8.5
Income Statement Assumptions for Kohl's

2002 Sales year

	Actual	Forecast	Forecast	Forecast	Forecast	Forecast	Forecast	Forecast	Forecast	Forecast
Forecasting Assumptions										
Company Name										
Forecast Horizon										
Estimated Price/Share=$42.87										
Fiscal Year End Date	2/2/2002	2/2/2003	2/2/2004	2/2/2005	2/2/2006	2/2/2007	2/2/2008	2/2/2009	2/2/2010	2/2/2011
Implied Return on Equity	0.199	0.208	0.223	0.229	0.232	0.232	0.226	0.220	0.214	0.19
Income Statement Assumptions										
Sales Growth	21.7%	24.7%	23.0%	19.6%	17.2%	15.4%	14.0%	12.9%	12.0%	5.0
Cost of Goods Sold/Sales	65.7%	65.7%	65.7%	65.7%	65.7%	65.7%	65.8%	65.8%	65.9%	65.9
R&D/Sales	0.0%	0.0%	0.0%	0.0%	0.0%	0.0%	0.0%	0.0%	0.0%	0.0
SG&A/Sales	20.8%	20.6%	20.4%	20.2%	20.0%	19.8%	19.8%	19.8%	19.8%	19.8
Dep&Amort/Avge PP&E and Intang	8.0%	9.1%	10.1%	11.2%	12.3%	13.4%	14.5%	15.6%	16.7%	17.8
Interest Expense/Avge Debt	5.9%	6.0%	6.0%	6.0%	6.0%	6.0%	6.0%	6.0%	6.0%	6.0
Non-Operating Income/Sales	0.1%	0.0%	0.0%	0.0%	0.0%	0.0%	0.0%	0.0%	0.0%	0.0
Effective Tax Rate	38.0%	38.1%	38.2%	38.3%	38.3%	38.3%	38.3%	38.3%	38.3%	38.3
Minority Interest/After Tax Income	0.0%	0.0%	0.0%	0.0%	0.0%	0.0%	0.0%	0.0%	0.0%	0.0
Other Income/Sales	0.0%	0.0%	0.0%	0.0%	0.0%	0.0%	0.0%	0.0%	0.0%	0.0
Ext. Items & Disc. Ops./Sales	0.0%	0.0%	0.0%	0.0%	0.0%	0.0%	0.0%	0.0%	0.0%	0.0
Pref. Dividends/Avge Pref. Stock	0.0%	0.0%	0.0%	0.0%	0.0%	0.0%	0.0%	0.0%	0.0%	0.0

expense and some other items, the forecast of the income statement item is based on its relation to a balance sheet item.

When forecasting a firm's expense ratios you should always compare them with their industry peers. As we discussed in Chapter 5, you can load a peer firm or an industry composite into eVal from the Data Center sheet.

Cost of Goods Sold

The ratio of Cost of Goods Sold (COGS) to Sales describes how much of every sales dollar is spent directly on providing the product or delivering the service. When forecasting this item think about how the firm's products or services are viewed in the product market. Can they charge a price premium over their competitors? Is this premium sustainable in the long run? Are there manufacturing efficiencies to be gained that will lower production costs? The effects of competition are first seen in this line item: As a firm is forced to lower its prices in response to competitors' price reductions this ratio will increase. Much of the ratio analysis of profitability that we discussed in Chapter 5 is designed to help you forecast this item. In addition, you may find some guidance for this forecast by reading the firm's MD&A and earnings announcements. Note that the discussion in the MD&A may be pitched in terms of the Gross Profit Margin, defined as

$$\text{Gross Profit Margin} = 1 - \text{COGS/Sales}$$

Finally, remember that a pure price increase, with no other changes, will increase the gross profit margin, which reduces the COGS/Sales ratio.

Along with the firm's own past, the COGS/Sales ratio of a few close competitors is a good place to start when forecasting this ratio. If the firm has a low COGS/Sales ratio relative to its peers then you need to think about whether or not it can sustain this advantage. If you are analyzing a young firm with no clear cost structure yet exhibited in the data, then using a more mature firm's COGS/Sales ratio to guide your forecasts is a good idea. If the firm has exhibited some economies to scale that have caused the COGS/Sales ratio to decline in recent years then ask yourself how much longer you expect this trend to continue.

Research and Development Expenses

While there is no necessary relation between Research and Development (R&D) Expenses and Sales, many firms budget their R&D expenditures in exactly this way. For instance, Gillette has a stated goal of growing R&D expenditures at the same rate as sales, so the ratio of R&D to Sales should remain constant for Gillette. Be particularly cognizant of the stage in a firm's life cycle when forecasting this item. Start-up firms will invest a much larger fraction of their sales in R&D with the intent of bringing this percentage down over time. Also, there may be a relation between the firm's R&D spending and the price premium implied in your COGS forecast. A firm whose strategy is to continually develop new products and sell them at a premium will have a higher R&D to Sales ratio and a lower COGS to Sales ratio than a firm which copies other firms' products and sells them at a discount. For example, a hallmark of IBM is its research and development activity—it has the largest number of patents granted per year for any firm in the United States for the last six years running. This strategy is reflected in their ratios: IBM's ratio of R&D Expense to Sales has been fairly constant at about 6 percent, and its gross margin is about 38 percent. In contrast, Dell Computer invests only 1.5 percent of its revenue in R&D but its gross margin is only 22.5 percent—clearly a different strategy than at IBM.

You should be aware of opportunistic accounting related to R&D on software. Software development costs can be capitalized as an asset once the product is "technologically feasible"—whatever that means—so these expenditures will not show up in R&D expense immediately. Given the vagueness of this definition, companies have considerable flexibility when choosing whether to allocate expenditures to R&D, in which case they are expensed immediately, or to software development, in which case they are classified as an asset and then amortized to expense over a number of years.

Selling, General and Administrative Expenses

Selling, General and Administrative (SG&A) expenses have some components that move directly with sales, such as commissions paid to the sales force, and other components that are only weakly related to sales, such as the clerical staff salaries. The fixed components will give this ratio some economies of scale, so it may decline as a percentage of Sales if Sales grow. Working against this effect, however, is the fact that many of these expenditures are highly discretionary. For example, when Sales are high the firm may invest in management training programs but when Sales are low they may cut back on these types of discretionary expenditures. Examine how this ratio has changed in the past in response to changes in the sales growth rate for evidence of economies of scale. In addition, the MD&A discussion might give you some clues about future movements in this ratio. In particular, cost-cutting initiatives are frequently aimed at this line item.

Depreciation and Amortization

The ratio of Depreciation and Amortization to Average (net) Property, Plant and Equipment (PP&E) and Intangibles is forecasted based on the relation between the balance sheet amounts and the income statement amounts. For firms who use straight-line depreciation and who replace assets at roughly the same rate as they depreciate them, this ratio is approximately constant and equal to one over *half* the average useful life of the assets (half because in steady state the assets are roughly halfway through their useful life so net PP&E is roughly half gross PP&E). But there are some minor problems with this approach that can't be helped given the typical data that is available as an input to eVal. The general idea is that straight-line depreciation and amortization expenses are charged off uniformly over the asset's life. But in this case what we really want to use is *Gross* PP&E and Intangibles in the denominator of this ratio, not the *net* amount. However, while you can usually find the gross PP&E balance somewhere in the financial statement footnotes, you can rarely find the gross intangibles balance, and neither amount is shown on the face of the balance sheet. The distortion that this introduces is minor for stable firms but large for growing firms because their asset age is changing over time. For a growing firm this ratio increases as the mix of assets changes from mostly new assets to assets that are, on average, halfway through their useful life. To deal with this we recommend finding the disclosure in the financial statement footnotes that gives the total gross balance and net balance of PP&E. From this you can compute the proportion of gross PP&E to net PP&E and then multiply the ratio given in eVal by this amount to get an estimate of the ratio of depreciation and amortization expense to *gross* PP&E and Intangibles (note that we are assuming that the age mix in Intangibles is the same as the age mix in PP&E). One over this amount is an estimate of the useful life of the assets. Enter one over *half* of the useful life estimate as your terminal year forecast. Is this a cool recipe or what?

Another problem that frequently arises when forecasting Depreciation and Amortization is that the line item is not shown on the income statement and so is coded as zero by some standardized data providers. If you get the actual financial statements you can typically find the depreciation and amortization amounts on the Statement of Cash Flows, but this is of only limited value because you don't know what income statement line item the company lumped these expenses into. They could be included as part of COGS, as part of SG&A or, most likely, divided between these two line items. The Media General data included with eVal subtracts depreciation and amortization from COGS if it isn't shown explicitly on the income statement. If you know which line item contains the depreciation and amortization expense then you can correct the financial statements in eVal by moving the balance to the "depreciation and amortization" line item. Otherwise, all you can do is skip this item and pick it up implicitly in your forecasts of COGS and SG&A.

To forecast the depreciation and amortization expense ratio you should think about the type of assets that the firm must deploy to generate sales and how long these assets are expected to last. The footnote that describes the firm's accounting policies typically gives the useful lives of their major types of assets. If the firm primarily uses just one type of asset then this disclosure is a great guide for your forecast (for example, if the asset has a 10-year useful life then forecast 20 percent) but more commonly all you learn is that buildings have a 20–40 year life, equipment has a 5–10 year life, and computers have a 2–4 year life. In addition, the intangible asset "goodwill" is no longer amortized over any period. Instead it is treated as a permanent asset (like land) and each year the accountants ask if it has been "impaired." The consequence of this accounting treatment is that it is virtually impossible to forecast when the consumption of goodwill will show up as an expense in the financial statements. Practically speaking, all you can do is look at how the firm has handled goodwill impairment in the past and hope that this provides a guide to the future.

Interest Expense

The ratio of Interest Expense to Average Debt is the firm's average interest rate on all debt combined. The past rate at which the firm has borrowed is a good indicator of the future borrowing rate, unless you forecast a large change in either the firm's default risk or macro-level interest rates. You may also want to read the debt footnote and see what rate the firm has borrowed at most recently. As a reminder, we warned you in Chapter 5 to beware of interest income that is netted against the company's interest expense. This will make the past interest expense look extremely low when computed as a percentage of average debt. If this is the case then you should find the amount of interest income and move it into the non-operating income line item on the financial statements. Another complication arises if a firm has convertible debt. Convertible debt carries a lower interest rate because of the value of the conversion option. The easiest method of dealing with this problem is to assume that the firm will issue straight debt in future years at the going market rate of interest (see Chapter 12 for more detail on this issue).

Non-Operating Income

Non-Operating Income includes such things as dividends received or interest income on investments, the write-down of assets, and other miscellaneous income. Because this item represents a mix of many things, none of which have obvious drivers, we ask you to forecast it as a percentage of sales with the idea that the amounts for these items vary roughly with the firm's size. If the past amounts of non-operating income are significant then you should go back to the actual financial statements and figure out what is in this item.

If the non-operating income is interest or dividends from a financial asset you need to think about whether that asset will exist in the future. For example, a firm might have an unusually large cash balance if it has recently raised capital but not yet spent it, and this cash balance will beget some interest income. If you believe that the cash will soon be invested in operating assets, then the interest income will soon disappear. Alternatively, the asset might be an investment in another company that was made for strategic reasons and is not expected to change in the near future.

In this case, the dividend income or equity method income is likely to continue in the future, but will bear no relation to the level of company sales, and you will want to forecast the non-operating income as a dollar amount and input the result directly on eVal's Financial Statements sheet. The general point is that income rarely falls from the sky, even non-operating income; rather, it takes assets to produce it. Make sure that you know where these financial assets are on the balance sheet—they may be in Cash and Marketable Securities, they may be in Investments, or they may be lumped in with something else—and keep track of the relation between the balance of these assets and your forecast of non-operating income.

Other items that frequently show up as part of non-operating income are asset write-downs, impairment charges, and restructuring charges (note that expenses are entered as negative numbers in eVal). While all these charges sound like one-time events, it is actually quite common for companies to record expenses like these year after year. If you see a string of impairment and restructuring expenses in a company's past financial statements then it is very likely that they will continue in the future. In effect, the company is moving normal operating charges into this line item. If this is the case, then your forecasts should treat them as recurring expenses. In addition, if you anticipate a significant asset write-down in the future, possibly because you believe the company's accounting is currently too aggressive, then you should work out more precisely how the write-down will affect this ratio.

Effective Tax Rate

A firm's Effective Tax Rate is the ratio of the Tax Expense to earnings before income taxes (~~EBIT~~). As a ballpark figure, the statutory tax rate for most firms in the United States is 35 percent. To this you add a few percentage points for state and local taxes and possibly deduct a few percentage points for the tax advantages that come from having foreign operations, if your company should be so lucky. The firm's tax footnote contains a great table that explains why the effective tax rate differs from the statutory 35 percent. In accounting language, the items appearing in this table are called "permanent differences" to distinguish them from the "timing differences" that create deferred taxes, as discussed later. You should look through this table with an eye for things that might change in the future. For example, if a company is planning to move its operations from California, with a flat corporate tax rate of 8.84 percent, to Kansas, with a flat corporate tax rate of 4 percent, it will save 4.84 percent on its effective tax rate (but it will give up the ocean view).

If the firm is losing money (pre-tax) then its current effective tax rate may be a very poor indicator of its future tax rate. Suppose, for example, that you are examining a young company that has yet to show a profit. The company's losses create net operating loss carryforwards, which can be used to reduce taxes in the future if they become profitable, but can only be booked as assets in the year of the loss under strict conditions. So our young company will probably have an effective tax rate close to zero. But if you forecast that the company will become profitable, then you need to increase the effective tax rate in the future. The company will be able to keep the effective tax rate near zero for a few years beyond the point that it turns profitable by using its net operating loss carryforwards to offset the profit, but eventually profitable companies must pay taxes. We hate to send you there, but the only place you can learn about all this stuff is in the tax footnote. Grab your flashlight and carry a stick.

Minority Interest

Minority Interest represents the claim on the income of the consolidated firm by the shareholders in the majority-owned subsidiaries. For most firms this is zero because they own 100 percent of their subsidiaries, so there are no minority share-holders to make a claim, and you can skip to the next item. However, ignoring this line item for firms that actually have a minority interest can lead to big mistakes, so we include a line for it on eVal's Forecasting Assumptions sheet. These minor-ity shareholders have a claim to some portion of the subsidiary's income, which is being reported as part of the consolidated total. We ask you to forecast this amount as a percentage of after-tax income. But since the size of the minority interest claim varies with the subsidiary's income and not the parent company's income, there is no necessary reason that this line item will remain constant. It is generally very difficult to get much information about the subsidiary's income, however, so this scaling variable is the best we can do. If the subsidiary's income moves roughly with the parent's income, then this percentage will be fairly constant.

Other Income

Other income is a bit of a catchall line item. This item differs from the "Non-Operating Income" because it is after-tax. You might find the after-tax effects of investment gains/losses or equity method investments here. If this item is non-zero then you really need to read the actual financial statements to figure out what the company or standardized data providers have put here and whether you be-lieve it will continue in the future. As with non-operating income, we ask you to forecast this as a percentage of Sales simply to capture the idea that these items tend to increase with the size of the firm, not because sales is really the driver of these costs. This line item is also another good place to tuck any major adjust-ments that you might make to the financial statements. For instance, if you want to forecast a large write-off, possibly because you think the company's account-ing practices are aggressive, then you can enter the after-tax effect on this line item and keep it nicely separated from the rest of your forecasts.

Preferred Dividends

The ratio of Preferred Dividends to Average Preferred Stock is quite similar to the ratio of Interest Expense to Debt discussed earlier. This ratio gives the preferred dividend rate, which can usually be found in the financial statement footnotes, or can be inferred from the statement of shareholders' equity. You may notice that the balance sheet of some firms shows preferred stock outstanding yet shows 0 per-cent for this ratio in the past data. This occurs because some standardized data providers do not give the preferred stock dividend in their database, so our default entry is zero. If you see a historical balance of preferred stock, then you should get the firm's complete financial statements to look up the historical dividend rate and input the preferred dividends manually on the Financial Statements sheet in eVal.

Some Final Thoughts about Forecasting the Income Statement

The result of your income statement assumptions is a forecast of the firm's entire sequence of future income statements. For each line item, you should think once again about the transition from the firm's most recent historical performance to its performance in the next few years, through its transition to your terminal year forecasts. As a rough guide, you might think of the near-term performance as being driven by firm-specific activities, such as a rapid expansion plan or a cost-cutting initiative, and the long-term performance as being driven by industrywide and economywide forces, such as competition or technological innovations. Do your forecasts paint a reasonable picture of how the firm might evolve? You will undoubtedly feel more confident about your near-term forecasts than your long-term forecasts; this is simply the reality of forecasting in an uncertain world.

You aren't completely done with your income statement assumptions. These assumptions and the balance sheet assumptions together imply financial ratio and cash flow consequences, and these consequences might be unrealistic. If this is the case, as it usually is after just the first pass, then you need to revisit your income statement assumptions once again.

Expense Forecasts for Kohl's

As an example, we will develop a set of expense forecasts for Kohl's. As input to these forecasts, you may want to refer back to the ratio analysis of Kohl's in Chapter 5. The forecasts are summarized in Figure 8.5.

Kohl's has shown a steady improvement in its gross margin over the past few years. In their 2001 MD&A they attribute the most recent margin improvement to a shift in sales mix to a slightly greater weighting on women's clothes, which carry higher margins than their average product. We also noted in Chapter 5 that Kohl's margins are much better than Target's, their closest competitor (Target's ticker is TGT). Since the margin improvement was not attributed to economies of scale and since we don't anticipate a significant shift in the product mix in Kohl's stores, we anticipate no further margin improvements in the near future. Because Kohl's is still relatively young and new, we forecast that they can withstand competitive pressure for the next five years, but then competition will slowly eat away at their margins. As a guide for our long-run forecast, we note that in fiscal 2001 Target's COGS/Sales ratio is about 68 percent and Saks' (ticker = SKS) is about 67 percent. Assuming that Kohl's margins will move slowly toward the margins of these other stores, we forecast a terminal year ratio of 66 percent. We let eVal smooth years 6 through 10 to this value.

Kohl's has steadily improved its SG&A/Sales ratio each year. In their 2001 MD&A they state that their goal is to reduce this amount by .2 percent per year. Noting that they have achieved this goal for at least the past five years, we forecast that they will continue to do so for the next five years and then reduce the ratio another .2 percent in the terminal year to reflect long-term efficiency gains. ✓

Kohl's ratio of Depreciation and Amortization to the average balance of *net* PP&E and Intangibles is 8 percent in the most recent year and has fluctuated between 7.6 percent and 8.2 percent over the past five years. Because Kohl's is a rapidly growing firm this ratio will change in a very predictable manner as their growth slows and their asset base is, on average, closer to the 50 percent accumulated depreciation of a stable company (that is, the assets are halfway through their useful life). From the financial statement footnotes we learn that the ratio of *gross* PP&E to *net* PP&E is about 1.2. Multiplying the 8 percent ratio by 1.2 gives roughly 10 percent, meaning that the assets have an average useful life of about 10 years. Given the mix of buildings, which have a relatively long life, with store fixtures, which have a relatively short life, this seems like a reasonable estimate. When Kohl's is in steady state and its asset mix is approximately halfway through its useful life at all times, the ratio of Depreciation and Amortization to *net* PP&E and Intangibles will be one over half of the useful life, or 20 percent. We forecast that this ratio will increase smoothly from its current level of 8 percent to a terminal value of 20 percent.

Kohl's most recent Interest Expense as a percentage of the average Debt balance is 5.9 percent. This may seem a bit low, but Kohl's has over a half billion dollars in subordinated convertible debt that, because of its conversion option, has an effective interest rate of only 2.75 percent. Most recently, they issued senior debt at 6.3 percent. We forecast that they will have an effective interest rate of 6 percent in the future, which is the same as Target's most recent rate.

Non-Operating Income for Kohl's is interest income on their short-term investments. For the past two years, this interest income has been approximately 2.8 percent of the average balance of cash and marketable securities. We do not anticipate that non-operating income will grow at the same rate as Sales because we believe that Kohl's will use these balances to build new stores. Instead, we think non-operating income will remain approximately 2.8 percent of the cash and marketable securities balance, a reasonable interest rate on this low-risk investment. In the next section we will forecast that the cash and marketable securities balance will remain at 1.3 percent of Sales so, putting this all together, we get

$$\text{Non-Operating Income/Sales} = \text{Non-Operating Income/Cash} \times \text{Cash/Sales}$$

or

$$2.8\% \times 1.3\% = .0364\%$$

This rounds to zero, which is what we ultimately forecast for non-operating income.

Finally, Kohl's effective tax rate has declined slightly because of lower state taxes in recently entered markets, as discussed in their MD&A. However, the largest new market that they are just about to enter is California, which has one of the highest state income taxes, so we expect this ratio to increase slightly in the future. Target pays an average of 3.3 percent in state taxes (net of the federal tax

FIGURE 8.6
Balance Sheet Assumptions for Kohl's

	A	B	C	D	E	F	G	H	I
	File Edit View Insert Format Tools Data Window eVal Help								
	A3	=							
1	**Forecasting Assumptions**								
2	Go To User's Guide		Change Forecast Horizon						
3									
5	Company Name	Kohl's Corporation							
6	Forecast Horizon	10 Years							
7	Estimated Price/Share=$42.87								
8		Actual	Actual	Actual	Actual	Actual	Forecast	Forecast	Forecast
9	Fiscal Year End Date	1/31/1998	1/30/1999	1/29/2000	2/3/2001	2/2/2002	2/2/2003	2/2/2004	2/2/2005
10									
11	Implied Return on Equity		0.182	0.181	0.191	0.199	0.208	0.223	0.229
27	Balance Sheet Assumptions:								
28	**Working Capital Assumptions**								
29	Ending Operating Cash/Sales	1.4%	0.8%	0.9%	2.6%	4.5%	1.3%	1.3%	1.3%
30	Ending Receivables/Sales	7.6%	7.4%	11.1%	11.1%	11.2%	11.2%	11.2%	11.2%
31	Ending Inventories/COGS	25.2%	25.2%	26.4%	24.7%	24.3%	23.3%	22.3%	21.3%
32	Ending Other Current Assets/Sales	0.4%	0.6%	1.0%	1.1%	1.3%	1.3%	1.3%	1.3%
33	Ending Accounts Payable/COGS	7.4%	8.7%	11.2%	9.9%	9.7%	10.7%	11.7%	12.7%
34	Ending Taxes Payable/Sales	1.3%	1.3%	1.4%	1.6%	1.7%	1.7%	1.7%	1.7%
35	Ending Other Current Liabs/Sales	3.1%	3.2%	3.4%	3.1%	3.5%	3.5%	3.5%	3.5%
36	**Other Operating Asset Assumptions**								
37	Ending Net PP&E/Sales	24.5%	25.3%	29.7%	28.1%	29.4%	29.1%	29.1%	29.1%
38	Ending Investments/Sales	0.0%	0.0%	0.0%	0.0%	0.0%	0.0%	0.0%	0.0%
39	Ending Intangibles/Sales	1.0%	0.7%	0.4%	0.2%	0.1%	0.1%	0.1%	0.1%
40	Ending Other Assets/Sales	0.9%	1.1%	3.8%	3.1%	3.4%	3.4%	3.4%	3.4%
41	**Other Operating Liability Assumptions**								
42	Other Liabilities/Sales	0.8%	0.8%	0.7%	0.7%	0.6%	0.6%	0.6%	0.6%
43	Deferred Taxes/Sales	1.5%	1.5%	1.5%	1.4%	1.5%	1.5%	1.5%	1.5%
44	**Financing Assumptions**								
45	Current Debt/Total Assets	0.1%	0.1%	3.3%	0.6%	0.3%	0.3%	0.4%	0.4%
46	Long-Term Debt/Total Assets	19.2%	16.1%	16.9%	20.6%	22.2%	23.2%	24.2%	25.2%
47	Minority Interest/Total Assets	0.0%	0.0%	0.0%	0.0%	0.0%	0.0%	0.0%	0.0%
48	Preferred Stock/Total Assets	0.0%	0.0%	0.0%	0.0%	0.0%	0.0%	0.0%	0.0%
49	Dividend Payout Ratio	0.0%	0.0%	0.0%	0.0%	0.0%	0.0%	0.0%	0.0%
50									
51									
52									

User's Guide / Financial Statements / **Forecasting Assumptions** / User Worksheet / Ratio Analysis / Graphics
Ready

benefit, as disclosed in the 2001 annual report), so we will increase Kohl's effective tax rate .1 percent a year for the next three years to bring it in line with Target's rate of 38.3 percent.

We can't do very meaningful ratio analysis on these forecasts yet, because many ratios depend on balance sheet items. Moreover, our forecasts of PP&E and Debt will affect the depreciation and interest expense lines.

8.4 BALANCE SHEET FORECASTS

The next set of assumptions will construct the balance sheet forecasts. They are organized into assumptions about the Net Operating Assets, consisting of working capital, other operating assets, and other operating liabilities; and assumptions about Financing. The Net Operating Assets are forecasted as a percentage of Sales (or as a percentage of COGS) because they are the assets that generate the sales. In contrast, the financial obligations are forecasted as a percentage of total assets. As a guide to the balance sheet assumptions, Figure 8.6 shows this portion of the forecasting assumptions sheet in eVal.

8.5 WORKING CAPITAL ASSUMPTIONS

Working Capital requirements are driven largely by the operating cycle of the firm. Consequently, all the forecast assumptions in this section are linked to either Sales or COGS. A firm's past working capital requirements, and your forecasts of its future requirements, are a statement about the firm's operating efficiency. An improvement in operating efficiency means the firm can generate the same level of gross profit with fewer net assets tied up in working capital.

Operating Cash

Every firm requires some amount of Operating Cash. A typical amount might be 3 percent of Sales, but firms vary widely in their holdings of cash and cash equivalents. If your firm has traditionally held a large amount of cash relative to their peers, then they probably don't need all this cash for daily operations; rather, part of the balance is really an investment in financial assets. As we discussed in Chapter 5, if the past operating cash balance appears larger than you think necessary for operations, you need to get the as-reported financial statements and make an estimate as to how much of the line item is really operating cash and how much is an investment in financial assets. Once you have an estimate of the amount of true operating cash and the amount of financial assets, you have a few choices about how to proceed. Assuming you think the firm is going to hang onto the financial assets, you can continue to forecast a high ratio of Operating Cash to Sales and then include the interest income from the financial assets in non-operating income. Alternatively, you can reclassify the financial assets into the Investments line item and forecast its balance separately.

A wilder alternative for dealing with financial assets is to liquidate them in the first forecast period, which you can do in eVal by assuming a sufficiently low ratio of operating cash to sales, which will in turn imply proportionately lower levels of debt and equity. In many cases this will imply a large stock repurchase. On the surface this might seem absurd since it is probably unlikely that the firm will make such a large stock repurchase in the next period. But from a valuation point of view, the present value of a future stream of interest income is equivalent to the liquidation value of the financial assets, so either approach will yield the same valuation (if done carefully). Liquidating the financial assets immediately has the advantage of getting the financial assets out of the picture so we can focus on forecasting the operating variables. For this reason, the liquidation alternative is the most common choice in a traditional discounted cash flow valuation.

Receivables

The ratio of Receivables to Sales depends directly on the company's collection policy and their customers' ability to pay. A ratio of .25, for instance, means the average receivable was outstanding for .25 of a year, or about 90 days. This is approximate because sales and collections fluctuate through the year, but you get the idea. Insofar as receivable credit is effectively granting the customer an interest-free loan, this is an important strategic decision the firm makes, and one you should think carefully about when forecasting. If the firm's past values of this ratio are constant, then this reflects a consistent collections policy that is unlikely to change in the near future. If the ratio is changing significantly or differs drastically from competitors' ratios, however, then you will need to investigate further. Ask yourself, What is the firm's relative bargaining power with its customers? A small firm that supplies a large firm might see a favorable Receivables to Sales ratio disappear quickly when economic times get tight. To see a great example of this phenomenon, load Salton (ticker = SFP) into eVal. Salton makes the famous George Foreman Grill ("it's a lean, mean grillin' machine!") and other small appliances. They sell the bulk of their goods to a few large retail chains, such as Kmart and Wal-Mart, not generally known for the generous terms they provide their suppliers. Indeed, between 1999 and 2002 Salton saw the average time it took to collect its receivables go from 50 days to 80 days as these big customers slowly put on the squeeze.

Inventories

The ratio of Inventories to COGS is very similar to the receivables ratio, except that both the numerator and the denominator are computed using historical costs rather than selling prices. The other principle difference is that the company can acquire inventories without selling them, which would increase the numerator without the commensurate increase in the denominator. For that reason an increasing Inventory to COGS ratio is traditionally considered to be a warning sign that the company is having trouble selling its goods. Of course, the common retort is that they are stocking up for a new product release that will send sales skyrocketing. When forecasting this ratio, think about why it might differ from its historical past. Do you anticipate the company implementing a "just-in-time" inventory handling system and thus lowering the required amount of inventory? Alternatively, do you anticipate that the firm's customers or suppliers have so much bargaining power that they will force the firm to hold the inventory for increasingly longer periods? Was there some unusual event in the most recent fiscal year that caused the ratio to differ significantly from its normal level?

Other Current Assets

Other Current Assets include tax refunds, prepaid expenses, and other miscellaneous items. We ask you to forecast this item as a percentage of sales because it tends to increase with the size of the firm, so this ratio should be fairly stable. But if this is a large amount you really need to look at the published financial statements and see what is included in this line item and decide if it does indeed move with sales.

Accounts Payable

The ratio of Accounts Payable to COGS is the mirror image of the Receivables ratio for the firm's suppliers (with respect to their accounts with the company). It reveals how quickly the firm is paying for the inventory it purchased. Since this is an interest-free loan to the firm, the higher this ratio the better, assuming of course that the firm is capable of paying the loan back. You may forecast that the ratio will increase if you believe that the firm has sufficient power over its suppliers that it can delay paying its bills. When times get tight in the automotive industry, for example, the Big 3 automakers don't renegotiate the contract terms with their suppliers—they simply delay paying them for significant periods of time.

Taxes Payable and Other Current Liabilities

Taxes Payable frequently show up as a current liability simply because the firm owes taxes as of the end of the fiscal quarter, but they don't have to pay them until a later date. Other Current Liabilities includes dividends declared but not yet paid, customer deposits, unearned revenue, and other miscellaneous liabilities that will be paid within a year. We ask you to forecast these items as a percentage of sales because they tend to increase with the size of the firm, so this ratio should be fairly stable. But as with Other Current Assets, if the amounts in these categories are significant, you should read the financial statements to see precisely what they are and decide if you think the past ratios are good predictors of the future.

8.6 OTHER OPERATING ASSETS AND LIABILITIES

The key issue for this set of assumptions is determining the size of the firm's future investment in long-lived assets necessary to produce the forecasted sales. Consequently, these items are forecasted as a percent of sales. Your forecasts of these ratios are a statement about the firm's expected production strategy. If the firm outsources much of its production, its investment in assets will be significantly smaller than the investment that is necessary for a more vertically integrated operation. Of course, since outsourcing captures a smaller portion of the value chain, the firm should earn correspondingly smaller margins.

PP&E

To forecast the ratio of PP&E to Sales you should consider the firm's existing capacity relative to your forecast of sales growth. Firms tend to add capacity in large lumps, so as you analyze the firm's past ratio of PP&E to Sales, be aware of whether the past ratio amounts were generated by assets operating at full or partial capacity. A good source of information for forecasting this item is the discussion of liquidity and capital resources in the MD&A; in fact, firms often give estimates of future capital expenditures here. And capital-intensive industries, such as steel or auto-making or airlines, often give capacity utilization statistics in their Selected Data Schedule (Item 6 on Form 10-K). Finally, you can get industry-level statistics on growth rates in investments in different classes of assets from the Bureau of Economic Analysis fixed asset tables.

It is common for PP&E to rise rapidly during a company's early years and then remain relatively constant thereafter. But note that this pattern does not imply that the *ratio of PP&E to Sales* will rise and then flatten out. If the company's sales are also rising rapidly in the early years, this ratio could remain constant throughout the growth and maturity phases of a firm's life cycle. What you really need to think about is whether there are significant economies to scale that the firm will enjoy as it grows. As California Pizza Kitchen expands across the country, its investment in PP&E will necessarily grow at the same rate as sales because there are very few scale economies in a restaurant chain (having a restaurant in Nebraska has little effect on the cost of opening a restaurant in Oregon). Alternatively, once Iridium puts the necessary satellites in place for its global phone system, sales can grow significantly without additional investment in PP&E.

Investments

Investments are primarily made up of equity holdings by the firm in other companies. If this amount is significant for your company, then read the financial statements and figure out exactly what this investment represents. We forecast this item as a percentage of sales but there may be no structural reason for the size of the investment to be related to sales. For example, the book retailer Barnes & Noble (ticker = BKS) owns approximately 36 percent of Barnes & Noble.Com (ticker = BNBN), which sells books over the Internet. There is no particular reason that Barnes and Noble's investment in this Internet business will increase in lock-step with sales at retail outlets. You have to ask yourself how much additional capital will Barnes & Noble invest in this enterprise? If you examine the financial statements of Barnes & Noble.Com you will see that they have been losing money pretty steadily, so additional capital may well be required.

Intangibles

Intangibles are all those assets that can't be physically touched. To be included in the accounting system usually the intangible must have been acquired in an arm's-length transaction by the firm. So *purchased* patents, copyrights, licenses, and trademarks would be included, but *internally developed* versions of the same things are not. What you really need to forecast is *purchased* intangibles but, unfortunately, companies that purchase lots of intangible assets generally develop lots of them internally as well. To make matters worse, the biggest purchased intangible is "goodwill," defined to be the excess of the purchase price in a corporate acquisition over the fair market value of the identifiable assets (tangible and intangible) received. Because it is created only by an acquisition, goodwill tends to arrive in large and unpredictable lumps. Goodwill, plus the rather arbitrary distinction between purchased and internally developed intangible assets, makes forecasting intangibles very difficult. As with investments, there is no particular reason why this item should remain a constant percentage of sales; we use this ratio only because larger firms tend to have more intangibles than smaller firms.

Other Assets and Other Liabilities

Other Assets includes many items; some examples are long-term receivables, pre-opening expenses for retail stores, and pension assets. Other Liabilities include pension liabilities and other miscellaneous non-current liabilities. See the financial statement footnotes for specifics if your firm has a significant amount for these items.

Deferred Taxes

To forecast deferred taxes you need to think about the firm's tax "timing differences." You may have noticed that when we forecasted the firm's effective tax rate we considered "permanent differences" that caused the rate to differ from the statutory 35 percent, but did not take into consideration the timing of the tax payments. For example, a firm might have accelerated tax deductions because of an investment in a certain type of asset. In this case, not only does the firm get to deduct the cost of the investment, but they also get to deduct most of it in the first few years of the asset's useful life. Accountants capture this effect in the balance of deferred taxes, so named because accelerated deductions today mean higher taxes tomorrow when the deductions run out. The firm's specific deferred tax items are described in the footnotes to the financial statements. The principal source for deferred tax liabilities is usually the timing difference between depreciation on PP&E and the tax deductions for these investments. Early in the life of an asset this will result in deferred tax liabilities (representing the future increase in tax payments when the accelerated tax deductions for the PP&E are exhausted); later this effect will reverse and the liability will shrink back to zero. But as long as the firm is replacing its assets, this liability will remain. If the firm maintains its assets at a fixed level then the deferred taxes will remain a constant percentage of total assets; the ratio will increase slightly if the asset base is growing. But if you forecast that the firm will shrink its asset base, this ratio will fall dramatically. This is because without new acquisitions of assets, new tax deductions are not generated, causing tax payments to increase and the liability to fall.

Some Final Thoughts about Forecasting the Net Operating Assets

The key statistic coming out of the working capital, other asset, and other liability assumptions is the Net Operating Asset Turnover ratio (defined as Sales over Net Operating Assets), which is given on the Ratio Analysis sheet in eVal. This statistic summarizes your forecasts of the net operating assets that a firm will need to put in place in order to create the sales that you forecasted. Because a firm's asset turnover is largely determined by its production technology this ratio typically changes very slowly over time, if it changes at all. Therefore, if your forecasts show this ratio changing dramatically, go back and make sure that you have good reasons for the specific forecasts you have made.

Forecasting Net Operating Assets for Kohl's

Forecasts for Kohl's are shown in Figure 8.6. Most of Kohl's working capital ratios have remained relatively constant over the past five years (recall from Chapter 5 that the large increase in their receivables collection period that occurred four years ago is caused by a change in accounting, not underlying economics). We also noted in Chapter 5, however, that Target Stores has a much better Net Operating Asset turnover ratio than Kohl's, ranging between 2.6 and 3.2 versus Kohl's most recent value of 2 · 1.

Starting with the working capital assumptions, we forecast that in the next year Kohl's will bring down their balance of operating cash to the level of Target Stores, which is 1.3 percent of sales in fiscal 2001. We hold their receivables ratio constant because this has changed very little over the past three years. We forecast that, as Kohl's grows they will be able to negotiate better deals with their suppliers, including more timely delivery of inventory and longer payment periods. The fiscal 2001 inventory-holding period at Target Stores is 58 days; at Kohl's it is 81 days. We forecast that Kohl's will reduce this ratio by approximately 10 days by 2005, which means that the ratio of inventory to COGS will decrease 1 percent a year for the next three years. (This takes a bit of trial and error in eVal to figure out.) Similarly, Target Stores pays its Accounts Payable in 52 days during fiscal 2001; Kohl's pays them in 34 days. We forecast that Kohl's will increase this by 10 days by 2005, which implies that the ratio of Accounts Payable to COGS will increase by 1 percent per year over the next three years. The Other Current Assets and Current Liabilities are not described in any greater detail in Kohl's financial statements. We forecast that these items, along with the Current Taxes Payable balance, will remain the same percentage of Sales as in the most recent year. None of the items is large enough for this rather naive assumption to do serious damage.

The biggest remaining Net Operating Asset that we still need to forecast for Kohl's is PP&E. This is a bit tough because Kohl's uses a mix of owned and leased stores, and many of the leased stores are accounted for as operating leases (meaning that they are not part of PP&E; rather, they simply generate rent expense in COGS). Small changes in the mix of owned versus leased stores can have a huge effect on this ratio. Fortunately, we are saved by a disclosure in Kohl's MD&A that they plan to spend $740 on capital expenditures in 2002. A little guesswork and a lot of toggling between the Forecasting Assumptions sheet and the Cash Flow Analysis sheet in eVal reveals that the forecast of 29.1 percent for PP&E to Sales results in approximately $740 million in capital expenditures in fiscal 2002. Since this value is within the range of Kohl's historical past and since the relation between stores and sales is so strong for this type of business, we maintain this ratio until the terminal period. In the terminal period we reduce it one more percentage point in recognition of the fact that comparable store growth will continue to lower this ratio even after the system of stores is fully developed. We assume that all the remaining forecasting assumptions will stay constant at their levels in the most recent year. This is partly a cost-benefit trade-off; we can't get much information on these items and they aren't a particularly large slice of the pie.

The result of our Net Operating Asset assumptions for Kohl's is that the Net Operating Asset Turnover ratio increases from 2.1 in the most recent year to 2.3 in the terminal year.

8.7 FINANCING ASSUMPTIONS

The main consideration for this set of assumptions is the firm's long-term capital structure. What is the mix of debt and equity that the firm will employ to support the level of net operating assets you have forecasted? The optimal capital structure for a firm takes into account the risk that debt financing brings with it, as well as debt's tax advantages. Volumes have been written in corporate finance textbooks about optimal capital structure. See, for example, Brealey and Myers (2000) (see References, section 8.9). When forecasting this item you should examine the firm's capital structure in the recent past and the capital structure of other firms in the same industry. In the liquidity section of the MD&A, firms will sometimes discuss their target capital structure; if so, you should use this in your forecasts. Each of the items in this section is forecasted as a percent of Total Assets.

Current Debt and Long-Term Debt

Current Debt is short-term borrowing plus the current portion of long-term debt that is due within a year. Long-Term Debt, combined with the current debt above, is the firm's total debt financing. These liabilities, unlike the other non-current liabilities above, are represented by contractual claims to debt capital providers. As such, they are financing liabilities rather than operating liabilities. Details of a firm's debt contracts are given in the footnotes to the financial statements. Particularly noteworthy is the discussion of short-term borrowing, the allocation of total debt to current and non-current portions, and the schedule of future maturities of existing debt.

Minority Interest

Minority Interest represents the claim of shareholders in the firm's partially owned subsidiaries. There is no immediate reason why this amount should remain a constant percentage of Total Assets other than that larger firms tend to have larger minority interests, if they have them at all. You could make a more informed estimate of this amount if you knew that the firm intended to acquire a less than 100 percent interest in another company, or if you knew the firm would not be making any more acquisitions of less than 100 percent, so that this amount might decline as a fraction of total assets. But in all honesty, it is hard enough to forecast a firm's future acquisition activity without having to also estimate the percentage of ownership they will acquire when they acquire less than 100 percent.

Preferred Stock

Preferred Stock is more like long-term debt than equity when it comes to forecasting the value of the firm's common equity. Details of the preferred stock holdings can be found in the financial statement footnotes. You may want to forecast that this item remains a constant dollar value, rather than a constant percentage of total assets, unless the firm specifically says that it intends to continue issuing preferred stock.

Some Final Thoughts on Forecasting the Financing Ratios

The end result of this set of forecasts will be a leverage ratio, defined either as total capital to equity or debt to equity. Like the net operating asset turnover ratio, these ratios tend to be very stable for a firm over time, probably because the optimal capital structure of a firm is driven by fairly stable economic factors. Do not fall into the trap of believing (and forecasting) that a firm will increase its return on equity simply by borrowing to increase its leverage. Remember that more debt begets more interest expense; increasing leverage increases ROE only if the return the firm earns on the new capital exceeds the after-tax cost of debt. Note that the Forecasting Assumptions sheet in eVal automatically takes this into account—you forecast the interest rate in the income statement assumptions and this amount is applied to the forecasted debt balance.

You have now constructed the forecasted balance sheets for your company. The turnover ratio assumptions determine the net operating assets, and the financing assumptions determine the financial obligations. The common equity is therefore determined: common equity equals net operating assets less financial obligations.

Dividend Payout Ratio

The Dividend Payout Ratio shown historically is the percent of net income that is paid out as cash dividends. But note that your preceding forecasts completely determine future net income and future total common equity. Hence, your forecasting assumptions already imply the net amount of new common equity that will be issued or discharged (through a dividend or stock repurchase). The dividend payout ratio assumption determines what retained earnings will be, but with a compensating adjustment to paid in common capital (net) that sets common equity to the level implied by your previous forecasting assumptions. That is, since the future equity balances are already determined, this assumption can only change the composition of the equity. Nonetheless, it is a useful item to forecast, because later, when performing a cash flow analysis, you will be asked to think about the reasonableness of the firm's implied stock issuance activity, and the more they pay out in dividends the more they need to issue in new equity to finance future growth.

Forecasting Kohl's Financial Obligations

As noted in Chapter 5, Kohl's currently has a relatively low debt to equity ratio at 0.4 as compared to Target Stores or the industry average, both of which are a bit more than 1. Kohl's management might be tempted to raise their ROE by increasing their leverage, given that they have a positive spread between RNOA and the net borrowing cost, but a significant increase in leverage would likely cause their future borrowing rate to increase as well. There is no discussion in Kohl's MD&A about changes in leverage, and it has been relatively constant for the past few years. For this reason, we are reluctant to make drastic changes in this amount. We forecast that the Current Debt/Total Asset ratio and the Long Term Debt/Total Asset ratio will steadily increase to 1.5 times their most recent level, ending at terminal values of .45 percent and 33.3 percent, respectively. This will result in a terminal year debt to equity ratio of 0.85.

8.8 PRO FORMA ANALYSIS OF FORECASTS

Wait! You aren't done yet! Once you get to the bottom of eVal's Forecasting Assumptions sheet you have completed your *first pass* at forecasting a complete set of financial statements. You now need to do some ratio and cash flow analysis on these future financial statements to see how reasonable they really are. Go back to the Ratio Analysis and Cash Flow Analysis sheets in eVal and look at what your forecasts imply for the future ratios and cash flows. Is this what you meant to forecast? Are the implied ROEs and margins consistent with industry norms? If the turnover or leverage ratios are changing significantly, be sure that this is what you really mean because typically these ratios are relatively stable over time.

Pro Forma Analysis of Kohl's Forecasts

If you have been busy inputting the Kohl's forecasts that we have made in the previous sections, then you can now examine the implications of those forecasts by returning to the Ratio Analysis and Cash Flow Analysis sheets. (If your forecasts have gotten messed up, possibly because you loaded in Target Stores for comparison, then restart eVal and reproduce the forecast assumptions shown in Figures 8.5 and 8.6.) The first thing that jumps out when analyzing the pro forma financial ratios for Kohl's is that the terminal ROE forecast is 21 percent, well above any reasonable estimate of their cost of equity capital. Since we don't believe Kohl's has a permanently sustainable competitive advantage, and there are no major accounting distortions that will permanently inflate the ROE, this forecast seems a bit too rosy. Where did we go wrong? After looking over all the financial ratios and pro forma cash flow statements, we see two things that need some adjustment. First, even though we forecast that competitive pressures would increase the COGS/Sales ratio a bit, the net effect of our other forecasts is that the operating margin decreases to 5.5 percent in the terminal period. This is well above the 4 percent operating margin of Target Stores and far above the industry average of about 2.6 percent. If we increase the terminal COGS/Sales ratio to 68 percent that brings the net operating margin down to 4.3 percent. Second, even though our financing forecasts increased the debt to equity ratio from 0.4 to 0.85, we didn't increase the forecasted borrowing rate. If we increase the terminal period Interest Expense/Average Debt to 7 percent, the terminal ROE is 14.7 percent, a much more reasonable long-term forecast.

We already did some Cash Flow Analysis when we reverse-engineered the PP&E/Sales forecast to hit the capital expenditure amount that Kohl's mentioned in their MD&A. Beyond this, everything else looks reasonable. After the first few years the pro forma cash from operations is sufficient to fund their capital investment needs. Each year they are forecasted to issue debt and retire equity, which is exactly what we are forecasting that they will do as they increase their leverage ratio.

8.9 LINKS AND REFERENCES

Forecasting for the Love Boat: Royal Caribbean Cruises in 1998

This is the second part of a two-part case set in the cruise industry in 1998. This part of the case focuses on forecasting the next three years of financial statements for Royal Caribbean Cruises. It provides input files for eVal and lots of macroeconomic and industry data that you can use along with Royal Caribbean's 10-K and excerpts from Carnival Cruise's 10-K, its main competitor. This case is available on the eVal website.

Other References and Links

Brealey, R. and S. Myers, *Principles of Corporate Finance:* Boston, MA: Irwin/McGraw-Hill, 2000.

D. Nissim and S. Penman, "Ratio Analysis and Equity Valuation: From Research to Practice," *Review of Accounting Studies* 6 (2001), pp. 109–154.

- Bureau of Economic Analysis—www.bea.gov

   In addition to GDP data, this site's fixed asset surveys describe, by industry, quantities of fixed assets, amount spent, net holdings, average age, etc., of investments in many classes of assets. For example, this site gives the amount the electrical machinery industry spent on metalworking machinery (lots) versus farm tractors (very little).

- Bureau of Labor Statistics—www.bls.gov

   This is a good source for wages and productivity statistics and also has fascinating surveys on consumer spending patterns.

- Congressional Budget Office—www.cbo.gov

   This is a good source for economic forecasts of GDP and its major components.

- Conference Board—www.conference-board.org/

   This site has leading indicators for GDP growth and some interesting consumer confidence data.

- Yahoo!Finance—http://finance.yahoo.com/

- eVal website—www.mhhe.com/eval

CHAPTER NINE

The Cost of Capital

9.1   INTRODUCTION

The forecasted financial statements describe an infinite series of future flows of value, either residual income flows or cash flows. In order to combine all these flows into a single estimate of the value today, we need a discount rate, commonly referred to as the firm's cost of capital. This chapter explains what it is we are trying to estimate with the cost of capital and it gives some advice about how to make the estimate. But we should be truthful at the outset: There are no good answers to these questions. None of the standard finance models provide estimates that describe the actual data very well. The discount rate that you use in your valuation has a large impact on the result, yet you will rarely feel very confident that the rate you have assumed is the right one. The best we can hope for is a good understanding of what the cost of capital represents and some ballpark range for what a reasonable estimate might be.

This chapter is closely linked to the next chapter on valuation models. You can probably read either one first: Your choice is to read about the discount rate used in the valuation models without yet fully understanding the models or to read about the models without yet fully understanding the discount rate, one of the most important inputs for the models.

eVal calculates the firm's equity value using residual income models and discounted cash flow models. For both models it computes the value of the equity directly by discounting the residual income or cash flow each period by the cost of equity capital. eVal also gives you the option to compute the value of the firm to all investors, both equity and non-equity capital providers combined. Computing the value of the equity directly requires only one valuation input: the cost of equity capital. However, computing the value to all investors requires that you also estimate the cost of debt capital and the cost of preferred equity capital, and then weight these pieces correctly to derive a weighted average cost of capital. We begin with the cost of equity capital because it is conceptually the easiest to describe, and it is a necessary input to any valuation model.

9.2   COST OF EQUITY CAPITAL

At its most basic level, the cost of equity capital is the expected rate of return that equity investors could earn on their next best alternative investment with an equivalent level of risk (that is, the opportunity cost of the equity capital). The "equivalent risk" portion of this statement is where the problems lie. What is the correct measure of risk? Risk has something to do with investors' distaste for the uncertainty in future payoffs, but how should we quantify this distaste? Should we quantify risk only by reference to the volatility in the company's underlying cash flows, or should we rely on market prices to infer risk? Should our measure of risk take into consideration the fact that we may or may not hold a diversified portfolio of equity securities? How we estimate the cost of equity capital—the expected return on an investment with "equivalent risk"—depends on the answers to these and other questions.

What Is Risk?

The discount rate that we use in our valuation model serves two purposes. It must account for the time value of money and it must account for the risk of the investment. The time value of money, absent any risk, is a straightforward concept. It is why banks pay interest on savings accounts and charge interest on loans. If risk was not an issue, we could use the risk-free interest rate, say the yield on a 10-year U.S. Treasury Bond, as our cost of equity capital. Unfortunately, risk is very much an issue.

The forecasted financial statements are your best estimates of how the future will unfold for the company, but it is certainly possible that the actual outcomes could be better or worse. And even if reality plays out exactly as you forecasted, the market still may not value the firm as you think it should. In short, the payoff to investing in any equity is uncertain. Further, investors generally dislike uncertainty. (What would you rather have: $1 million for sure or a 50/50 gamble between $0 and $2 million?) A fundamental measure of risk would quantify the amount of uncertainty and the investors' distaste for different levels of uncertainty, and then combine these measures in a model of investor decision-making. But while developing a fundamental measure of risk works great on paper, in practice it is very difficult to quantify an investment's level of uncertainty and extremely difficult to quantify investors' distaste for it. Consequently, the standard approach sidesteps the issue by looking at how the market has historically compensated investors for bearing risk. We don't attempt to measure the fundamental risk directly; rather, we measure the compensation that was offered in exchange for bearing it.

Because investors dislike uncertainty, they will hold a risky security only if they are compensated for doing so; higher risk investments must offer higher expected returns. We measure risk as the additional expected return beyond the risk-free rate that the security offers. The idea is simply that the risk-free rate captures the time value of money, so everything else in the expected return must be compensation for risk. To measure the expected return for different levels of risk we identify different "risk classes" or "risk factors" and then compute the average past realized returns for firms in each class. The amount that the average return in a risk class exceeds the risk-free rate is the "risk premium" for firms in that risk class. The trick, then, is to identify risk classes that group together firms with similar fundamental risk, even though we are punting on actually measuring the fundamental risk itself.

One issue that plays a big part in any discussion of risk is the idea of diversification. A particular equity investment may feel very risky because your estimates of the firm's future cash flows seem quite uncertain, but if the company is only one investment in a large portfolio, then even though its individual payoffs may seem risky, this risk could be diversified away in the portfolio. Consider, for instance, a small bank in Wisconsin, whose cash flows fluctuate with the general health of the economy, and are particularly sensitive to the local Wisconsin economy. By itself, this investment may feel like it is relatively risky. But if you hold this investment in a portfolio of stocks that include banks and collection agencies in other states, then the collective cash flows to all these investments may be considerably less volatile than the cash flows to our little Wisconsin bank. If the general economy is good then banks generate great cash flows; if the general economy is bad then the collection agencies generate great cash flows. And if something uniquely bad happens to the Wisconsin economy then something uniquely good may well happen in another state's economy. Diversification lowers risk. Before you conclude that a particular company has uncertain cash flows and is therefore very risky and warrants a high discount rate, think about the source of the uncertainty. If the source can be diversified away in a portfolio, then the market is probably not willing to compensate you for bearing the risk.

As a practical answer to the question "what is risk?" we offer two models that identify classes of firms that are considered equally risky. The first model is the Capital Asset Pricing Model (CAPM) and the second model is based on the size of the firm.

Capital Asset Pricing Model

Our first pass at quantifying risk is derived from the Capital Asset Pricing Model (CAPM). Without diving into a semester-long class on the subject, the CAPM says that a firm's expected stock return is given as

$$r_e = r_f + \beta(r_m - r_f)$$

where

r_e is the expected stock return for the firm; equivalently, it is the firm's cost of equity capital.

r_f is the risk-free rate of return.

r_m is the expected return on the market portfolio.

β is the firm's "beta," which measures the sensitivity of the firm's returns to the market's returns.

One assumption underlying the CAPM is that every investor holds a mix of the risk-free bond, which returns r_f, and the entire market portfolio, which is uncertain but returns r_m in expectation. The only source of risk that cannot be diversified away in the market portfolio is variation in the market return and, consequently, the only thing that distinguishes one equity security from another is β, the degree to which the security moves with the market. Firms with high βs are more risky than firms with low βs and firms with the same β are equally risky. Putting it all together, the firm's cost of equity capital is r_e: The risk-free rate r_f captures the time value of money, the market risk premium $(r_m - r_f)$ captures the compensation for marketwide risk, and β captures the individual firm's exposure to marketwide risk.

To use this model you need an estimate of the risk-free rate, an estimate of the market risk premium, and a firm-specific estimate of β. The risk-free rate, measured by the yield on the 10-year U.S. Treasury Bond, has ranged between 4 and 7 percent during the last five years. To get the latest value go to the site Yahoo!Finance major US indices. Another estimate of the risk-free rate is the historical yield on the 20-year U.S. Treasury Bond, which has averaged 5.2 percent over the past 75 years (Ibbotson 2001).

The expected risk premium $(r_m - r_f)$ is much more difficult to estimate. This is the amount that investors expect to earn as compensation for bearing the risk of owning the market portfolio. It is the compensation for risk that is currently impounded into the current equity prices, so if you think that equity prices are unusually high, this is equivalent to saying that you think the expected risk premium is unusually low. Historically, the difference between the long-run realized market return and the risk-free return has been somewhere between 2 and 8 percent, but the exact estimate is quite sensitive to the time period of stock return history that is included and how broadly the "market" is defined. For instance, defining the market portfolio as the S&P 500 index, the average risk premium was 7.6 percent over 1926–1998 (Ibbotson Associates 1998). However, if the market portfolio is defined to include all publicly traded companies and the risk premium is computed over the 1964–1994 period, the average is 5.2 percent (Fama and French 1997). In addition, the standard deviation of this estimate is 2.7 percent, which means that there is a 32 percent chance that the true value lies more than one standard deviation above or below this average. In other words, there is a 68 percent chance that the true value is in a range between 2.5 percent and 7.9 percent, and a 32 percent chance it is even more extreme than these endpoints. None of this should make you feel very confident about your estimate of the expected risk premium.

If the estimate of the expected risk premium is shaky, the estimate of the firm-specific β is even worse. This is typically estimated by regressing the realized r_e on the realized r_m for the past five years of monthly returns. What we are shooting for is a measure of how closely the firm's equity price moves with the broader market. Since the market movement is the only source of risk in the CAPM, a firm with a stronger correlation with the market is a riskier investment. As a benchmark, a firm that perfectly tracked the market would have a β of 1; a β of .5 would be very low and a β of 1.5 would be very high, by historical standards. The trouble

TABLE 9.1 **Long-Run Industry Beta Estimates**

Industry	Beta	Industry	Beta
Pharmaceutical products	0.92	Shipping containers	1.03
Medical equipment	1.17	Construction materials	1.13
Health care	1.56	Insurance	1.01
Computers	1.04	Precious metals	0.78
Electronic equipment	1.38	Miscellaneous	1.26
Business services	1.34	Transportation	1.21
Measuring and control equipment	1.29	Rubber and plastic products	1.21
Consumer goods	0.97	Fabricated products	1.31
Restaurants, hotel, motel	1.32	Apparel	1.24
Alcoholic beverages	0.92	Chemicals	1.09
Personal services	1.25	Recreational products	1.34
Construction	1.28	Shipbuilding, Railroad Equipment	1.19
Retail	1.11	Candy and soda	1.24
Entertainment	1.35	Petroleum and natural gas	0.85
Food products	0.87	Nonmetallic mining	0.98
Agriculture	1.00	Tobacco products	0.80
Machinery	1.16	Business supplies	1.11
Printing and publishing	1.17	Textiles	1.12
Aircraft	1.26	Banking	1.09
Coal	0.96	Telecommunications	0.66
Defense	1.04	Utilities	0.66
Wholesale	1.15	Real estate	1.17
Trading	1.16	Steel works, etc.	1.16
Electric equipment	1.15	Automobiles and trucks	1.01

Source: Fama and French 1997.

with estimates of firm-specific βs is that they change drastically over time for no apparent reason. For example, IBM's β estimate was 1.5 in 1966 and .85 in 1969; it was .51 in 1995 and 1.2 in 1998. Surely IBM's fundamental risk didn't change this much during these two three-year periods. Because of this instability, it is not uncommon to use the average β in the firm's industry rather than the firm-specific estimate. But there is also evidence that industry β estimates are themselves unstable, with an average standard deviation of .12 (Fama and French 1997), meaning that there is approximately a 32 percent chance that the true β for an industry with an estimate of 1 could be lower than .88 or higher than 1.12. To compensate for this variation, our best advice is to use an industry β that has been computed over a long time period. Table 9.1 gives industry β estimates computed over 1964-1994.

Another source for β estimates, computed for individual stocks over the most recent five-year horizon, is yahoo!finance. Enter the company ticker symbol and select "Profile" from the resulting screen. If you want to see the industry β computed over the same five-year period, hit the Ratio Comparison link (this takes you to the Multex Investor site). Putting this all together in an example, as of July

2002 the firm-specific estimate of β for Kohl's is 1.06. The industry β for the past five years for the Retail–Department and Discount is .95, and the long-run β estimate for the Retail industry from Table 9.1 is 1.11. If, based on all this, we conclude that our best guess for β is 1.10, and if we combine this with a 4.5 percent risk-free rate (based on 10-year Treasury note in July 2002) and a 7.6 percent risk premium (based on the S&P 500 historical average), we get a cost of capital estimate for Kohl's of

$$r_e = 4.5\% + 1.10 * 7.6 \text{ percent} = 12.86\%$$

Recall, however, that the risk premium and the β estimate are noisy. If we allow a one-standard deviation up or down for each of these estimates, then there is still a 32 percent chance that the true r_e is below 9.3 percent or above 17.0 percent. So don't feel too smug about your fancy CAPM-derived estimate of the cost of equity capital.

Another reason to question the CAPM estimate is that it fits the actual data very poorly. The CAPM says that the only systematic thing causing different firms to have different stock returns is their beta. So you would think that if you estimated firms' betas at a point in time and then tracked the subsequent stock returns, you should find that firms with higher beta estimates would, on average, have higher subsequent stock returns (as compensation for the extra risk). Unfortunately, many studies have shown that this relation is very weak. Further, you may ask yourself, Why are we relying on market prices to tell us about the firm's risk in the first place? The whole premise of this book is that securities can be mispriced and that we can discover the mispricing by our careful analysis. Finally, there is a difference between the realized risk premium over the past 75 years and the expected risk premium going forward. Back in 1926 it would have been difficult to know that the U.S. economy would turn out to be such a huge success story. Part of the difference between the market return and the risk-free rate over this period is simply due to good luck. For this reason we are inclined to use the lower estimate of 5.2 percent for the risk premium, taken from the Fama and French study. Consistent with this lower estimate, the average cost of equity capital from the 12 countries that have had public exchanges for the longest period of time (approximately 1900–2000) is about 5 percent over the risk free rate (Dimson, Marsh, and Staunton 2000).

The Size Model

Our second pass at quantifying the risk of an "equivalent investment" is quite simple. Firms of similar size, as measured by their market value, are considered to be in the same risk class. That is, the firm's expected return is

$$r_e = r_f + r_{size}$$

where

r_e is the expected stock return for the firm; equivalently, it is the firm's cost of equity capital.

r_f is the risk-free rate of return.

r_{size} is the expected return in excess of the risk-free rate for the firm's size decile.

This model is motivated by the empirical observation that small firms have historically higher returns than large firms, so the higher return, it is argued, must be compensation for higher risk. The knock on this model is that there is no good explanation for why the size of the firm should drive its non-diversifiable risk. A large firm may have more resources to adapt to changing conditions than a small firm, but isn't a portfolio of small firms very much like a single large firm with many divisions? Table 9.2 describes 10 size deciles and gives each decile's historical return in excess of the risk-free rate of 5.2 percent, its historical β estimate, and the return in excess of the CAPM-estimated expected return, each estimated from all publicly traded firms over 1926–2000.

The first thing to note from Table 9.2 is that the returns increase monotonically as you go from the largest firms (in the first decile) to the smallest firms (in the 10th decile). Further, the increase is dramatic: the smallest firms have earned returns in excess of the risk-free rate that are more than double the returns earned by the largest firms. The market has clearly treated these firms as riskier, rewarding investors handsomely, on average, for their willingness to bear this risk. Small firms look riskier from a CAPM perspective as well, with β increasing monotonically from the largest decile of firms to the smallest decile.[1] But interestingly, even after controlling for the CAPM risk, small firms still have higher returns than large firms, as the final column in Table 9.2 shows. You can combine the CAPM model and the Size model using the data in the last column. First estimate the CAPM expected return for your firm as described in the previous section. Then add to this the return in excess of the CAPM return, or the "size premium," as given in the last column of Table 9.2.

Kohl's market capitalization as of July 2002 was approximately $21 billion, placing it in the largest decile of firms in Table 9.2. Applying the Size model to Kohl's and using 4.5 percent as our current estimate of the risk-free rate, we get

$$r_e = 4.5\% + 6.84\% = 11.34\% \quad \checkmark$$

If we add the size premium to the CAPM estimate for Kohl's (computed above), we get

$$r_e = 4.5\% + 1.1 * (7.6\%) - 0.2\% = 12.66\%$$

Does size really measure risk? Should you set your discount rate higher for smaller firms? The empirical evidence in Table 9.2 would certainly say yes. The evidence is taken from market prices, however, so if markets are not completely efficient, maybe we should be more circumspect. Suppose that there was no dif-

---

[1]While small firms are large in number, they are small in "weight," as measured by their market capitalization. The largest decile of firms is, by definition, only 10 percent of the total count of firms, yet they make up over 70 percent of the total market capitalization in 2000. So even though 9 of the 10 deciles of firms have an average β estimate greater than 1, the grand average is still 1.

20 yr Tr. Ibbotson 1926-2000

TABLE 9.2 **Size-Decile Returns in Excess of Risk-Free Return and CAPM Return**

Decile	Market Value of Largest Company in Decile ($ millions)	Return in Excess of Historical Riskless Rate of 5.2%	Historical Beta	Return in Excess of CAPM Return
1	524,352	6.84%	0.91	−0.20%
2	10,344	8.36	1.04	−0.31
3	4,144	8.93	1.09	0.47
4	2,177	9.38	1.13	0.62
5	1,328	9.95	1.16	0.93
6	840	10.26	1.18	1.08
7	538	10.46	1.24	0.88
8	333	11.38	1.28	1.47
9	193	12.17	1.34	1.74
10	85	15.67	1.42	4.63

Source: Stocks, Bonds, Bills, and Inflation, 2001 Yearbook, Ibbotson Associates (2001).

ference in the fundamental risk of large or small stocks, but market participants consistently undervalued small stocks. Each year the small stocks would perform better than the large stocks. Their market value would increase and they would move out of the lowest size decile, and a new crop of small stocks would be born to take their place. If this was the case then we would see small stocks generating larger returns than large stocks, but it wouldn't be because they were any riskier than large stocks, it would be because the market was inefficiently pricing the small stocks. This story isn't too hard to imagine; small stocks get little analyst coverage, are not held by many institutions, and generally fly under the radar of most investors. It seems like a prime place to find market inefficiency.

What Number Do I Put in eVal?

Ultimately there is no good answer to the question "what is the cost of equity capital?" As a practical matter, we want to be able to compare the valuations of different firms on a risk-adjusted basis. If we evaluate 10 firms and then sort them based on the amount we think they are undervalued, we want this sort to reveal relative mispricing, not just differences in the riskiness across the 10 firms. In addition, if we can get the discount rate to adequately control for risk, then we can separate the forecasting exercise from the discounting exercise. We can input our best guesses for the forecasting assumptions without trying to make these estimates compensate for risk as well.

Rather than take the CAPM estimate as truth or the Size model estimate as truth, we prefer that you use these models as guides, combining the resulting estimate with your own intuition and some common sense. You might want to ask yourself what rate of return you personally would require on an investment with this firm's level of risk? How much extra return beyond the risk-free rate seems reasonable, given the riskiness of the firm's future payoffs, and evaluated in light of the diversification you have in your portfolio?

The default value for the cost of equity capital in eVal is 10 percent, found on the Valuation Parameters sheet. You can think of it as 5 percent for the risk-free rate and 5 percent for the risk premium; at least it is easy to remember!

There is one constraint on your cost of equity capital input; it must be greater than your assumed terminal growth rate in sales. If this isn't the case then you are assuming that the firm will grow faster than the discount rate forever. This makes the perpetuity formula in the valuation models invalid; effectively the value of such a firm is infinite. If you mistakenly violate this condition, eVal will display the error message "Error! cost of equity capital <= growth rate" in red on the relevant valuation sheet. For more discussion, see the section on terminal value forecasts in Chapter 7.

9.3   COST OF NON-EQUITY CAPITAL

The only reason you need to consider the cost of non-equity capital is if you are interested in computing the value of all investors' claims on the firm, commonly referred to as the *entity value,* rather than just the equity value. This is also a necessary computation if your approach to valuing the equity is to first value the whole entity and then subtract from this the value of the non-equity claims.

The Valuation Parameters sheet has an optional section for you to enter the cost of capital from debtholders and preferred stockholders. We strongly encourage you to use the same estimates here as you input for the terminal period interest and preferred dividend assumptions on the Forecasting Assumptions sheet. For instance, if your terminal period estimate of the firm's interest rate is 6 percent we highly recommend inputting 6 percent on the optional Valuation Parameters sheet for the Cost of Debt. In the short term a firm may have debt outstanding that has a coupon interest rate different from its market interest rate. It would be quite odd, however, to forecast that forever into the future the company will somehow manage to issue debt at a rate different from its market rate. Similarly, the Cost of Preferred Stock should probably match your terminal inputs for this item on the Forecasting Assumptions sheet. Note that the value of the equity is already determined by your forecasts and your assumption about the cost of equity capital. Consequently, as you change your assumptions about the cost of debt or the cost of preferred stock you will change the entity value and the value of the non-equity claims, but the net effect will hold the equity value constant.

Just as with the cost of equity capital, your inputted costs of non-equity capital in the optional section should not be smaller than your forecasted terminal period sales growth rate. If it is, then the perpetuity formula we use to compute the present value of the free cash flows to these capital providers is invalid and an error flag will show up on the valuation sheet. Think about what it would mean for the cost of debt to be lower than the growth rate forever. In the terminal period the growth rate drives the growth in debt, so debt would be growing faster than it was being discounted back and the present value would be infinite (or infinitely negative, depending on whether you are the firm or the debt holder). If your forecasts violate this condition, you will see the message "Error! cost of capital $\leq$ growth rate" on the associated valuation sheet.

9.4   WEIGHTED AVERAGE COST OF CAPITAL

To compute the entity value (as opposed to the equity value) you need a discount rate that reflects the cost of capital from all providers: equity, preferred stock, and debt. Another way to think about this is that we are trying to estimate the cost of equity capital for a hypothetical firm that has the net operating assets of the actual firm but does not have the debt claims or preferred stockholder claims. Consequently, this rate is sometimes referred to as the cost of capital for the unlevered firm, or the expected return on net operating assets (not to be confused with the actual return on net operating assets, as computed in Chapter 5). To see this, examine the basic accounting equation:

$$\text{Net Operating Assets} - \text{Debt} - \text{Preferred Stock} = \text{Common Equity}$$

$$\text{Net Operating Assets} = \text{Common Equity} + \text{Debt} + \text{Preferred Stock}$$

$$\text{Net Operating Assets} = \text{Unlevered Equity}$$

To compute the cost of capital for this hypothetical unlevered firm, a logical approach is to take a weighted average of the cost of equity capital, the cost of preferred stock, and the after-tax cost of debt. The *weighted average cost of capital (WACC),* labeled r_w, does just this. It is computed as

$$r_W = \frac{r_e P_e + (1 - tx)r_d P_d + r_{ps} P_{ps}}{P_e + P_d + P_{ps}}$$

where

tx is the firm's estimated effective tax rate.

r_e is the firm's estimated cost of equity capital.

r_d is the firm's estimated cost of debt capital.

r_{ps} is the firm's estimated cost of preferred stock capital.

P_e is the estimated value of the firm's common equity.

P_d is the estimated value of the firm's debt.

P_{ps} is the estimated value of the firm's preferred stock.

The value r_w is the cost of a dollar of additional capital, holding the firm's capital structure constant. Imagine the firm raising the dollar by issuing common equity, preferred stock, and debt in exact proportions to their market values. The weighted average cost of capital is the natural benchmark for the firm's return on net operating assets, which is the return before any consideration of the firm's financing costs.

Note that the weights used to compute r_w are based on the estimated values of the equity, preferred stock, and debt, not their book values, not their current market values, and not some estimate of their future values in some future capital structure.[2] But this raises a problem. The formula makes reference to P_e, the value of the common equity, yet P_e is exactly what we are trying to find. How can we weight the different costs of capital based on their estimated values if we don't yet know the estimated value of equity? We sidestep this issue by using the estimate of P_e already found in the model that valued the equity directly. With P_e, P_d and P_{ps} determined, the value of the entity is simply the sum of these three components. eVal then searches for the value of r_w that discounts the forecasted future free cash flows to all investors back to this predetermined amount. In this way we find an internally consistent solution for the weighted average cost of capital and the estimated equity value. This approach is completely valid: Given the same series of forecasted financial statements, all valuation models, correctly applied, should yield the same estimate.

What Is Constant and What Is Changing?

In the previous sections we estimated the cost of equity capital, the cost of preferred stock, and the cost of debt as constants—a single rate that is used to discount flows to each of these capital providers throughout time. We then combined these values using estimates of the value of the equity, preferred stock, and debt to construct the weighted average cost of capital. However, what if you forecast that the firm's capital structure will change in the future? For instance, suppose you think that the company will drastically increase its ratio of debt to equity in the future. Based on the formula above, if you were to compute the weighted average cost of capital in the future, it would be different from the r_w based on the current capital structure. Should you base your estimate of r_w on the current capital structure or on the forecasted future capital structure, or should you use a different discount rate each period?

Technically, to be consistent with the assumption of constant costs of capital, the r_w should change with the changing capital structure. But an alternative point of view is that the different costs of capital should change as the capital structure changes in such a way as to hold r_w constant. Recall the r_w can also be thought of as the expected return on the net operating assets of the company, or the expected return on unlevered equity. The idea behind this alternative view is that the fundamental driver of the firm's risks and returns is its net operating assets and that these risks and returns will remain constant regardless of how the supporting capital structure changes. Unfortunately, this issue will never be resolved because the unlevered equity is not a naturally occurring market security, so its return cannot

---

[2]The weighted average cost of capital given here is "after-tax," meaning that the cost of debt has been adjusted down to account for the tax shield of interest (i.e., the $(1 - tx)$ part in the formula). By accounting for the tax deductibility of interest in the discount rate, we do not adjust the free cash flow estimates for the tax benefits of interest. An alternative approach found in some texts is to define WACC on a "pre-tax" basis (i.e., without the $(1 - tx)$ adjustment in the formula) and then add the tax deduction associated with interest to the free cash flows. This issue is discussed in greater detail in Chapter 10.

be observed. And given the difficulty in estimating the cost of equity capital discussed earlier, it seems fruitless to compound this difficulty by trying to estimate how the cost of equity capital will change in the future.

Rather than take a stand on this issue, we simply require that r_w be consistent with the value of the equity when it is computed directly. By solving for a single r_w that reconciles with the estimated value of equity, we force it to be a constant when, technically speaking, it should change with the capital structure. But practically speaking, changing the r_w estimate each period has no effect on the estimated equity value, which is our main concern. Further, because the capital structure remains constant in the terminal period, whether the r_w is constant or changing also has very little effect on the estimated entity and non-equity values. Think of the single weighted average cost of capital reported in eVal as an average of the different, theoretically correct, r_w estimates.

If you see the message "Error! there is no internally consistent weighted average cost of capital" then eVal is telling you that your assumptions do not allow a feasible solution. For example, if your assumptions imply an equity value of $10 and a debt value of negative $12, then you need an entity value of negative $2 to reconcile these two amounts. But if your forecasts imply positive flows of free cash flow, then the entity value cannot be negative, regardless of how high you set the discount r_w. The cases that lead to this error message are rather bizarre, so if you see the message, there is probably something very wrong with your forecasting assumptions.

9.5   LINKS AND REFERENCES

- Yahoo! Finance major US indices— http://finance.yahoo.com/m1?u
- Yahoo! Finance—http://finance.yahoo.com/
- Multex Investor—http://www.multexinvestor.com/

seems to be Reuters

moodys

Elroy Dimson, Paul Marsh, and Mike Staunton, "The Millennium Book: A Century of Investment Returns." London: ABN-AMRO and London Business School, 2000.

Eugene Fama and Kenneth French, "Industry Costs of Capital," *Journal of Financial Economics* 43 (1997), pp. 153–193.

Ibbotson and Associates, *Stocks, Bonds, Bills, and Inflation*, 2001 Yearbook (Chicago: 2001).

bondsonline.com

CHAPTER TEN

Valuation

10.1 INTRODUCTION

You have now completed the hard work in valuation. The forecasts you developed in Chapters 7 and 8 describe the future evolution of net distributions to equity holders. The cost of equity capital you chose in Chapter 9 determines how valuable uncertain cash flows in the future are to you today. All that remains is to combine the forecasts with the discount rate to compute the present value of the net distributions to equity holders. Why then are there so many pages in this chapter?

It turns out that there are a number of different ways to compute the value of equity. Each of them leads to the same answer, but does so in a manner that sheds a different light on the source of value creation. Further, various user groups have historically preferred different models: Accounting types like the residual income models, and finance types like the discounted cash flow models. If all you care about is the final answer, any of the models will do. But we have a smorgasbord of models for you to choose from, should you wish to see the answer presented in a particular way that you prefer because of some other class or life experience.

There are two features that distinguish valuation models. First, the flow variable, the thing that is being discounted, can be either free cash flows or accounting residual income flows (we give precise definitions below). Second, we can compute the value of the flows to equity holders directly, or we can first compute the value of the flows to all investors and then back into the value of the equity claim by subtracting the value of the flows to non-equity capital providers. But if we work carefully (and eVal is *very* careful), if we feed each model the same inputs, each yields exactly the same result. The forecasted financial statements and discount rate assumption *determine* the value; all we have to do is discover it.

All the models we describe allow for the possibility that the firm will live forever, so all models sum over time from the present, labeled time zero, to infinity. It takes a really long time to add up an infinite number of terms one at a time, so at some point in the future, known as the terminal year, we need a more succinct way of expressing the present value of the flows in the remaining years. All the models solve this problem the same way so we defer the discussion of the present value calculations until the end of the chapter and present each model as an infinite sum of terms. But don't worry about this; there is a nifty solution to this problem.

10.2   RESIDUAL INCOME VALUATION MODELS

Although actually quite old, the residual income model has recently come back into vogue on Wall Street. Its primary advantage is that it expresses value directly in terms of the financial statements that you worked so hard to estimate, rather than translating these amounts into free cash flows. Define *residual income* RI_t in period t as

$$RI_t = NI_t - r_eCE_{t-1}$$

where

 NI_t is net income available to common equity for the period ending at date t.

 r_e is cost of equity capital.

 CE_{t-1} is common shareholders' equity at date $t-1$ (i.e., one year earlier than the NI_t date).

Residual income is the amount that net income exceeds the capital charge on the book value of common equity invested in the firm. If the firm could deposit its book value in a bank account at the beginning of the year and earn interest at the rate r_e, it would earn r_eCE_{t-1} for the year. Residual income is the amount that NI_t exceeds or falls short of this benchmark. In this sense, it is "residual."

The *residual income model* computes value as the sum of the initial book value of common equity plus the present value of future residual income flows. Both the book value and the net income component of residual income are accrual account-ing constructs, which may make you incredulous about this model. How can the model work when we know that a firm's accounting book value is an imperfect measure of its market value and that earnings is an imperfect measure of value cre-ation? How can these numbers be used to estimate a firm's market value? The key is to recognize that if book value is understated then future residual income will be overstated, and by precisely enough to correct for the erroneous book value. For example, if a firm has a missing asset, one that the accounting rules don't recog-nize, then the asset isn't included in CE_{t-1} but it produces NI_t, making RI_t positive. In a later section we will illustrate how all this adds up perfectly.

The easiest version of this model is the one that values the common equity directly.

Residual Income to Common Equity

The algebraic statement of this model is

$$P_e = CE_0 + \sum_{t=1}^{\infty} (1 + r_e)^{-t}RI_t$$

where

 P_e is the estimated market value of common equity as of the last financial statement date (i.e., time 0).

CE_0 is common shareholders' equity as of the last financial statement date.

RI_t is residual income, equal to $NI_t - r_eCE_{t-1}$, as defined above.

r_e is the cost of equity capital.

The model starts with the initial stock of accounting value CE_0 and adds to it the discounted sum of expected future residual income flows. The reason a firm's market value P_e might be greater than its accounting book value is because it is forecasted to earn positive residual income in the future. To get a feel for this model, imagine a savings account with $100 in it and a 10 percent interest rate. The book value of this investment, by any reasonable accounting measurement, would be $100. Further, if 10 percent is the market rate of interest on saving accounts then the return on a similar investment with equivalent risk is probably also 10 percent, so assume $r_e = 10$ percent. In this case, regardless of deposits or withdrawals (made at the beginning of each year), the earnings each period will be 10 percent of the beginning book value, which is exactly the capital charge r_eCE_{t-1}, so residual income in all future periods is zero. Thus, the value of the savings account is $100. If, however, the savings account paid 11 percent interest in some years, yet the discount rate remained 10 percent, then the savings account would earn "residual income" in the these years and its market value would exceed $100. Pretty simple.

Figure 10.1 shows the residual income valuation to common equity for Kohl's computed on 9/3/2002 for the fiscal year that ended on 2/2/2002, using the default eVal forecasts. To see this in eVal, first enter 9/3/2002 as the Valuation Date on the Valuation Parameters sheet and then return to the User's Guide and hit the View Residual Income Valuation button. Each column shows the net income and beginning common equity for the fiscal year, taken directly from the Financial Statements sheet. Residual income is computed from these inputs and then discounted each period, using the default cost of equity capital of 10 percent. The present value of each period's residual income is added up for the first 20 years and then for all the years beyond 20 (this computation is discussed later). The result is added to the book value of common equity as of 2/2/2002 to arrive at the $12,057,789 thousand, labeled as the "Forecast Equity Value Before Time Adjustments."

In the previous savings account example, the key comparison was between the discount rate and the rate of interest the account paid. More generally, in a real company the key comparison is between the forecasted ROE and the cost of equity capital r_e. To see this, multiply and divide RI_t by CE_{t-1} so that

$$RI_t = (NI_t - r_eCE_{t-1}) = (ROE_t - r_e)CE_{t-1}$$

where ROE_t is computed on beginning common equity. The expression says that residual income equals the excess of ROE_t over the cost of equity capital times the beginning common equity book value for the period. If you forecast that the firm's ROE will exceed its cost of equity capital then residual income will be positive. Stated another way, a firm is worth more than the book value of its common equity only if it is expected to earn an ROE in excess of its cost of equity capital.

FIGURE 10.1   **Residual Income to Common Equity**

Valuation based on eVal defaults as of 9/3/2002 for 2/2/2002 fiscal year end.

	A	B	C	D
1	**Residual Income Valuation**	**($000)**		
2	Go To User's Guide	View Valuation to Common Equity		
3		View Valuation to All Investors		
4	**Company Name**	Kohl's Corporation	NI and CE taken	
5	Most Recent Fiscal Year End	2/2/2002	from Financial	
6	Date of Valuation	9/3/2002	Statements sheet	
7	Cost of Common Equity	10.00%		
8				
9	Fiscal Year of Forecast	2/2/2003	2/2/2004	2/2/2005
11	**Valuation to Common Equity**			
12	Net Income	590,761	700,011	818,802
13	Common Equity at Beginning of Year	2,791,406	3,355,453	3,982,450
14	Residual Income	311,620	364,466	420,557
15	Present Value of Residual Income	283,291	301,212	315,970
16	Present Value Beyond 20 Years	3,831,760		
17	Present Value of First 20 Years	5,434,623		
18	Common Equity as of			
19	2/2/2002	2,791,406	$= 364{,}466/(1+.10)^2$	
20	Forecast Equity Value Before Time Adj.	12,057,789		
21	Forecasted Value as of Valuation Date	13,402,735		
22	[= 590,761 − .10(2,791,406)] Claims	(1,147,681)	$= 311{,}620/(1+.10)^1$	
23	Equity	12,255,054		
24	Common Shares Outstanding at BS Date	332,167		
25	Equivalent Shares at Valuation Date	332,167		
26	Forecast Price/Share	**$36.89**		
27				
28				

◄ ◄ ► ►│ Graphics / Cash Flow Analysis / Valuation Parameters \ **Residual Income Valuations** / DCF Valuations / EPS Fo │ ◄

Ready

Remembering from previous chapters that ROE was our premier measure of profitability, this equation says that profitability creates value.

This expression also demonstrates that size by itself does *not* create value. If $ROE_t = r_e$ then residual income is zero regardless of the value of CE_{t-1}. Similarly, growth in CE_t, by itself, does not create value. However, if ROE_t is forecast to exceed r_e in the future, then a firm wants to grow to be as big as possible. Think of it this way: If you forecast that a firm's ROE will always equal its cost of equity capital in the future, then you are really forecasting that the firm will always engage in zero net present value projects. If this is the case, then it doesn't matter how big or small those future projects are; none of them will create value. If you forecast that ROE_t will exceed r_e in the future, however, then you are saying that the firm has positive net present value projects in the future. In this case you want the projects to be as big as possible; in this case, growth is good. Wall Street analysts frequently confuse the value of growth with the value of profitability when assessing equity securities. Many research reports extol the huge growth potential of a company without explaining how the firm will ever turn the growth into profitability. If the company can't earn a return that is at least as great as its cost of capital, being a big firm just means that it will destroy value faster than a small firm will. We suspect that analysts like rapidly growing firms because such firms are likely to require investment-banking services, not because they think they are fundamentally good investment opportunities.

The residual income model has many desirable features. For one thing, it is written in terms of the accounting variables that you worked so hard to forecast. The net income and common equity variables come straight from the forecasted financial statements in eVal. More fundamentally, the residual income model describes value in an economically appealing way. Value is driven by profitability and growth. Much of the previous discussion in this book has been aimed at building your intuition for how economic forces and accounting distortions will act on a firm's profitability and growth. By expressing value as a function of these two drivers, the residual income valuation model exploits this intuition.

Finally, because the residual income model is written in terms of accounting numbers, we will use it in the next chapter to describe some popular valuation statistics such as the market-to-book ratio, the price-to-earnings ratio, and the PEG ratio.

Bad Accounting and the Residual Income Valuation Model

Because the residual income model is stated in terms of accounting values, you may worry that distorted accounting measurements will make the model invalid or inaccurate. But as the next example illustrates, the model is surprisingly resilient to accounting errors. Suppose that the sequence of forecasted common equity and net income, before any consideration of accounting errors, is CE_0, NI_1, CE_1, NI_2, CE_2, NI_3, CE_3 . . . , so that the residual income model yields

$$P_e = CE_0 + \frac{NI_1 - r_e CE_0}{(1 + r_e)} + \frac{NI_2 - r_e CE_1}{(1 + r_e)^2} + \frac{NI_3 - r_e CE_2}{(1 + r_e)^3} + \cdots$$

Now suppose that you are sure that $K of value is missing from CE_0, possibly because of an R&D investment that cannot be capitalized but is forecasted to pay off in NI_1. You could set out to correct for this error in the accounting model by adding K to CE_0 and subtracting if from your estimate of NI_1; that is, you could recognize the value creation in the current book value rather than waiting for it to materialize in future earnings. In this case the valuation would be

$$P_e = (CE_0 + K) + \frac{NI_1 - K - r_e(CE_0 + K)}{(1 + r_e)} +$$

$$\frac{NI_2 - r_e CE_1}{(1 + r_e)^2} + \frac{NI_3 - r_e CE_2}{(1 + r_e)^3} + \cdots$$

noting that the addition of K to CE_0 increased book value at date 0 but that book value at date 1 is back to normal because of the subtraction of K from NI_1. Simple algebra demonstrates that the two valuations are equal. At first blush this may seem impossible. Shouldn't moving K to the present increase the value estimate, since money has time value? But look carefully at the second term in the second equation; not only has K been deducted from date 1 earnings, but the capital charge is also higher by r_eK, thus perfectly correcting for the time value of this manipulation. And you don't even have to forecast *when* the K of additional value will show up in future earnings. Suppose you estimated that the additional value was going to materialize in year 2 rather than year 1, so that your corrected forecasts yielded the following value estimate:

$$P_e = (CE_0 + K) + \frac{NI_1 - r_e(CE_0 + K)}{(1 + r_e)} +$$

$$\frac{NI_2 - K - r_e(CE_1 + K)}{(1 + r_e)^2} + \frac{NI_3 - r_eCE_2}{(1 + r_e)^3} + \ldots$$

With some hard work you can show that this again equals the original amount (feeling like this is an algebra test?). By including a capital charge in the definition of residual income, the model perfectly corrects for accounting distortions. Consequently, you really don't need to get involved in correcting the financial statements for accounting distortions; if your forecasts anticipate the unraveling of the accounting distortion, the model will do the rest.

You *should not* conclude from this discussion that it isn't important that you understand accounting. Your forecasts of the future are probably based on observations of the firm's past, and if that past is distorted by poor accounting then you need to be aware of this. For instance, if the firm has generated unusually high income by capitalizing more expenses than is appropriate, and thus deferred their recognition on the income statement, you need to be aware that future income will suffer when these capitalized expenses start to flow to income (as they surely must in an accrual accounting system).

Residual Income to all Investors

This version of the model is less commonly used, but reconciles nicely with the other valuation models. It computes the value of common equity by first computing the value to all capital providers combined, commonly labeled as the *entity value,* and then subtracting from this the value of debt and preferred stock claims. It computes the value of each of these claims as the sum of a beginning balance and the present value of a flow of future residual amounts, just like the previous model.

To express this model algebraically we need to remind you of some earlier notation. In Chapter 5 we defined NOA_t as the net operating assets of the firm, computed as the total assets less the operating liabilities. Next define L_t as the accounting value of the debt (current and non-current combined) and PS_t as the accounting value of the preferred stock (in Chapter 5 we lumped debt and preferred stock together and labeled them "Net Financial Obligations," but here we will value each separately). By the basic accounting equation common equity CE_t is given as

$$CE_t = NOA_t - L_t - PS_t$$

In Chapter 5 we also defined NOI_t as the net operating income, computed after tax. The quickest way to compute NOI_t is to start with net income available to common equity holders NI_t and then add back the after-tax interest that flows to debtholders $(1 - tx)I_t$ and the preferred dividend flows to preferred shareholders PD_t. That is,

$$NOI_t = NI_t + (1 - tx_t)\,I_t + PD_t$$

where

tx_t is the firm's effective tax rate in year t.

NOI_t is the amount the firm earned before expenses related to capital providers.

The idea behind the model is that all investors together own NOA_0 and the future stream of after-tax operating income NOI_t. We can therefore compute the value of the entity as the initial balance of NOA_0 plus the present value of the future residual NOI_t stream. Denoting the weighted average cost of capital as r_w, we define *residual net operating income* as

$$RNOI_t = NOI_t - r_w NOA_{t-1}$$

Note the similarity with residual income defined in the previous section as $RI_t = NI_t - r_e CE_{t-1}$. To compute residual net *operating* income, NI_t is replaced with NOI_t and CE_{t-1} is replaced with NOA_{t-1}.

The *entity value* P_f is then given as

$$P_f = NOA_0 + \sum_{t=1}^{\infty} (1 + r_w)^{-1} RNOI_t$$

All investors together own the "unlevered" firm, valued at P_f. To find the value of the equity holders' claim we need to subtract from P_f the value of the debt claim and the value of the preferred stock claim. And in the spirit of residual income valuation, the value of the debt claim is computed as the initial balance of L_0 plus the present value of the future "residual interest expense," $I_t - r_d L_{t-1}$, where r_d is the cost of debt capital. Similarly, the value of the preferred stock claim is computed as the sum of the initial balance PS_0 and the present value of the future "residual preferred dividends," using the cost of preferred stock capital r_{ps} as the discount rate. Denoting the debt value as P_d and the preferred stock value as P_{ps}, we get

$$P_d = L_0 + \sum_{t=1}^{\infty} (1 + r_d)^{-t}(I_t - r_d L_{t-1})$$

and

$$P_{ps} = PS_0 + \sum_{t=1}^{\infty} (1 + r_{ps})^{-t}(PD_t - r_{ps} PS_{t-1})$$

The entity value is the sum of the value of the common equity, the value of the preferred stock, and the value of the debt:

$$P_f = P_e + P_{ps} + P_d$$

so we can solve for the value of the common equity as

$$P_e = P_f - P_{ps} - P_d$$

This may seem like the long way around to get to a common equity valuation. The advantage of this indirect approach to valuing the equity is that it focuses your attention on the value of the net operating assets and future net operating income of the firm. The idea is that we should first work hard on valuing the entity, since this is the fundamental source of value for the firm, and then worry about how the value gets allocated between the capital providers.

Figure 10.2 illustrates the residual income valuation to all investors for Kohl's as of 9/3/2002 for the fiscal year that ended on 2/2/2002, using the default eVal forecasts. To see this in eVal, hit the View Valuation to All Investors button on the Residual Income Valuations sheet (and be sure you have the valuation date set to 9/3/2002). The figure shows how eVal computes the value of the debt, the value of the preferred stock (which is zero because Kohl's doesn't have any preferred stock), and the entity value. In each case the value is computed as a beginning balance plus the present value of a residual flow. The figure illustrates a few of the computations. We refer you back to Chapter 5 for the precise definitions of Net Operating Income and Net Operating Assets. Note that the flows to each capital provider are discounted at a different rate: debt is valued using the cost of debt capital (8%), preferred stock is valued at the cost of preferred stock (9%) and the entity value is computed using the weighted average cost of capital (shown as 9.6%, but in reality it is 9.5978% in this example). By subtracting the value of the debt and the value of the preferred stock from the entity value, we arrive at $12,057,789 thousand for the Forecast Equity Value Before Time Adjustment. Note that this is exactly the same amount that we found using the residual income to common equity model in the previous section.

The Tax Shield on Interest

If you have been following all this very carefully, you may have noticed that some money went missing. By definition,

$$NOI_t = NI_t + I_t(1 - tx_t) + PD_t$$

NOI_t is the income that flows to the entire entity. Similarly, NI_t is the income that flows to equity holders, I_t (*without* the $1 - tx_t$ adjustment) is the income that flows to debt holders, and PD_t is the income that flows to preferred stock holders. But what about the $-tx_t I_t$, *the tax shield on interest?* Where did it go? You can think of another agent in our story. For every I_t dollars that the firm sends to debt holders in the way of interest, the government sends $tx_t I_t$ dollar to the firm in the way of tax deductions (because interest is tax deductible). We could value the tax shield on interest separately and then add the result to an estimate of the entity value before any consideration of the tax shield. While this might seem like the most logical approach, the most common approach is to build the value of the tax shield into the entity value by adjusting the weighted average cost of capital. Recall from Chapter 9 that the weighted average cost of capital was a mix of the cost

FIGURE 10.2   Residual Income to All Investors

Valuation based on eVal defaults as of 9/3/2002 for 2/2/2002 fiscal year end.

	A	B	C	D	
1	**Residual Income Valuation**	**($000)**			
2	Go To User's Guide	View Valuation to Common Equity			
3		View Valuation to All Investors			
4	**Company Name**	Kohl's Corporation			
5	Most Recent Fiscal Year End	2/2/2002			
6	Date of Valuation	9/3/2002			
7	Cost of Common Equity	10.00%			
8					
9	Fiscal Year of Forecast	2/2/2003	2/2/2004	2/2/2005	2/2
53	**Valuation to all Investors**				
54	Cost of Debt	8.00%			
55	Cost of Preferred Stock	9.00%			
56	After Tax Weighted Average Cost of Capital	9.60%			
57					
58	Interest Expense to Debtholders	72,510	86,560	102,020	
59	Beginning Book Value of Debt	1,111,838	1,336,502	1,586,240	
60	Residual Interest Expense	(16,437)	(20,360)	(24,879)	
61	Present Value of Residual Interest Income	(15,219)	(17,456)	(19,750)	
62	Value of Debt	(285,758)			
63					
64	Dividends to Preferred Stockholders	0			
65	Beginning Book Value of Preferred Stock	0			
66	Residual Income to Preferred Stock	0			
67	Present Value of Residual Income	0			
68	Value of Preferred Stock	0			
69					
70	Net Operating Income	635,695	753,653	882,024	
71	Beginning Net Operating Assets	3,903,244	4,691,956	5,568,690	
72	Residual Income to all Investors	261,070	303,328	347,552	
73	Present Value of Residual Investor Income	238,207	252,528	264,006	
74	Entity Value	11,772,031			
75	Less Value of Debt	285,758			
76	Less Value of Preferred Stock	0			
77	Forecast Equity Value Before Time Adj.	12,057,789			
78		13,402,735			
79		0			

Annotations in figure:

- taken directly from Financial Statements sheet
- $72,510 - .08(1,111,838)$
- $-16,437/(1+.08)^1$
- $= 261,070/(1+.096)^1$
- 1,111,838 + sum of present values of residual interest expense
- = NI + (1−tx)Int. Expense + Pfd. Div.
  = 590,761 + (1−.38)72,510 + 0
- = CE + Pfd. Stk + LT Debt + ST Debt
  = 2,791,406 + 0 + 1,095,420 + 16,418
- = 3,903,244 + sum of present values of residual income to all Investors
- = 635,695 − .096(3,903,244)

Read

of equity capital r_e, the cost of preferred stock capital r_{ps} and the *after-tax* cost of debt capital $(1 - tx)r_d$. Using the after-tax cost of debt lowers the weighted average cost of capital that is used to discount the flows to the entity and therefore raises the entity value. Figure 10.3 illustrates the accounting variables and discount rates that each model uses.

FIGURE 10.3 **The Variables in Each Residual Income Valuation Equation**

entity value		common equity value		preferred stock value		debt value		tax shield
P_f uses	=	P_e uses	+	P_{ps} uses	+	P_d uses		
NOA_t	=	CE_t	+	PS_t	+	L_t		
and NOI_t	=	NI_t	+	PD_t	+	I_t	−	$tx_t I_t$

and discounts using

r_w	=	r_e	+	r_{ps}	+	r_d

weighted average of r_e, r_{ps}, and $(1-tx)r_d$

Value of $tx_t I_t$ is incorporated into entity value by using $(1-tx)r_d$ in r_w computation.

If it strikes you as a bit magical that using the after-tax cost of debt capital is all it takes to get the value of the tax shield on interest built into the entity value, your skepticism is justified. To be theoretically valid, we would need to add some additional assumptions, namely, that the tax rate and leverage ratios remain constant. But as discussed in Chapter 9, we side-step this whole issue by allowing eVal to find the internally consistent weighted average cost of capital for you. You input the cost of equity capital, the pre-tax cost of debt capital, and cost of preferred stock capital on the Valuation Parameters sheet, and eVal figures out the weighted average cost of capital that makes everything balance.

The tax shield on interest is an issue only when valuing the common equity using this indirect approach. When valuing the equity directly, interest payments and the associated tax deductions are just another type of expense that is tax-deductible, no different from cost of goods sold or marketing expenses.

10.3 DISCOUNTED CASH FLOW VALUATION

The *discounted cash flow (DCF) model* focuses on free cash flows rather than earnings flows. eVal computes the DCF model two ways: based on the free cash flows to common equity holders only and based on the free cash flows to all investors—common equity holders, preferred stock holders, and debt holders. With the "all investor" approach, the common equity is valued indirectly as the entity value less the value of the debt and preferred stock claims (just like the residual income to all investors model given in the previous section). The valuation attribute that drives the DCF model, in either form, is Free Cash Flow. Chapter 6 described in detail how this amount could be computed in many different, yet equivalent, ways. These derivations are shown in eVal on the Cash Flow Analysis sheet; you can jump straight to them by hitting the View FCF Computations button. We will give a few formulas for free cash flows here, but we refer you back to Chapter 6 for the details.

DCF to Common Equity

The *free cash flow to common equity* is the primary building block of all our valuation models. It is the net cash distributions to equity holders, labeled D_t. We can compute this amount directly as cash dividends plus stock repurchases less equity issuances. Alternatively, we can use the clean surplus relation and compute D_t based on net income and the change in common equity. That is,

$$CE_t = CE_{t-1} + NI_t - D_t$$

implies that

$$D_t = NI_t - (CE_t - CE_{t-1})$$

This is the cash flow that ultimately determines the value of a common equity claim. Discounting these flows at the cost of equity capital gives us the mother of all valuation models, the *DCF to Common Equity Model,* shown formally as

$$P_e = \sum_{t=1}^{\infty} (1 + r_e)^{-t} D_t$$

where

D_t is the net cash distributions to equity holders, computed as
$NI_t - (CE_t - CE_{t-1})$.

r_e is the cost of equity capital.

Your forecasted financial statements describe net income and common equity forever into the future. From these amounts we compute D_t, and discount these flows at rate r_e. Nothing could be simpler, really. The knock on this model is that it is hard to develop much intuition for future D_t flows. D_t is the distribution of wealth to equity holders, which typically happens much later than the actual creation of wealth. Further, past D_t is a poor predictor of future D_t, so you really need to rely on the financial statements to derive forecasts of future D_t. Your intuition alone won't get you very far.

Since they are all equivalent, it is hard to argue which of the four valuation models is the "original version." Nonetheless, this model is probably the first, most basic, expression of the value of an equity security. The formal derivations of the other models typically start here.[1]

Figure 10.4 illustrates the DCF valuation to common equity for Kohl's as of 9/3/2002 for the fiscal year that ended on 2/2/2002, using the default eVal forecasts. To see this in eVal, hit the View Valuation to Common Equity button on the DCF Valuations sheet (after changing the valuation date to 9/3/2002 on the Valu-

---

[1]It takes little work to derive the residual income model from the DCF to common equity model. Start with the DCF model and write D_t as $NI_t - (CE_t - CE_{t-1})$. For each future date, substitute for NI_t the value $RI_t + r_e CE_{t-1}$. The first term in the summation (when $t=1$) is $(1+r_e)^{-1}[RI_1 + r_e CE_0 - CE_1 + CE_0] = CE_0 + (1+r_e)^{-1}RI_1 - (1+r_e)^{-1}CE_1$. The second term in the summation (when $t=2$) is $(1+r_e)^{-2}[RI_2 + r_e CE_1 - CE_2 + CE_1] = (1+r_e)^{-2}RI_2 + (1+r_e)^{-1}CE_1 - (1+r_e)^{-2}CE_2$. Adding these two terms together gives $CE_0 + (1+r_e)^{-1}RI_1 + (1+r_e)^{-2}RI_2 - (1+r_e)^{-2}CE_2$. As you can see, we are building the residual income model term by term. Every time we add another term in the summation we add in the appropriately discounted RI_t term and cancel the last term in the previous sum. Since the summation is infinite, the last term is pushed out infinitely far into the future, and hence has zero present value.

FIGURE 10.4 DCF to Common Equity

Valuation based on eVal defaults as of 9/3/2002 for 2/2/2002 fiscal year end.

	A	B	C	D
1	**DCF Valuations**	**($000)**		
2	Go To User's Guide	View Valuation to Common Equity		
3		View Valuation to All Investors		
4	**Company Name**	Kohl's Corporation		
5	Most Recent Fiscal Year End	2/2/2002		
6	Date of Valuation	9/3/2002		
7	Cost of Common Equity	10.00%		
8				
9	Fiscal Year of Forecast	2/2/2003	2/2/2004	2/2/2005
11	**Valuation to Common Equity**			
12	Free Cash Flow to Common Equity	26,714	73,014	135,204
13	Present Value of FCF	24,285	60,343	101,581
14	Present Value Beyond 20 Years	6,183,403		
15	Present Value of First 20 Years	5,874,386		
16	Forecast Equity Value Before Time Adj.	12,057,789		
17	Forecasted Value as of Valuation Date	13,402,735		
18	Less Value of Contingent Equity Claims	(1,147,681)		
19	Value Attributable to Common Equity	12,255,054		
20	Common Shares Outstanding at BS Date	332,167		
21	Equivalent Shares at Valuation Date	332,167		
22	Forecast Price/Share	**$36.89**		
23				
24				
25				

Annotations:

$$= NI_1 - (CE_1 - CE_0)$$
$$= 590,761$$
$$\quad - (3,355,453 - 2,791,406)$$

$$= 73,014/(1+.10)^2$$

$$= 26,714/(1+.10)^1$$

Sheet tabs: Graphics / Cash Flow Analysis / Valuation Parameters / Residual Income Valuations / **DCF Valuations** / EPS Fo

Ready

ation Parameters sheet). Figure 10.4 illustrates the computation of net distributions to common equity holders, labeled as the Free Cash Flow to Common Equity, and a few present value computations for individual years. For details on the computation of free cash flow to common equity, we refer you to Chapter 6, and to the Cash Flow Analysis sheet in eVal. The present value from the first 20 years is added to the present value from beyond 20 years to arrive at the Forecast Equity Value Before Time Adjustments. The details of the present value computations and the time adjustments are discussed in a later section. Note that the final result, before time adjustments, is $12,057,789 thousand, exactly the same result we reached using the residual income models.

DCF to All Investors

When someone in practice says "the DCF model," this is the model they typically have in mind. This model is the warhorse of traditional finance. Unfortunately, because the computation of the *free cash flow to all investors* is rather involved, and because "all investor" models require a weighted average cost of capital that is consistent with the other costs of capital, it is the rare user who can successfully compute the DCF to all Investors model without error. By automating the required computations, eVal makes sure you don't mess up along the way.

Because of the long history this model has enjoyed, a number of different ways to compute the free cash flow to all investors have emerged. We summarize two methods here; we refer you to Chapter 6 for more detailed explanations or to the Cash Flow Analysis sheet in eVal for an example using Kohl's for the year ended 2/2/2002. The free cash flow to all investors, denoted here as C_t, is computed as

$$C_t = NOI_t - (NOA_t - NOA_{t-1})$$

In words, the free cash flow to all investors equals the net operating income less the increase in net operating assets. This should feel right. All investors together claim the cash flows that emanate from the use of the net operating assets. Free cash flow differs from NOI_t because accrual accounting recognizes some NOI_t dollars that are not yet cash dollars, which necessarily means they are still in NOA_t. Subtracting the increase in NOA_t from NOI_t leaves us with the cash that the entity generated from its operations over the period.

You can also compute the free cash flows directly from data given on the Statement of Cash Flows. Just ask yourself, what cash went to each investor group? The company sent equity holders the net distribution D_t (that is, common dividends plus stock repurchases less equity issuances). The firm sent debt holders interest, but received the benefit of the tax deduction on interest $I_t(1-tx_t)$, and less any increase in principle, denoted ΔL_t. The firm sent preferred stock holders preferred dividends PD_t less any new issuances, denoted ΔPS_t. Putting it all together, we have

$$C_t = D_t + I_t(1-tx_t) - \Delta L + PD_t - \Delta PS_t$$

If you suffer from insomnia and enjoy the finger exercises that only algebra can provide, you can show that this expression for C_t equals the previous one.[2]

Armed with the free cash flow to all investors C_t, we can now compute the *entity value*—the value of the operations to all investors before distinguishing between claimants. Denoting the weighted average cost of capital as r_w and the entity value as P_f, we have

$$P_f = \sum_{t=1}^{\infty} (1 + r_w)^{-t} C_t$$

And, yes, this version of P_f is exactly equal to the P_f computed using the Residual Income to all Investors model shown in the previous section. To compute the value of the common equity claim, we subtract from P_f the value of the debt P_d and preferred stock P_{ps}. In the spirit of discounting cash flows, each of these non-

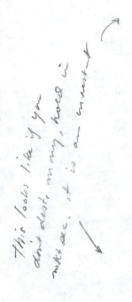

This looks like if you don't deal an any, hold in mkts ac. it is an invarment

---

[2]Here is the proof. By definition $NOI_t = NI_t + PD_t + I_t(1-tx_t)$ and $\Delta NOA_t = \Delta CE_t + \Delta L_t + \Delta PS_t$. Substitute these expressions for NOI_t and $(NOA_t - NOA_{t-1})$ in the first C_t expression. Next, note that by the clean surplus relation $NI_t = D_t + \Delta CE_t$. Substitute this in for NI_t, cancel the plus and minus ΔCE_t and you have the second expression for C_t.

common-equity claims is itself valued based on the cash flows it receives. Denoting the pre-tax cost of debt as r_d and the cost of preferred stock as r_{ps}, we have

$$P_d = \sum_{t=1}^{\infty} (1 + r_d)^{-t}(I_t - \Delta L_t)$$

and

$$P_{ps} = \sum_{t=1}^{\infty} (1 + r_{ps})^{-t}(PD_t - \Delta PS_t)$$

The value of P_d and P_{ps} computed based on cash flows is exactly the same as the value computed in the previous section based on residual flows. Putting it all together, we compute the value of the common equity as

$$P_e = P_f - P_d - P_{ps}$$

Finally, we can mix and match between the residual income model and the discounted cash flow model. For instance, it is not uncommon to compute the value of the debt P_d or the value of the preferred stock using a residual income model, with the added assumption that all future residual flows to these claimants are zero. In other words, the value of the debt and the value of the preferred stock are simply their current book values L_0 and PS_0, respectively. The value of the common equity is then the entity value computed using free cash flows to all investors less the book value of the debt and the book value of preferred stock.

Figure 10.5 illustrates the DCF valuation to all investors for Kohl's as of 9/3/2002 for the fiscal year that ended on 2/2/2002, using the default eVal forecasts. To see this in eVal, hit the View Valuation to All Investors button on the DCF Valuations sheet (after setting the valuation date to 9/3/2002). The figure shows the free cash flows each period to debt, to preferred stock (zero in Kohl's case), and then to all investors. Note that the value of debt, the value of preferred stock, and the entity value are each computed using a different discount rate. In particular, the entity value is computed using the weighted average cost of capital of 9.6% (actually, it is 9.5978%). This amount was derived by eVal as the rate that equates the equity value when computed directly with the equity value when computed indirectly as the entity value less the value of the debt and the value of the preferred stock. Note that the result of $12,057,789 thousand, labeled as the Forecast Equity Value Before Time Adjustment, is exactly the same result as in the other three valuation models.

Tax Shield on Interest

Just as in the residual income to all investors model, we need to worry about the tax shield on interest. When the firm pays I_t interest to the debt holders the government gives the firm a tax deduction worth $t_x I_t$. This is why the interest is after-tax in the C_t computation:

$$C_t = D_t + I_t(1-tx_t) - \Delta L + PD_t - \Delta PS_t$$

But notice that the $-tx_t I_t$ flow, *the tax shield on interest,* isn't getting discounted in the P_e, P_{ps} or P_d formulas. To see this clearly, Figure 10.6 shows the cash flows

FIGURE 10.5 **DCF to All Investors**

Valuation based on eVal defaults as of 9/3/2002 for 2/2/2002 fiscal year end.

	A	B	C	D
1	**DCF Valuations**	**($000)**		
2	Go To User's Guide	View Valuation to Common Equity		
3		View Valuation to All Investors		
4	**Company Name**	Kohl's Corporation		
5	Most Recent Fiscal Year End	2/2/2002		
6	Date of Valuation	9/3/2002	= Int. Expense – increase in Debt	
7	Cost of Common Equity	10.00%	= 72,510 – 224,664	
8				
9	Fiscal Year of Forecast	2/2/2003	2/2/2004	2/2/2005
53	**Valuation All Investors**			
54	Cost of Debt	8.00%		
55	Cost of Preferred Stock	9.00%		
56	After Tax Weighted Average Cost of Capital	9.60%	= –152,154/(1+.08)²	
57				
58	Free Cash Flow to Debt	(152,154)	(163,178)	(170,262)
59	Present Value of FCF to Debt	(140,884)	(139,899)	(135,160)
60	Value of Debt	(285,758)		
6_	= NOI – increase in NOA = 635,695 – 788,712 taken from Cash Flow Analysis	0	= –163,178/(1+.08)²	
6_	ck d Stock	= –123,082/(1+.096)²		
66	Free Cash Flows to Investors	(153,016)	(123,082)	(73,856)
67	Present Value of FCF to Investors	(139,616)	(102,469)	(56,102)
68	Entity Value	11,772,031		
69	Less Value of Debt	285,758	sum of present values of FCF to Investors	
70	Less Value of Preferred Stock	0		
71	Forecast Equity Value Before Time Adj.	12,057,789		
72	Forecasted Value as of Valuation Date	13,402,735		

that are being discounted to compute P_e, P_{ps} and P_d. How, then, can the sum of P_e, P_{ps} and P_d equal the entity value P_f, which discounts the full C_t flows? The answer is that the value of the tax shield is incorporated into the entity value through the discount rate r_w. Recall from Chapter 9 that the weight average cost of capital is a mix of the cost of equity r_e, the cost of preferred stock r_{ps}, and the *after-tax* cost of debt $(1-tx)r_d$. Using the after-tax cost of debt lowers the weighted average cost of capital, which raises the present value of the C_t flows in the P_f formula.

While it is relatively easy to see how lowering the weighted average cost of capital a bit will raise the entity value a bit, it is perhaps surprising that the adjustment is exactly the right amount to capture the value of the tax shield. In fact, we are hiding some complications from you. For this to really work out, we would need to assume that the tax rate and the leverage ratio remain constant, yet eVal allows you to forecast whatever tax rates and leverage rates you like. Rather than constrain your forecasts, we side-step this whole issue by allowing eVal to find the internally consistent weighted average cost of capital for you. You input the cost

FIGURE 10.6 The Variables in Each DCF Valuation Equation

entity value		common equity value		preferred stock value		debt value	tax shield
P_f		P_e		P_{ps}		P_d	
cash flows	=	cash flows	+	cash flows	+	cash flows	cash flows
C_t	=	D_t	+	$PD_t - \Delta PS_t$	+	$I_t - \Delta L_t$	$- \quad tx_t I_t$

discounted using

| r_w | = | r_e | | r_{ps} | | r_d | |

weighted average
of r_e, r_{ps}, and $(1-tx)r_d$

Value of $tx_t I_t$ is incorporated into entity value by using $(1-tx)r_d$ in r_w computation.

of equity capital, the pre-tax cost of debt capital, and cost of preferred stock capital on the Valuation Parameters sheet, and eVal figures out the weighted average cost of capital that makes everything balance. For more information, see the discussion of the weighted average cost of capital in Chapter 9.

Figuring out how to value the tax shield on interest is an issue only when we want to first value the whole entity and then back into the value of the common equity. If we value the free cash flows to equity directly, then interest and its tax deduction are built into our financial statement forecasts and play out through net income and the book value of equity just like any other expense. What this means is that any debate about valuing the tax shield on interest (and academics love to debate this issue) is really just a debate about how to get the entity value to equal the sum of the debt value, preferred stock value, and common equity value.

Figure 10.7 summarizes all four valuation models. The columns describe what is being valued, the equity, the debt, or the preferred stock; and the rows describe which valuation attribute is being used, free cash flow or residual income. To compute the infinite sum of flows, each expression makes use of the perpetuity formula discussed in the next section.

10.4 PRESENT VALUE COMPUTATIONS

All four valuation models given above compute value as the present value of an infinite series of flows of the valuation attribute, either residual income or free cash flow. Since it is impossibly time consuming to compute the present value of an infinite series term by term, all valuation models compute the present value term by term up to the *terminal year* and then compute the present value beyond the terminal year using the formula for a growing perpetuity. In case you have forgotten, the present value of a growing perpetuity of payments, starting with $K one year from now and growing at rate g forever after, discounted at rate r, is given by the following formula:

$$\frac{K}{(1+r)} + \frac{(1+g)K}{(1+r)^2} + \frac{(1+g)^2K}{(1+r)^3} + \frac{(1+g)^3K}{(1+r)^4} + \ldots = \frac{K}{(r-g)}$$

FIGURE 10.7   **Summary of Valuation Equations**

	Equity Valued Directly as P_e	*Equity Valued Indirectly as* $P_e = P_f - P_d - P_{ps}$		
	Value of Common Equity P_e	Value of Whole Entity P_f	Value of Debt P_d	Value of Preferred Stock P_{ps}
Residual Income Cash Flows (Valuation Attribute)	$\sum_{t=1}^{T-1} \dfrac{D_t}{(1+r_e)^t} + \dfrac{D_T}{(r_e-g)(1+r_e)^{T-1}}$	$\sum_{t=1}^{T-1} \dfrac{C_t}{(1+r_w)^t} + \dfrac{C_T}{(r_w-g)(1+r_w)^{T-1}}$	$\sum_{t=1}^{T-1} \dfrac{I_t-\Delta L_t}{(1+r_d)^t} + \dfrac{I_T-\Delta L_T}{(r_d-g)(1+r_d)^{T-1}}$	$\sum_{t=1}^{T-1} \dfrac{PD_t-\Delta PS_t}{(1+r_{ps})^t} + \dfrac{PD_T-\Delta PS_T}{(r_{ps}-g)(1+r_{ps})^{T-1}}$
	$CE_0 + \sum_{t=1}^{T-1} \dfrac{RI_t}{(1+r_e)^t} + \dfrac{RI_T}{(r_e-g)(1+r_e)^{T-1}}$ where $RI_t = NI_t - r_e CE_{t-1}$	$NOA_0 + \sum_{t=1}^{T-1} \dfrac{RNOI_t}{(1+r_w)^t} + \dfrac{RNOI_T}{(r_w-g)(1+r_w)^{T-1}}$ where $RNOI_t = NOI_t - r_w NOA_{t-1}$	$L_0 + \sum_{t=1}^{T-1} \dfrac{RIT_t}{(1+r_d)^t} + \dfrac{RIT_T}{(r_d-g)(1+r_d)^{T-1}}$ where $RIT_t = I_t - r_d L_{t-1}$	$PS_0 + \sum_{t=1}^{T-1} \dfrac{RPD_t}{(1+r_{ps})^t} + \dfrac{RPD_T}{(r_{ps}-g)(1+r_{ps})^{T-1}}$ where $RPD_t = PD_t - r_{ps} PS_{t-1}$

D_t is cash flow to common equity;
C_t is cash flow to all investors;
L_t is the debt balance at time t
CE_t is the shareholders' equity at time t;
NOI_t is the operating income for the period ending at time t, net of tax
I_t is the interest expense for the period ending at time t,
NI_t is the net income for the period ending at time t;
NOA_t is the net operating asset balance at time t

PD_t is preferred dividend at time t
PS_t is preferred stock balance at time t
g is the perpetual growth rate
r_e is the cost of equity capital
r_d is the cost of debt capital
r_{ps} is the cost of preferred stock capital
r_w is the weighted average cost of capital:

$$r_w = \frac{r_e P_e + (1-tx)r_d P_d + r_p P_{ps}}{P_e + P_d + P_{ps}}$$

The left-hand side of the formula shows the sequence of terms that continue in perpetuity in the present value computation and the right-hand side of the formula shows the very simple result.

Before the terminal year, your forecasts can be as wild as you like. Each year's forecasts will imply a flow of valuation attributes, however unusual, and the model will compute the present value of each year's flow. Starting with the terminal year, however, your forecasts are constrained to behave in a more predictable manner. Sales growth is fixed at the rate you input into eVal in the terminal year and this becomes the g in the perpetuity formula. Profit margins, asset turnovers, and leverage ratios are also assumed to remain constant after the terminal year. These forecasts imply well-defined financial statements forever into the future, and they are financial statements that will generate residual income flows and free cash flows that will grow forever at rate g. Once everything is safely growing at this known rate, we can compute the present value of the subsequent flows using the formula given above.

In previous chapters we noted that your terminal growth forecast should not exceed the discount rate; otherwise, the present value is infinite. In terms of the formula given above, if g is greater than r then the result is negative, but you shouldn't try to attach any meaning to this. The formula is simply not valid when g exceeds r. At the other extreme g can be negative, implying that the value flows are decaying rather than growing; $g = -1$ implies that the firm liquidates in the next period.

Let's use the growing perpetuity formula to rewrite the residual income to common equity model. The model given earlier is

$$P_e = CE_0 + \sum_{t=1}^{\infty} (1 + r_e)^{-1}RI_t$$

Now suppose that, starting in year T, the financial statement forecasts imply that residual income will be RI_T and then grow at rate g forever after. We can now compute the present value as

$$P_e = CE_0 + \sum_{t=1}^{T-1} (1 + r_e)^{-t}RI_t + \frac{RI_T}{(r_e - g)(1 + r_e)^{T-1}}$$

The first two terms are the present value for years 1 through $T-1$ and the last term is the present value for years T and forever after. To understand the formula for a growing perpetuity in this setting, you need to think carefully about when the different residual income flows take place. The residual income in year T is RI_T, it is $RI_T(1+g)$ in year $T+1$, and so on, growing forever at rate g. If we were standing in year $T-1$ and wanted to compute the present value of this growing perpetuity, we would apply the formula and get

$$\frac{RI_T}{(r_e - g)}$$

But we want the present value at time 0, not time $T-1$, so we need to discount back $T-1$ more years. To do this we divide by $(1+r_e)^{T-1}$, as shown in the denominator of the last term.

All the other valuation models handle the present value computations exactly the same way. After the financial statement forecasts become sufficiently stable, insofar as they imply a smooth sequence of future free cash flows or residual income flows, the perpetuity formula kicks in to compute the remaining present value. As a summary, Figure 10.7 gives the precise definition of each model.

So what is the value of T, the terminal year? In eVal, it is always 23 years. This may not seem like the most obvious choice, so let us explain. On the Forecasting Assumptions sheet the longest horizon you can pick for making detailed forecasts is 20 years. After 20 years it is assumed that all relationships stabilize and grow at the terminal sales growth rate. However, many of the forecasting assumptions in eVal are based on relationships between income statement amounts and average balance sheet amounts, so it takes two more years for all the relationships among the financial statements to stabilize and yield steady sequences of cash flows and residual income flows. If you pick the 5-year or 10-year forecasting horizon the cash flows and residual income flows stabilize sooner, but we still get the same present value if we discount each year individually until we get out to year 23.

In general, you should be very cautious about using the perpetuity formula too soon. Many of the financial statement relationships change around the transition from the finite horizon to the steady state that follows after the terminal year. Because year T is the starting value for an infinite stream of future values, even a small error in the year T cash flow or residual income flow gets greatly amplified, resulting in a big mistake in the valuation. As an example, suppose that you use a

5-year finite forecasting horizon, so that year 6 is the terminal year and all financial statement line items are forecast to grow at rate g beginning in year 7 and forever after. Using the residual income model, the perpetuity starts with RI_7—this is the amount you put in the numerator of the terminal value calculation. One of the most common mistakes we see on home-grown valuation spreadsheets is to assume that $RI_7 = (1+g)RI_6$. This is a tempting answer because year 6 is probably the last column on the spreadsheet. Why is this answer generally wrong? By definition $RI_7 = NI_7 - r_eCE_6$ which equals $(1+g)NI_6 - r_eCE_6$ since all the financial statement line items are governed by the growth rate g *starting in year 7*. But note that $(1+g)RI_6 \neq (1+g)NI_6 - (1+g)r_eCE_5$ which isn't generally equal to $(1+g)NI_6 - r_eCE_6$ because CE_5 and CE_6 occur before year 7 and so they are not constrained in any way. Because the terminal value calculation is important, yet tedious, we let eVal handle the calculation.

Adjusting the Present Value to the Present

Figure 10.8 illustrates eVal's present value computations for the DCF to Common Equity and the Residual Income to Common Equity models. The amounts are from Kohl's, valued as of 9/3/2002 for the fiscal year ended 2/2/2002, using the default forecasting settings. Consider the DCF to Common Equity, shown in the top panel. eVal adds the Present Value of the First 20 Years and the Present Value Beyond 20 Years to arrive at the Forecasted Equity Value before Time Adjustment. Comparing the two amounts shows that a little less than half the total value of the cash flows arrives in the first 20 years. But now compare this to the Residual Income model in the bottom half of Figure 10.8.

The Residual Income model also shows values for the first 20 years and beyond 20 years, but they aren't the same as the DCF model. In particular, the value beyond 20 years is much smaller and, if we consider the Value of Common Equity as of 2/2/2002 as part of the value during the first 20 years, then the Residual Income model shows a significantly greater portion of value arriving much earlier than the DCF model. Both models arrive at the same Forecasted Equity before Time Adjustment but why do they allocate the value differently across time? The answer reveals a fundamental difference in the way the two models characterize value creation. The Residual Income model counts the balance of common equity as value already owned and counts net income as value created, regardless of the actual cash flow. The DCF model, in contrast, waits for the actual cash to arrive. Another way to say this is that the DCF treats investment as a consumption of value (cash is leaving the firm) while the Residual Income model treats investment as a store of value (assets are put on the books). The two models ultimately get to the same total value because they are based on the same underlying financial statement forecasts, but they differ drastically on when they say the value is created.

Regardless of which model you are working with, it is useful to think about when the model says that value is being created. In most cases you are probably more confident about your forecasts during the first 20 years than you are about your forecasts beyond 20 years, so if most of the value is concentrated more than 20 years away, then you might be less confident in your valuation. Are we more

FIGURE 10.8

Kohl's Present Value Computations

Valuation based on eVal defaults as of 9/3/2002 for 2/2/2002 fiscal year end.

	Valuation to Common Equity	
11	**Valuation to Common Equity**	
12	Free Cash Flow to Common Equity	26,714
13	Present Value of FCF	24,285
14	Present Value Beyond 20 Years	6,183,403
15	Present Value of First 20 Years	5,874,386
16	Forecast Equity Value Before Time Adj.	12,057,789
17	Forecasted Value as of Valuation Date	13,402,735
18	Less Value of Contingent Equity Claims	(1,147,681)
19	Value Attributable to Common Equity	12,255,054
20	Common Shares Outstanding at BS Date	332,167
21	Equivalent Shares at Valuation Date	332,167
22	Forecast Price/Share	$36.89
23		

	Valuation to Common Equity	
11	**Valuation to Common Equity**	
12	Net Income	590,761
13	Common Equity at Beginning of Year	2,791,406
14	Residual Income	311,620
15	Present Value of Residual Income	283,291
16	Present Value Beyond 20 Years	3,831,760
17	Present Value of First 20 Years	5,434,623
18	Common Equity as of	
19	2/2/2002	2,791,406
20	Forecast Equity Value Before Time Adj.	12,057,789
21	Forecasted Value as of Valuation Date	13,402,735
22	Less Value of Contingent Equity Claims	(1,147,681)
23	Value Attributable to Common Equity	12,255,054
24	Common Shares Outstanding at BS Date	332,167
25	Equivalent Shares at Valuation Date	332,167
26	Forecast Price/Share	$36.89
27		

confident in the residual income model than in the DCF model because it records valuation creation sooner? The answer is absolutely not. One model can be derived algebraically from the other and so it would be silly to be more confident in the left-hand side of an equation than in the right-hand side. Whatever uncertainty you have in your forecasts about book value and net income translates into exactly the same amount of uncertainty in future net distributions to common equity holders.[3]

[3]Lundholm and O'Keefe (2001) provide careful discussion of this issue, along with a list of common errors in the implementation of each model that generate apparent, but not real, differences between the residual income model and DCF models.

So far we have discussed the present value calculations as of the end of the fiscal year for the most recent financial statements, which is 2/2/2002 in the Kohl's example, and have worked our way down Figure 10.8 to the line labeled the Forecast Equity Value Before Time Adjustment. There are two more present value adjustments that take us to the next line, labeled Forecasted Value as of Valuation Date. First, the present value computation treats the cash flows and residual income flows as though they are realized on the last day of the fiscal year. In reality, wealth is created somewhat more evenly throughout the year. To correct for this we multiply the value estimate by $(1+r_e/2)$. This effectively moves the flows forward six months in time. Second, you will typically want to compute the value as of the day you are thinking of trading the stock, not the last day of the last fiscal year. You can enter whatever valuation date you like on eVal's Valuation Parameters sheet; the default is the current date. eVal then computes the fraction of the year (ρ) between the inputted date and the fiscal year end, and multiplies the value estimate by $(1+r_e\rho)$ to get the present value as of the inputted date. This adjusts your valuation estimate for the passage of time between the last set of financial statements and the date entered. As time passes you get closer to the estimated future values, so their present value increases. In the Kohl's example in Figure 10.8 the valuation date is 9/3/2002, which is 58.6 percent of the way through the next fiscal year. Putting these two time value adjustments together, and using the default cost of equity capital in eVal of 10 percent, the adjustment to go from the Forecasted Equity Value before Time Adjustment to the Forecasted Value as of Valuation Date is

$$12{,}057{,}789(1+.10/2)(1+.10(.5861)) = 13{,}402{,}735$$

There are two other adjustments we need to make before we get to the final estimate of price per share. These are discussed in the next section.

10.5 VALUING CONTINGENT CLAIMS AND OTHER ADJUSTMENTS

The value of *contingent claims* represents your estimate of the value of other potential claims on the firm that are not currently recognized in the financial statements or in your estimates. These might be stock warrants, the convertible component of a debt issue or, most commonly, employee stock options. Firms frequently grant stock options to their employees with an exercise price equal to the current market price at the date of the grant. Because the accountants are typically unwilling to estimate the option value of this grant, they make no entry in the accounting system to reflect the granting of the option. Later, if the stock price increases and the employee exercises the option, the company simply treats it as issuing stock at the initial exercise price. Consequently, the value of the current equity claims should reflect the possibility that the firm will issue equity at below-market prices sometime in the future. Forming a precise estimate of this loss in value can be quite complicated. We will describe how to compute a lower bound for this value, how to approximate it more accurately using the **Contingent Claims Calculator** in eVal, and then discuss some limitations to both of these approaches.

We will focus on estimating the value of employee stock options; the other types of contingent claims can be estimated in similar fashion. Start by reading the firm's financial statement footnote on employee stock options. Here they tell you the number of options outstanding in different ranges of option exercise prices. If the option can be exercised at a low price and the stock is currently trading at a high price, then each option is worth *at least* the difference between these two amounts. That is, the option is "in the money" by the difference between these two amounts. But this represents only a lower bound on the value of the option because it doesn't account for the fact that the stock price might increase even more before the option must be exercised. How likely this is to occur depends on the life of the option and on the volatility in the stock price. There are a number of ways to put all these puzzle pieces together and form an option pricing model. eVal offers you a calculator that uses the most popular solution: the Black-Scholes Option Pricing Model. Let

S = current stock price.

K = exercise or "strike" price.

y = long-term forecasted annual dividend yield.

r = annual risk-free interest rate.

t = number of years before the option expires.

σ = standard deviation of the annualized continuously compounded stock return.

N($\bullet$) = cumulative standard normal distribution function.

The Black-Scholes formula is then

$$optionvalue = Se^{-yt}N(d_1) - Ke^{-rt}N(d_2)$$

where

$$d_1 = \frac{\ln(\frac{S}{K}) + \left(r - y + \frac{\sigma^2}{2}\right)t}{\sigma\sqrt{t}} \quad \text{and } d_2 = d_1 - \sigma\sqrt{t}$$

Without attempting to derive the specific form of this model, we offer some observations about it. First, note that the option's value increases with the gap between the current stock price S and the option's exercise price K. The deeper the option is in the money, the more valuable it is. Second, the option's value increases with t, the number of years remaining before the option expires, and with σ, the stock price volatility. Third, the option value decreases with the dividend yield y because future dividends decrease the future stock price, all else equal. Actually evaluating this formula by hand would be quite difficult because the function N($\bullet$) is itself quite complicated. Instead, the Contingent Claims Calculator on the Valuation Parameters sheet in eVal takes your inputted parameters and does the calculation for you.

Most of the inputs to the Contingent Claims Calculator are obvious, but the one that you may not have a good feel for is the standard deviation of the stock return. A good source for this data item is the employee stock option footnote. Companies provide an estimate of this amount because they are required to estimate the value of options issued to employees during the current fiscal year and report the impact on earnings-per-share if this amount would have been expensed in the period. A ballpark figure is 30 percent, which is the default amount given in the Contingent Claims Calculator.

A problem with the Black-Scholes estimate given by the Contingent Claims Calculator is that real live employees frequently do not behave exactly like the model says they should. In particular, it has been shown that employees overwhelmingly exercise their options well before the option's expiration date. This doesn't make sense, from the model's point of view, because the option still has additional value right up to the expiration date. From the common equity holder's point of view, however, this is good news because less value is being given away to the employees. It also means that the Black-Scholes estimate might be too high. Your final estimate might be something higher than the simple difference between the current stock price and the exercise price and something less than the full Black-Scholes amount given in the Contingent Claims Calculator.

Generally the company reports a range of exercise prices and gives the weighted average of the exercise price, years to expiration, and other details for each set of options in the range. You need to estimate the value of the options separately for each exercise price and corresponding number of shares under option at that exercise price. In Figure 10.9 we illustrate the inputs to the Contingent Claims Calculator using the stock option footnote from Kohl's 10-K for the year ended 2/2/2002.

To use the data from Kohl's footnote in the Contingent Claims Calculator, we need to assume that all the options in an exercise price range have the weighted average exercise price and years remaining on the contractual life. We also take the risk-free interest rate, the dividend yield, and the volatility estimates from the Kohl's footnote. The net result is that the outstanding options have a Black-Scholes value of $1,147,681 thousand, or over a billion dollars, as shown in Figure 10.8 for the line labeled Less Value of Contingent Equity Claims. A billion dollars is a little over 5 percent of Kohl's market capitalization at the end of fiscal 2001.

Five percent of the market capitalization is a lot of money to be missing from the financial statements, and Kohl's is by no means a heavy user of employee stock options when compared to many technology companies. Unless the accounting rules change and begin measuring the wealth consumption that the issuance of options represents, the only way to capture this effect is to estimate it separately and adjust our valuation accordingly.

This adjustment for contingent claims only captures the effect of existing contingent claims. What if you expect that the firm will continue to issue options or other contingent securities in the future? As we discuss in Chapter 12, the best way to handle this is to estimate the dollar value of the to-be-issued options and record them as an expense in your forecasted financial statements. In other words, fix the accounting for stock options to get the expense into your forecasts.

FIGURE 10.9
Estimated Value of Kohl's Options Outstanding as of 2/2/2002

	Exercise Price Range		
	$1.75 to $9.49	$9.50 to $35.49	$35.50 to $71.82
Options outstanding................................	7,253,245	5,940,700	8,059,851
Weighted average exercise price of options outstanding $	6.57 $	24.63 $	54.72
Weighted average remaining contractual life of options outstanding.......................................	3.4	11.3	13.9

Estimated Value of Options Outstanding (in thousands)*

Options with Exercise Price Range of $1.75–$9.49	$432,610
Options with Exercise Price Range of $9.50–$35.49	$322,270
Options with Exercise Price Range of $35.50–71.82	$392,801
Total Value ($000)	**$1,147,681**

*Other inputs to the Contingent Claims Calculator are a risk-free rate of 6%, a dividend yield of 0% and stock return volatility of 40%, as given in Kohl's 10-K, and a $65 current stock price, which was the price just after the fiscal year end.

Adjusting for Stock Splits and Stock Dividends

If the firm has undertaken a stock split or stock dividend (which is very different from a cash dividend), between the date of the financial statements you are using and the valuation date, then you need to adjust for this by inputting a *dilution factor* on the eVal Valuation Parameters sheet. For example, if your firm does a 2-for-1 stock split after the date of the financial statements, then the number of shares outstanding doubles, resulting in a dilution factor of 2. If we failed to account for the split, then our per-share valuation estimate and all of our EPS forecasts would be twice what they should be. To see a list of recent splits for a company, go to Yahoo! Finance, type the company's ticker, and select the Chart option under More Info. Alternatively, go to Multex Investor, enter the company ticker, and go to the bottom of the Highlights Report. You only have to adjust for splits since the most recent balance sheet date loaded in eVal. Don't include any splits made before that date.

What if the firm issues new shares for cash or as part of the acquisition of another company? Interestingly, you do not need to adjust for this *if* you believe the shares were issued at their true intrinsic value. In a stock split or stock dividend, the number of shares increases but nothing of economic value is added to the firm, so adjusting the number of shares completely captures the effect of this event. If the firm receives something of economic value in exchange for the shares, however, then value of the firm increases along with the number of shares. If the new shares are issued at a price equal to their intrinsic value then the increase in firm value exactly offsets the dilution caused by the increase in the number of shares. To make this perfectly clear, imagine a firm that consists of $100 in a bank account and has 1 share outstanding, so its intrinsic value is $100/share. If the firm issues another share for $100 and deposits it in the bank, the firm is now worth $200 and has 2 shares, so it is still worth $100 per share. Complications arise, however, if the firm issues the stock at $90 or $110. In this case there is a wealth transfer between the original owners and the new investors. Situations such as this raise thorny issues in valuation. Fundamentally, what is the value of an overvalued stock that can issue equity at its inflated price? We will ignore such complications in this chapter and take them up in a serious way in Chapter 12.

The last stock split for Kohl's was in April 2000, well before the 2/2/2002 fiscal year end, so we don't need to adjust the number of shares in our computations. Consequently, the Common Shares Outstanding at Balance Sheet Date and the Equivalent Shares at Valuation Date are the same amount in Figure 10.8.

Putting It All Together

The valuation formulas given in the first part of the chapter compute the present value as of the most recent fiscal year end, assuming that all cash flows and residual income flows happen on the last day of each year. We then adjusted this value up by a half-year's worth of time value because the flows typically happen evenly throughout the year, not on the last day. We also adjusted the value up to the date that we are actually doing the valuation (or whatever date we want), rather than the end of the most recent fiscal year. We then subtract the value of any contingent claims and adjust the number of shares for any stock splits or stock dividends that occurred between the fiscal year end and the valuation date. The final result is our forecast of the intrinsic price/share. This is what you think the stock is really worth. For Kohl's, the final result is $36.89/share, as illustrated on the last line of Figure 10.8. Recall that the valuation date is set to 9/3/2002, and we simply used the default eVal forecasts. This is less than half of the market price of Kohl's at 9/3/2002, so the market is expecting much better performance from Kohl's than is implied by the eVal defaults. Whether Kohl's can live up to these rather lofty expectations remains to be seen.

The Model Summary sheet in eVal gives a quick snapshot of the firm's historical performance, the profitability and growth implications of your detailed forecasts, and the resulting price per share estimate. It also shows the market-to-book and price-to-earnings ratios that are implied by your estimated price; these ratios are discussed in the next chapter.

If the value estimate is ridiculously far from the current market price and you feel reasonably confident in your forecasts, here are a few things to check. First, are you sure you have the correct number of shares outstanding? If there was a stock split after the fiscal year end then you may be off by 100 percent in your estimate. Second, what if the estimated price is negative? Literally, a negative price means that you would pay this amount to *not* have to own the stock. We allow eVal to arrive at this conclusion if it is the logical implication of your forecasts and cost of capital inputs, but we don't really expect you to get out your checkbook. If the estimated price is negative it means that the present value of the cash flows that the equity holders are forecasted to send *to* the firm is greater than the present value of the cash flows that the equity holders are forecasted to receive *from* the firm. If this was literally true then an equity holder might indeed be willing to pay to not have to own the stock. But since the firm can't force the equity holders to keep sending it money, and since equity holders are not liable to third parties for the firm's losses, the real lower bound on price is zero. If the price is negative you would simply refuse to own the stock, and you can do this for free. We let eVal report a negative price because it shows you the logical implications of your forecasts. If you really think the firm has positive value, you need to revise your forecasts accordingly. To identify the economic source of a price estimate that is negative, or far too low, look at the series of ROE forecasts. Value is destroyed each period that the ROE is below the firm's cost of equity capital. If this situation continues on for too long, or for periods with very high growth, the net result will be a negative stock price. Negative stock prices are discussed in more detail in Chapter 12.

eVal's Model Summary sheet also has a handy tool for conducting a sensitivity analysis of your valuation. You feed the model a horizon, a beginning ROE, a terminal ROE, a beginning sales growth rate, a terminal sales growth rate, and a cost of equity capital. The model then estimates the value of the firm by extrapolating a linear progression between the beginning and ending ROEs and the sales growth rates. You can use this to see how small changes in your estimates affect your valuation. You can also use this tool to do a "quick and dirty" valuation of a company that you might be interested in studying further.

10.6   LINKS AND REFERENCES

Four Models—One Valuation

This case gives a numerical example to illustrate how each valuation model works and gives you some practice doing the calculations by hand (before we let eVal take over for you). There is also a data file that can be imported into eVal so that you can verify that the answers you got by hand match the answers in cVal. The case is available on the eVal website.

EnCom Corporation

This case involves a fictitious company and illustrates how aggressive and conservative accounting can temporarily distort accounting rates of return. It also illustrates how the residual income valuation model is not affected by accounting distortions as long as we correctly forecast their reversal. This case is available on the eVal website.

Can Salton Swing?

This is a basic valuation case about the company who sells the George Foreman grill. The default forecast assumptions in eVal result in a value estimate of nearly $300, while the stock price has never been above $40. To reconcile these two facts the students must conduct a Dupont analysis and examine a questionable asset on Salton's books (the George Foreman trademark). The case comes with eVal input files for Salton and its competitors and is available on the eVal website.

Intel's Earnings Torpedo

This case is useful for introducing students to eVal, illustrating the basic mechanics of valuation, highlighting the key drivers of value and illustrating the basic equivalence between the residual income and free cash flow approaches to valuation. It also provides a classic illustration of the "earnings torpedo" phenomenon, whereby a richly priced growth stock exhibits a sharp price decline in response to a small earnings disappointment. The case comes with an eVal input file and is available on the eVal website.

- eVal website—http://www.mhhe.com/eval
- Yahoo! Finance—http://yahoo.finance.com
- Multex Investor—http://multexinvestor.com/home.asp

Russell Lundholm, and Terrance O'Keefe, "Reconciling Value Estimates from the Discounted Cash Flow Model and the Residual Income Model." *Contemporary Accounting Research* (2001) pp. 311–335.

$$\frac{P_0}{BVPS} = \frac{ROE - g}{r - g}$$

$$g = ROE(b)$$

$$g = ROE(1-b)$$

$$g = r - bROE$$

$$b = \text{plowback ratio} = 1 - POR$$

$$P_0 = \frac{EPS_1}{r} + PVGO$$

$$P_0 = \frac{1}{r} \times \frac{PVGO}{EPS_1}$$

$$\frac{EPS_1}{P_0} = r\left(1 - \frac{PVGO}{P_0}\right)$$

$$P_0 = \frac{EPS_1}{r}$$

CHAPTER ELEVEN

Valuation Ratios

11.1 INTRODUCTION

In Chapter 5 we converted the financial statement data into ratios in order to reveal underlying economic properties and to make the data comparable across companies and over time. For the same reason, we can more easily compare the valuation of different companies by scaling the value by some accounting data. In this section we derive the market-to-book ratio, the price-to-earnings ratio and a new innovation known as the PEG ratio, and we discuss what each ratio reveals about the market's expectations about the company's future. These ratios are commonly used summary statistics for a firm's valuation and each can be found on financial information portals, such as Multex Investor or Yahoo!Finance. After we discuss each ratio we will give some historical and current benchmarks to get you grounded.

We offer a word of caution before proceeding. As we found in the last chapter, a valuation generally depends on an infinite series of forecasted financial data. Only in very special cases is it possible to value a firm based on just its current book value or its current earnings. Consequently, it is unlikely that you will be able to take a quick look at the price-to-earnings ratio or market-to-book ratio and know if a firm is mispriced. Rather, these ratios can help you to make a quick assessment of the expectations built into a firm's current market price.

11.2 THE MARKET-TO-BOOK RATIO

This ratio divides the current market value of equity (P_e) by the book value of equity from the most recent financial statements (CE_0). If we start with the residual income to common equity model and divide everything by CE_0 we get

$$\frac{P_e}{CE_0} = 1 + \sum_{t=1}^{\infty} \frac{(ROE_t - r_e)\dfrac{CE_{t-1}}{CE_0}}{(1 + r_e)^t}$$

where ROE_t is defined relative to beginning equity: $ROE_t = NI_t/CE_{t-1}$.

The first thing to note from this formula is that if you forecast that $ROE_t = r_e$ every period in the future, then the firm is worth exactly its book value (CE_0). This is like a savings account; every period it pays interest at exactly its discount rate and so every period it is worth exactly the balance in the account. When firms have a market-to-book ratio greater than 1, the market expects that, on average, they will earn a ROE_t higher than r_e in the future.

Note that the $\frac{CE_{t-1}}{CE_0}$ term in the numerator is the *cumulative* growth in beginning common equity each period. In other words, in year 1 it equals 1, in year 2 it equals CE_1/CE_0, in year 3 it equals CE_2/CE_0 and so on. The numerator in our expression for the market-to-book ratio is therefore the firm's abnormal profitability $(ROE_t - r_e)$ times its cumulative growth in beginning book value (CE_t/CE_0). This simple observation speaks volumes. A firm is worth more than its book value only if it is expected to have an ROE_t greater than r_e (as we keep repeating). Assuming the firm is expected to meet this profitability threshold, growth and profitability are multiplicative. This means that really high valuations come about when firms have both high profitability *and* high growth.

To give you a few reference points, suppose that ROE is forecasted to be constant forever, and equity is forecasted to grow at rate g forever. In this case the market-to-book ratio can be simplified to

$$\frac{P_e}{CE_0} = 1 + \frac{ROE - r_e}{r_e - g}$$

Suppose the firm has a 10 percent cost of equity capital, a forecasted constant ROE of 20 percent, and a perpetual growth rate of 5 percent. By historical standards, these would be very rosy forecasts. Using the preceding formula gives a P_e/CE_0 ratio of 3. As a contrast, the market-to-book ratio for Kohl's is greater than 8 (as of 9/3/2002). Kohl's current ROE is close to 20 percent, so why such a high valuation ratio? One reason is that their growth has been about 25 percent per year over the past few years, and the market expects similar growth far into the future. Clearly Kohl's can't sustain that rate of growth forever, so our simplified formula isn't going to work in this case. But, loosely speaking, Kohl's is expected to be more than twice as valuable as the hypothetical firm with a 20 percent ROE and a 5 percent perpetual growth. We will give lots of historical statistics later in the chapter, but as a final benchmark, the median market-to-book ratio between 1962 and 2001 for all publicly traded companies was 1.5; the bottom 25 percent were below .93 and the top 25 percent were above 2.5.

The market-to-book ratio is a very useful summary measure. It gives you a quick sense of what the market must think about the future growth and profitability of the firm. Of course, like everything else in valuation, our intuition can be thwarted by distortions in accounting. A good example of this is Kellogg, the maker of breakfast cereals ("they're great!"). You may not think of Kellogg as a high flying, fast growing stock. And it isn't; annualized growth over the past five years is only about 5 percent. Nonetheless, it has a market-to-book ratio greater than 12! The story behind this is relatively simple. The great value of Kellogg is in its brands, yet none of this value is on Kellogg's balance sheet. Most of their brands have been developed internally over many years, and GAAP accounting doesn't capitalize internally developed intangible assets. Consequently, Kellogg's book value vastly understates its economic value, causing its current ROE to exceed 60 percent. If we plug a constant 60 percent ROE and a perpetual 5 percent growth rate into our simplified P_e/CE_0 model, assuming a 10 percent cost of equity capital, we get a market-to-book ratio of 13.

11.3   THE PRICE-TO-EARNINGS RATIO

This ratio divides the current market price per share by the past annual earnings per share, computed either as the most recent annual figure or as the sum of the past four quarters of earnings. It takes a fair bit of algebra, but you can derive the following expression from the residual income model:

$$\frac{P_e}{NI_0} = \frac{1 + r_e}{r_e}\left(1 + \sum_{t=1}^{\infty} \frac{\Delta RI_t}{(1 + r_e)^t NI_0}\right) - \frac{D_0}{NI_0}$$

where ΔRI_t is the *change in* residual income between date t and date $t-1$, D_0 is the net distribution to common equity holders, and NI_0 is the net income for period *zero* (the most recent historical financial statement date).

To see the intuition behind this ratio, ignore the D_0/NI_0 term for the time being; this is the dividend payout ratio for the current year, and it is typically less than 1. If $\Delta RI_t = 0$ forever (residual income is a constant) and $r_e = 10$ percent then the price-to-earnings expression is $(1+r_e)/r_e = 11$. The reason the price-to-earnings ratio typically differs from 11 is because of the summation term inside the brackets. Now look carefully at the summation term. It is the sum of the *changes* in residual income, scaled by the current period's net income, as opposed to the sum of the *levels* of residual income that you saw in the residual income model. So the price-to-earnings ratio will be greater than 11 if the market expects residual income to grow and it will be less than 11 if the market expects residual income to shrink. It doesn't matter whether the *level* of residual income is positive or negative—all that matters is the direction and size of the expected change. This is very different from the market-to-book ratio, which was large only if the expected *level* of residual income was large and positive.

What will cause residual income to grow? Obviously, growth in net income will contribute to growth in residual income, but the relation is subtler than this. For *residual* income to grow, net income must grow *faster than* book value grows. This is much tougher than simply growing net income. We can illustrate this better by stating the change in residual income in relative terms. Divide ΔRI_t by common equity at time $t-1$ to get

$$\frac{\Delta RI_t}{CE_{t-1}} = \left[(ROE_t - ROE_{t-1}) + g_{t-1}(ROE_t - r_e)\right]\Big/\left(1 + g_{t-1}\right)$$

where ROE_t is defined as NI_t/CE_{t-1} and g_{t-1} is the percentage growth in common equity from date $t-2$ to $t-1$. Suppose that $g_{t-1} = 0$, so that book value has not grown and the second term is zero. In this case, if the firm can deploy the existing book value more profitably, $(ROE_t - ROE_{t-1})$ will be positive and ΔRI_t will increase. Alternatively, suppose that ROE_t is greater than r_e by a constant amount each period. In this case the first term in brackets is zero but, since the firm has positive net present value investments, growing book value increases income faster than the increase in book value, so again ΔRI_t will increase.

One logical benchmark for the price-to-earnings ratio that we have already discussed is to assume that residual income is a constant in perpetuity and that the current dividend payout (D_0/NI_0) is zero, so that

$$\frac{P_e}{NI_0} = \frac{1 + r_e}{r_e}$$

If $r_e = 10$ percent then this gives a price-to-earnings ratio of 11, as discussed above. A related benchmark is the "forward price-to-earnings ratio," defined as P_e divided by the forecasted net income for next year, NI_1. In this case, assuming residual income is a constant perpetuity, we get

$$P_e = CE_0 + \frac{RI_1}{r_e} = CE_0 + \frac{NI_1 - r_e CE_0}{r_e} = \frac{NI_1}{r_e}$$

or

$$\frac{P_e}{NI_1} = \frac{1}{r_e}$$

If $r_e = 10$ percent then we get a price-to-forward-earnings ratio of 10. For all companies with positive earnings between 1962 and 2001, the median price-to-earnings ratio was 13.4; the bottom 25 percent were below 8.6 and the top 25 percent were above 21.9. If NI_0 is negative, the price-to-earnings ratio isn't really meaningful, so we have excluded these firms. But you can think of firms with negative earnings as having very high price-earnings ratios—in the sense that they have a positive price even though they have negative earnings. Clearly, these companies must return to profitability if they are to create value for their shareholders.

11.4 THE PEG RATIO

We have one more valuation ratio to discuss, the PEG ratio, which is an acronym for Price-Earnings to Growth. It is defined as follows:

$$\text{PEG Ratio} = \frac{\text{Price-to-Earnings Ratio}}{\text{Earnings Growth} \times 100} = \frac{P_e/NI_1}{\left(\dfrac{NI_2 - NI_1}{NI_1}\right) \times 100}$$

Note that the price-to-earnings ratio in the numerator is the forward ratio (the denominator is the forecast of next year's net income) and earnings growth rate is defined here as growth from one year ahead to two years ahead. The earnings growth rate is frequently defined over a longer period, say three to five years, but it still must be an annualized percentage. By defining it as given above, we can reconcile this ratio with a legitimate valuation model. As we will explain shortly, the benchmark for the PEG ratio is 1. Stocks with a PEG under 1 are considered undervalued and those with a PEG greater than 1 are considered overvalued (per the Yahoo! Education website).

This ratio is a rough heuristic. The idea is that the price-to-earnings ratio measures the amount of earnings growth that is reflected in the market price, so if we compare this ratio with forecasted earnings growth, we can see whether the market price correctly reflects the forecasted growth and thus determine whether a stock is underpriced or overpriced. This seems reasonable, but why is 1 the magic benchmark? Academics have searched for special cases of a more general valuation model that will make this formula true, but with only limited success. Here is one such case.

Define the forecasted "abnormal earnings" at time $t+1$ as

$$ae_{t+1} = NI_{t+1} - [NI_t + r_e(NI_t - D_t)]$$

This amount is "abnormal" in the following sense. You expect to earn in time $t+1$ the same net income as you did at time t, plus a "normal" level of earnings on any amount that you didn't distribute to equity holders $(NI_t - D_t)$. This is the amount in square brackets. The amount that NI_{t+1} exceeds or falls short of this amount is therefore "abnormal."

The PEG ratio follows from a valid valuation model when two conditions hold. First, net distributions to equity holders are forecasted to be zero one-year ahead $(D_1 = 0)$. This implies that forecasted abnormal earnings in year 2 are

$$ae_2 = NI_2 - (1 + r_e)NI_1$$

Second, forecasted net income and net dividends from year 3 forward are such that abnormal earnings is constant, and equal to the abnormal earnings in year 2, computed assuming $D_1 = 0$. That is,

$$ae_t = ae_2 \text{ for } t \geq 2$$

If these assumptions are met, then one can show that

$$P_e = \frac{NI_2 - NI_1}{r_e^2}$$

Constructing the PEG ratio from this simple valuation model gives

$$\frac{P_e/NI_1}{\left(\dfrac{NI_2 - NI_1}{NI_1}\right) \times 100} = \frac{1}{r_e^2 \times 100}$$

If r_e is 10 percent, then this gives a PEG ratio of 1. And if all these assumptions hold then stocks with a PEG ratio less than 1 are undervalued and stocks with a PEG ratio greater than 1 are overvalued.

As you can see, with some work we can beat the PEG ratio back into our world of theoretically valid valuation models. But the real question is, How reasonable are the assumptions that were necessary to get the job done? We had to assume that "abnormal earnings" is constant forever in the future, and equal to the abnormal earnings computed based on the forecasted earnings for the next two years. We also had to assume that net distributions to equity holders are forecasted to be zero next year. Finally, for the ratio to be benchmarked at 1, we needed to assume the cost of equity capital is 10 percent.

To put the underlying model that supports the PEG ratio into perspective, we can rewrite price in this special case as

$$P_e = \frac{NI_1}{r_e} + \frac{NI_2 - (1 + r_e)NI_1}{r_e^2}$$

Note that the first term is the price we would get by capitalizing next period earnings in perpetuity ($P_e = NI_1/r_e$). In the previous section, we showed that this case occurs when residual income is a constant perpetuity ($NI_t - r_e CE_{t-1}$ is constant for all t). The model supporting the PEG ratio adds to this a bonus for abnormal earnings between year 1 and year 2. In this sense, the model behind the PEG ratio incorporates future growth, which is exactly what the PEG ratio was intended to do. If you were an analyst trying to "sell" investors on a stock with high forecasted growth in the near term, the PEG ratio is a good tool because it makes such stocks look undervalued. There is no evidence, however, that such stocks are actually undervalued; they just look this way when evaluated using the PEG ratio. To warrant such a valuation, they must maintain the level of abnormal earnings implied by the near term growth rate indefinitely.

11.5 PUTTING SOME VALUATION RATIOS TOGETHER

The market-to-book ratio is simply a scaled version of the residual income model and is therefore clearly focused on measuring value. Because the price-to-earnings ratio scales by earnings in the most recent year, it is much more focused on expected growth. It is driven by how much residual income will increase in the future relative to today. And to wrap all of this up into a neat package, note that

$$\frac{P_e}{CE_0} = \frac{NI_0}{CE_0} \times \frac{P_e}{NI_0}$$

or

$$\text{Market-to-Book Ratio} = ROE_0 \times \text{Price-to-Earnings Ratio}$$

defining ROE_0 now as the return on *ending* equity.

Remember how we hammered away on the idea that value is created by a combination of profitability and growth? Here we see this once again. The market-to-book ratio is the product of profitability, measured as ROE_0, and growth, measured loosely by the price-to-earnings ratio.

The market-to-book and price-to-earnings ratios together give you a great snapshot of the market's expectations about the firm. To help you develop a feel for what a big or small ratio is, we have plotted the economywide market-to-book and price-to-earnings ratios each year from 1980 to 2001 in Figure 11.1.

FIGURE 11.1
Valuation Ratios for the U.S. Economy through Time

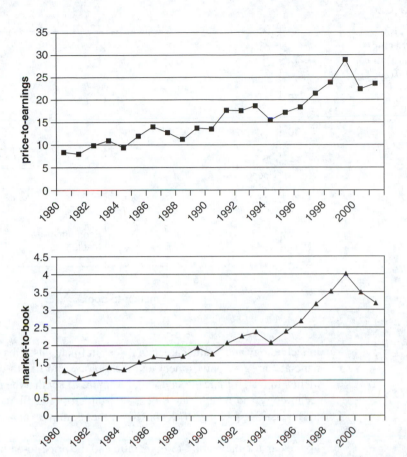

Two observations are immediately clear from the figure. First, valuations relative to fundamentals (net income and common equity) have been drifting steadily up over the past 20 years. This may be caused by steadily declining interest rates over the same period, increasingly optimistic estimates about future growth and profitability, or a steady decline in the ability of accounting measures to capture true value. Which interpretation is correct is unclear; different scholars and practitioners have championed each. The second observation is that the "dot-com bubble" reached its peak in fiscal 1999 and has been partially deflated. Whether there is still air left in the bubble remains to be seen. At the end of 2001 the economywide market-to-book ratio was about 3 and the economywide price-to-earnings ratio was about 25. Both amounts are roughly twice as high as the values during the 1980s.

The valuation ratios not only change over time, they also vary greatly across different sectors of the economy. Figure 11.2 plots the market-to-book and price-to-earnings ratios for each of the 8 Media General sectors. Note the huge difference between the financial sector and the technology or health care sectors. Not surprisingly, the market sees more growth potential and more future profitability

FIGURE 11.2
Median Sector
Valuation Ratios
as of 12/31/2002

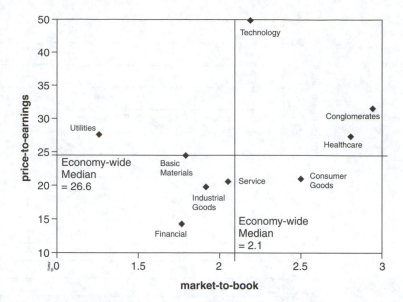

in technology and health care than it sees in financials. This doesn't mean that financials are a bad investment and technology and health care are good investments. In fact, if it means anything, it is more likely that the market is overpricing technology and health care stocks and underpricing financials. We will return to the issue of picking stocks based on these simple valuation ratios in the next section.

We can use the market-to-book ratio and the price-to-earnings ratio together to see how the market views different firms in an industry. Figure 11.3 plots the valuation ratio for some representative firms in the Retail Department Stores.

The figure is divided loosely into four regions. Firms that are low on both dimensions are labeled as *value* and firms that are high on both dimensions are labeled *glamour.* You can see from the figure that Kohl's is a solid glamour stock, consistent with its high growth and profitability. At the opposite extreme we have May Department Stores and Sears, which are in the value category. When compared to Kohl's and the other firms in the industry, the market sees little growth and limited profitability from these stores. The off-diagonal categories identify more unusual firms. Saks and Cole Myer both have very high price-to-earnings ratios, but relatively low market-to-book ratios. These types of firms are labeled *turnarounds* because they currently have very little earnings but, based on a big restructuring, a new CEO or blind faith, the market expects that they will have lots more earnings in the future. The future earnings growth may not coincide with a high ROE, so while the price-to-earnings ratio is very high, the market-to-book ratio is still low. At the other extreme we have *harvesters.* This industry doesn't have a solid example of this type of firm. Imagine a firm that has lots of profitability but only moderate growth. Without much anticipated growth

TABLE 11.1 **Portfolio Returns to Different Price-to-Fundamental Investment Strategies**

Next Year's Return	Market-to-Book Ratio	Price-to-Earnings Ratio	Book Value + .62 Residual Income
Return on Bottom 10% of Ratio	19.1%	20.7%	21.0%
Return on Top 10% of Ratio	11.8	11.8	11.1
Hedge Return	7.3	8.9	9.9

Note: Returns are for investments in the top or bottom 10% of the indicated ratio for all publicly traded firms between 1976–1995. The portfolio position is taken three months after the fiscal year end and held for 12 months. See Dechow, Hutton, and Sloan (1999) for details.

price-to-fundamental ratio, where the fundamental is either book value, earnings, or a combination of the two, and then buys firms with the lowest ratios and sells firms with the highest ratios. The portfolios are formed three months after the fiscal year end (to be sure that the book value and earnings data are publicly available) and are held for one year. The tests are conducted over a large sample of firms from 1976–1995. The first column of the table shows that the decile of firms with the lowest market-to-book ratio earned an average return of 19.1 percent while the decile of firms with the highest market-to-book earned an average return of only 11.8 percent. A hedge portfolio has no exposure to marketwide risk because it is equally long and short in the same dollar value of stocks, yet it would have returned 7.3 percent (it made 19.1 percent on the long position and lost 11.8 percent on the short position). The second column of the table shows a similar result for portfolios based on the price-to-earnings ratio. The hedge return to this strategy is 8.9 percent. The third column computes a crude "value" measure based on the current book value and residual income. It is defined as

$$V_e = CE_0 + .62RI_0$$

where the value .62 is based on an estimate of the average rate at which residual income mean-reverts in the entire economy. The strategy then computes the P_e/V_e ratio and forms portfolios. As shown in the table, the hedge return to this portfolio is 9.9 percent, with no exposure to marketwide movements in price.

These hedge returns are quite large by Wall Street standards. A hedge return is equally long and short in the same dollar amounts, so it is zero net investment, at least in principle. Of course, you can't walk into a brokerage house and open an account with zero dollars. But imagine that you invested your wealth in a fund that tracked the entire market and, in addition, you took the zero net position in the hedge portfolio described above. This combined strategy would beat the market return by almost 10 percent. A money manager who consistently beat the market by 10 percent would be a god on Wall Street, so is it really this easy? Not really. First, the actual transaction costs of taking a long position in 10 percent of the market and a short position in a different 10 percent of the market would be prohibitively costly. A truly implementable strategy would have to limit itself to a

FIGURE 11.3
**Valuation Ratios
for the Retail
Department Stores
Industry**

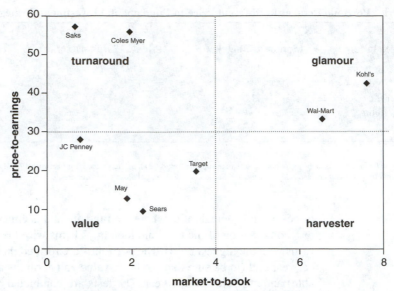

Ratios computed on 9/3/2002

the price-to-earnings ratio would be relatively low while the high ROE would generate a high market-to-book ratio. A true "harvester" would be a hypothetical combination of Sears, with its low growth expectations, and Wal-Mart, with its high profitability expectations.

Can You Make Money with These Ratios?

The market-to-book and price-to-earnings ratios both compare the current market price to an accounting measure of fundamental value. It is natural to ask whether or not firms that are extreme on either of these measures tend to move back to an average value. Do these statistics mean-revert? And further, if they do mean-revert, is it because the price corrects itself or is it because price correctly predicts future changes in the accounting fundamentals? If the correction is caused by future price changes then it may be possible to form a trading strategy based on these ratios.

Before giving you the answers to these titillating questions, we want to stress that the whole point of this book is to teach you how to develop a detailed forecast of the firm's future financial statements and then translate these forecasts into a value estimate. We expect you to arrive at a value estimate that is far superior to what you could get simply by looking at the company's earnings and book value and then comparing each to price. But with that thought in mind, the short answer to the questions is yes, historically you would have made a bit of money by trading solely on the market-to-book and price-to-earnings ratios.

Table 11.1 gives the details of three different investment strategies based only on the accounting book value and earnings. Each strategy sorts the firms on the much smaller set of firms, and this smaller set of firms may not have the same returns as those documented in Table 11.1. Further, while the hedge portfolio has no exposure to marketwide price movements, it still may have a significant exposure to other types of risk. What if all the long positions are in utility stocks and all the short positions are in technology stocks? It is certainly possible that utility stocks will go down and tech stocks will go up and you would lose a lot of money. The hedge portfolio is market-neutral but it certainly isn't without risk. In fact, the return to the market-to-book strategy is so thoroughly documented that many finance professors refer to it as a "risk factor," although it isn't clear exactly what fundamental risk such a strategy exposes one to. This is always the debate—is it an exploitable return or is it compensation for bearing risk? Finally, even if this profitable strategy was available in the past, there is no guarantee that it will be available in the future. If enough investors notice this pattern in the data and invest to profit on it, they will push the price of low price-to-fundamental stocks up and push the price of high price-to-fundamental stocks down, eliminating the hedge return in the process.

11.6   LINKS AND REFERENCES

Restaurant Industry in 2002

This case compares the price-to-book and price-to-earnings ratios for different firms in the restaurant industry. It is available on the eVal website.

- eVal website—http://www.mhhe.com/eval
- Multex Investor—http://www.multexinvestor.com/home.asp
- Yahoo!Finance—http://yahoo.finance.com
- Yahoo!Education—http://biz.yahoo.com/edu/

P. Dechow, A. Hutton, and R. Sloan, "An Empirical Assessment of the Residual Income Valuation Model," *Journal of Accounting and Economics* 26 (1999).

CHAPTER TWELVE

Some Complications

Up to this point, the valuation step has been straightforward. Given a series of forecast financial statements and the key valuation parameters, we just let eVal crank out the valuation. Unfortunately, life is not always this simple. In this chapter we discuss some of the most common complications that arise in the valuation step. We stress that eVal does not provide any "quick fix" solutions to these complications. Instead, it is up to you now, as an educated valuation specialist, to make sure that you anticipate these complications. Remember, as we have stated many times before, the maxim "garbage-in, garbage out" is the order of the day.

There are two primary categories of complications. The first category relates to negative values and the abandonment option. If you load a company that is losing money into eVal, you will typically find that the default valuation is negative. What does this mean? Stocks never have negative values in real life. This category of complications is the subject of section 12.2.

The second category of complications relates to value creation and destruction through financing transactions. eVal simply computes the intrinsic value of the company to the existing stockholders, assuming that they will be the only participants in all future net cash distributions. But what if the existing stockholders let some new stockholders invest in the company at a price that is different from intrinsic value? Whenever a company issues or repurchases common stock at a price other than intrinsic value, it creates or destroys value for the existing stockholders. This category of complications is the subject of section 12.3.

12.2 NEGATIVE VALUES AND THE ABANDONMENT OPTION

Negative Values

In Chapter 10 we discussed what it means for eVal to return a negative stock price. In this section we revisit this issue and offer some advice about how to deal with this unusual situation. A negative stock valuation is actually not an uncommon occurrence in eVal if you simply use eVal's default forecasting assumptions on a company with losses in its most recent year. Yet in the real world we never see negative stock prices. To understand why eVal generates negative stock prices,

FIGURE 12.1   eVal "Model Summary" for Sepracor

Model Summary		Sensitivity Analysis	
Go To User's Guide		Reset to Current	
Historical Data For:		**Forecast Horizon** 5 10 20	10 Years
SEPRACOR INC			
Most Recent Fiscal Year End:	12/31/2001	**This Year's ROE (%)**	89.18%
Average ROE (last five years)	-174.12%		
Sales Growth (last five years)	133.42%	**Terminal Year's ROE (%)**	75.72%
Forecast Data:		**This Year's Sales Growth (%)**	71.75%
Forecast Horizon	10 Years		
This Year's ROE	89.18%	**Terminal Year's Sales Growth (%)**	5.00%
Terminal Year's ROE	75.72%		
This Year's Sales Growth	71.75%	**Cost of Equity Capital (%)**	10.00%
Terminal Year's Sales Growth	5.00%		
This Year's Forecast EPS	-$4.87	**Estimated Price/Share**	-$928.89
Forecast 5 Year EPS Growth	53.16%		
Valuation Data:		Sensitivity analysis allows you to assess the impact of changing key	
Cost of Equity Capital	10.00%	assumptions on the estimated price per share. Note that the sensitivity	
Valuation Date	1/6/2003	analysis uses a linear smoothing algorithm to compute ROE and Sales	
Estimated Price/Share	-$930.86	Growth between the current year and the terminal year, so it may	
Estimated Price/Earnings Ratio	190.96	provide a different price estimate from your detailed analysis even	
Estimated Market/Book Ratio	231.63	with the same key forecasting assumptions.	

(handwritten margin notes: −492.64 @ 2/19/04; pull up through for 12/31/2002; −$442.38 @ 2/16/04 12/31/02)

let's look at a specific example. Figure 12.1 provides the "Model Summary" sheet for a company called Sepracor (ticker = SEPR) as of the end of fiscal 2001.

Sepracor is a biotechnology company that has many drugs under development but only a small number that are currently generating revenue. Consequently, sales revenues are smaller than the combined amount of R&D and SG&A expense, and Sepracor has reported substantial losses for the last several years. The valuation in Figure 12.1 was obtained using the default forecasting assumptions in eVal. Note that the estimated price/share is −$930.86. The summary of the forecast data indicates a current ROE of 89 percent and a terminal ROE of 75 percent. How can ROE be positive if the company is making losses? It turns out that the company has made such large cumulative losses that its common equity is negative. When we divide the negative earnings by the negative common equity, we get a positive ROE. But the positive ROE is clearly not meaningful when the equity base is negative.[1] You should always check that the book value of common equity is positive before trying to interpret the ROE. If we were to look into the details of the forecasted financials, we would see that Sepracor is forecast to have negative earnings, residual income, and cash flows for every future period—clearly a bleak future. We also see that sales are forecast to grow at 72 percent in the current year, trending down to 5 percent in the terminal year. When we combine the negative earnings, cash flows, and residual income with the aggressive sales growth, we get a huge negative valuation. According to our forecasts, Sepracor has a money-losing

---

[1]Note that we can still use the residual income valuation model when the book value of common equity is negative. We just can't divide earnings or residual income by a negative book value number and meaningfully interpret the resulting ratio.

FIGURE 12.2   eVal "DCF Valuations" for Sepracor

	A	B	C	D	E	F
A10	=B1b+bbU+bb4-bbd					
1	**DCF Valuations**	**($000)**				
2	Go To User's Guide	View Valuation to Common Equity				
3		View Valuation to All Investors				
4	**Company Name**	SEPRACOR INC				
5	Most Recent Fiscal Year End	12/31/2001				
6	Date of Valuation	1/6/2003				
7	Cost of Common Equity	10.00%				
8						
9	Fiscal Year of Forecast	12/31/2002	12/31/2003	12/31/2004	12/31/2005	12/31/2006
11	**Valuation to Common Equity**					
12	Free Cash Flow to Common Equity	(155,042)	(278,772)	(480,795)	(794,230)	(1,254,584)
13	Present Value of FCF	(140,948)	(230,390)	(361,229)	(542,470)	(778,998)
14	Present Value Beyond 20 Years	(32,824,658)				
15	Present Value of First 20 Years	(29,991,172)				
16	Forecast Equity Value Before Time Adj	(62,815,831)				
17	Forecasted Value as of Valuation Date	(72,662,212)				
18	Less Value of Contingent Equity Claims	0				
19	Value Attributable to Common Equity	(72,662,212)				
20	Common Shares Outstanding at BS Date	78,059				
21	Equivalent Shares at Valuation Date	78,059				
22	Forecast Price/Share	-$930.86				
23						

business model and plans to continue to grow the business, thereby losing even more money in the future.

Now look at Sepracor's forecasted future free cash flows on eVal's "DCF Valuation" sheet, which is reproduced in Figure 12.2. In 2002, Sepracor is forecast to have negative free cash flow to common equity of over $155 million. By 2006, the amount of negative free cash flow is forecast to grow to over $1.2 billion. This means that in order to keep operating the business consistent with our forecasts, enormous amounts of new common equity will have to be issued. If the existing stockholders act as forecast in our eVal model, then they will have to provide huge amounts of new equity injections into Sepracor, even though they will never get a positive cash dividend payment in return. Under this scenario, the value of the company to the existing stockholders is clearly negative, because of the negative present value of the additional cash infusions that they are forecast to make.

Why then do we never observe negative stock prices? The reason is that stockholders have limited liability. Management and creditors can never force the existing stockholders to pay more cash into the company, so the least that a stock can ever be worth is zero. This is where the eVal model doesn't jibe with reality. We have forecasted that stockholders will be willing to pay in additional cash indefinitely, and eVal took the present value of those negative cash flows to common equity holders, but in reality stockholders are likely to abandon the company and it will cease operations. The most obvious limitation of our forecasting model is that we have extrapolated Sepracor's past losses into the indefinite future. But in reality the stockholders of Sepracor hope that profitability will improve as drugs that are currently under development start generating revenues.

Given that we never observe negative stock prices in the real world, why do we allow them to arise in eVal? The reason is that we want you to see just how bad an investment in such a company would really be. How much value are you forecasting that the company can destroy as investors send good money chasing after bad? We know that the price will never actually be negative. Interpret the negative value estimate as the amount that investors would pay to *not have to own the stock.* This gives you a feel for just how bad the forecasted future of the company really is.

The present value computations in eVal assume that existing stockholders will finance any additional cash infusions implied by your forecasts. While we know that this is unrealistic, what if the existing management and stockholders are able to hoodwink new investors into providing the additional capital? While this would be a negative net present value proposition for the new investors, it is possible that the existing stockholders could make themselves better off at the expense of the new investors. This is one of the reasons why investment bankers who can "sell any deal" are able to charge such high fees. Figuring out the amount of wealth transfers between existing stockholders and new capital providers is complicated, and we will address this issue in more detail in section 12.3.

The Abandonment Option

We have now established that equity cannot have a negative value in practice because stockholders have limited liability. They are free to walk away from the company and cannot be forced to provide additional capital to fund money-losing operations or to pay creditors. This stockholder right is sometimes referred to as the "abandonment option." As with most options, the abandonment option has value. In this section, we will examine the abandonment option in more detail.

The Forecasting Assumptions we discussed in Chapter 8 are our "best guesses" for what we think the values will be in the future. They are each a point estimate of the most likely outcome rather than ranges of many possible outcomes. But in reality any number of possible outcomes could arise for most of our assumptions. To see how sensitive your forecasts are to some key assumptions, play with the Sensitivity Analysis tool on the Model Summary sheet in eVal (shown in Figure 12.1). As long as the range of reasonable valuations is symmetric around our most likely estimate, and all the valuations are positive, then the most likely valuation estimate is also the expected value of the investment. Unfortunately, the abandonment option can introduce significant asymmetries into the range of possible valuation outcomes. In particular, since equity values can never be negative, the left tail of the possible range of valuation outcomes is truncated at zero. The result is that the most likely point estimate valuation can seriously underestimate the true valuation when we take the abandonment option into consideration. We illustrate the effect of the abandonment option in Figure 12.3.

Figure 12.3 charts the probability distribution of possible valuation outcomes for three different scenarios. In each of the three scenarios, the most likely point estimate of value, represented by the peak of the valuation distribution, is $100. Sensitivity analysis reveals the range of other possible valuation outcomes. The first chart represents a "low variance" scenario, in which the range in possible valuation outcomes is quite closely clustered around the most likely estimate of $100. Note also that the range of possible outcomes is symmetric and all values are positive. This first scenario represents the typical case, in which the range of

FIGURE 12.3
Probability Distributions of Valuation Outcomes for Three Different Scenarios

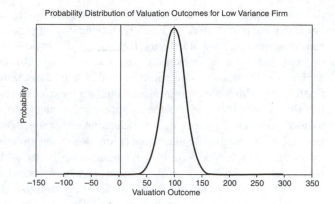

Probability Distribution of Valuation Outcomes for Low Variance Firm

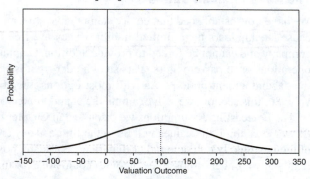

Probability Distribution of Valuation Outcomes for High Variance Firm
Ignoring the Abandonment Option

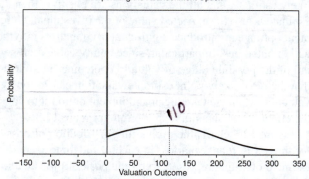

Probability Distribution of Valuation Outcomes for High Variance Firm
Incorporating the Abandonment Option

possible valuation outcomes is symmetric around the most likely point estimate valuation, all reasonable valuations are positive, and so the most likely point estimate valuation is our best estimate of the true valuation.

The second chart represents a "high variance" scenario, in which the range of possible valuation outcomes varies widely around the most likely point estimate of $100. As with the first chart, the range of possible outcomes continues to be symmetric around the most likely valuation estimate of $100, so the expected value is still $100, but a significant range of the possible valuation outcomes in the second chart falls below zero. As discussed above, all the negative valuations are unreasonable because the existing stockholders will not indefinitely continue to invest good money after bad; rather they will exercise their abandonment option and refuse to contribute additional capital.

The range of possible valuation outcomes, assuming that stockholders optimally exercise their abandonment option, is shown in the third chart of Figure 12.3. In this chart, the distribution of possible valuation outcomes is truncated at zero. All the possible negative valuation outcomes in the second chart are now concentrated at zero. Note that stockholders still keep all the upside in the case of very positive valuation outcomes, but they avoid the downside in the case of negative valuation outcomes. As a result, the expected valuation of the investment is now greater than the most likely point estimate of $100. In the particular case shown in the third chart, the expected value works out to be about $110. Thus, by using the most likely point estimate valuation, we would have undervalued the stock by about 10 percent.

What determines the value of the abandonment option? The third chart in Figure 12.3 should make it clear that the greater the probability of a negative valuation outcome, the greater the value of the abandonment option. The lower the most likely point estimate valuation and the greater the variance of possible valuation outcomes, the greater the probability of a negative outcome, and the greater the value of the abandonment option. Thus, the abandonment option tends to be the greatest in money-losing companies with great uncertainty in future outcomes. A company such as Sepracor is a very good example. Owning a share in this company is like owning an option on the small chance that they will strike it big on some new drug.

To determine whether there is an abandonment option in play, you should always conduct sensitivity analysis for a "worst-case" scenario. If this scenario yields a negative valuation, then the abandonment option has positive value. To make the analysis tractable, this worst-case valuation scenario should represent a plausible outcome—assumptions that you feel have maybe a 25 percent chance of occurring. You should also think about a representative "best-case" valuation scenario. By assigning probabilities to each of these scenarios and assigning a value of zero to the negative valuation outcomes, you can compute the expected value of the stock *after* incorporating the abandonment option. Table 12.1 provides some representative computations assuming that the most likely outcome has a probability of 50 percent and the best-case and worst-case scenarios each have probabilities of 25 percent.

The table provides four representative cases. The first two cases represent a "healthy" firm, with a most likely valuation outcome of $100. The second two cases represent a "distressed" firm, with a most likely valuation outcome of $0.

TABLE 12.1   **Value of Abandonment Option**

	Worst Case 25% probability	Most Likely Case 50% probability	Best Case 25% probability	Value without Abandonment Option	Value with Abandonment Option
Healthy Low Variance Firm	$50	$100	$150	$100	$100
Healthy High Variance Firm	−50	100	250	100	112.5
Distressed Low Variance Firm	−50	0	50	0	12.5
Distressed High Variance Firm	−150	0	150	0	37.5

The first and third cases represent a "low variance" firm, with the best-case and worst-case scenarios deviating from the most likely case by $50. The second and fourth cases represent a "high variance" firm, with the best-case and worst-case scenarios deviating from the most likely case by $150. We compute the value without the abandonment option by summing the products of each of the valuation outcomes with their respective probabilities. We compute the value with the abandonment option using the same procedure, but after assigning a value of $0 to all negative valuation outcomes.

For the first case of the healthy, low variance firm, even the worst-case valuation outcome is positive, so the abandonment option has no value. In the second case of the healthy, high variance firm, the worst-case outcome has a negative value, giving value to the abandonment option. The value without the abandonment option is $100 and with the abandonment option is $112.5, so the value of the abandonment option is $12.5. Higher variance results in a greater value for the abandonment option. In the third case of the distressed, low variance firm, the worst-case valuation outcome is again negative, giving a value of $12.5 to the abandonment option. In the fourth case of the distressed, high variance firm, the worst-case valuation outcome is very negative, resulting in an abandonment value of $37.5. Financial distress combines with high variance to give great value to the abandonment option. Note that in this fourth case, the value of the company with the abandonment option is $37.5, even though the most likely valuation outcome is zero. Ignoring the abandonment option can result in serious undervaluation.

12.3   CREATING AND DESTROYING VALUE THROUGH FINANCING TRANSACTIONS

Common Equity Transactions

The valuation computations in eVal assume that all future net cash distributions to common stockholders will accrue to the current common stockholders or, if the current shareholders sell their shares to someone else, that they will do so at the share's intrinsic value. In reality, this is often not the case. Companies frequently issue new shares of stock to new stockholders and repurchase shares of stock from existing stockholders, and do so at values that are wildly different from the stock's intrinsic value. An obvious question is whether these transactions can create or destroy value. The answer is a resounding yes, and there have been numerous spectacular cases in which companies have created or destroyed value for stockholders through transactions in their own common stock.

To keep things simple, we will start by assuming that we have created a valuation model in eVal that correctly forecasts the future net cash distributions to common stockholders; that is, it captures the share's intrinsic value. By discounting these future cash distributions, eVal arrives at the value of common equity to the existing stockholders as a group. eVal then divides by the number of common shares outstanding to arrive at the estimate of intrinsic value per share. As long as all the current stockholders continue to hold their stock and no new stock is sold, then the current stockholders will all realize this intrinsic value.

But what if some existing stockholders sell their stock to new stockholders? As long as these transactions take place at intrinsic value, no wealth is transferred between the selling stockholders and the buying stockholders. However, if these transactions take place at a price that differs from the intrinsic value, there is a wealth transfer between the old selling stockholders and the new buying stockholders. If trades take place above intrinsic value, the selling stockholders gain at the expense of the buying stockholders. Conversely, if trades take place below intrinsic value, the buying stockholders gain at the expense of the selling stockholders. These results should come as no surprise. After all, one of the key goals of eVal is to help you profit from buying underpriced securities and selling overpriced securities. The important point to emphasize at this juncture is that the value of the stock to ongoing stockholders continues to be the intrinsic value computed by eVal, regardless of the price at which trades take place between old and new stockholders.

But what if the company itself trades in its own stock? As long as these trades take place at intrinsic value, again there are no wealth transfers. But if these trades take place at a price different from intrinsic value, then there are wealth transfers between the existing stockholders and the stockholders transacting with the company. Table 12.2 summarizes the direction of the wealth transfers.

The important issue here is that the ultimate value of a stock to an ongoing stockholder is determined not only by the intrinsic value of the stock, but also by the extent to which the company transacts in its own stock at a price differing

TABLE 12.2 **Wealth Transfers in Stock Transactions**

	Company Repurchases Stock from Existing Stockholders	Company Sells Stock to New Stockholders
Transaction Takes Place at a Price Above Intrinsic Value	Wealth is transferred from ongoing stockholders to selling stockholders	Wealth is transferred from buying stockholders to ongoing stockholders
Transaction Takes Place at a Price Below Intrinsic Value	Wealth is transferred from selling stockholders to ongoing stockholders	Wealth is transferred from ongoing stockholders to buying stockholders

from intrinsic value. This means that the market value of a stock is a potentially important determinant of the value of the stock even to a stockholder with no plans to trade the stock. Two examples help to clarify this. First, consider the case of a company with an intrinsic value of common equity of $1,000 and 10 shares outstanding. The intrinsic value per share is $100. Next assume that this company is able to issue an additional 10 shares at $300 per share. The company has a revised intrinsic value of $4,000 and 20 shares outstanding, giving an intrinsic value of $200 per share. By issuing new shares at a price that exceeds intrinsic value, the company has created additional intrinsic value for ongoing stockholders.

As a second example, begin again with a company that has intrinsic value of common equity of $1,000 and 10 shares outstanding. But now assume that this company's stock is trading at only $50 per share. If this company repurchases 6 shares of its own stock, it will have a revised intrinsic value of $700 and 4 shares outstanding, giving an intrinsic value per share of $175. By repurchasing shares at a price below intrinsic value, the company has created additional intrinsic value for ongoing stockholders.

The above analysis has important implications for the valuation of an equity security. If the market value of the security differs from its intrinsic value, then we must consider the potential for the company to engage in transactions in its own stock to take advantage of this misvaluation. You can probably see that this argument has an element of circularity to it. If a company's market price is an important determinant of its intrinsic value, then we have to forecast market value to estimate intrinsic value. For this reason, stock prices can get caught up in speculative bubbles. But at the end of the day, these speculative bubbles simply transfer wealth from one set of stockholders to another. The intrinsic value of a firm's total common equity is still determined only by the present value of its future net cash distributions.

It is difficult to identify airtight examples of firms issuing or repurchasing equity at prices different from the intrinsic value because we never really know for sure what a firm's intrinsic value is. Nonetheless, we offer AOL's acquisition of Time Warner as a likely illustration. In January 2000 AOL was trading at a total market value of $164 billion, a value that was difficult to justify based on forecasts of their future cash flows. AOL cashed in on their high stock price by issuing shares of AOL stock in exchange for Time Warner's stock. Whereas AOL had mostly Internet assets and a customer base with fading loyalty, Time Warner had hard assets, including magazines, cable networks, and recording studios. The acquisition used AOL's overvalued stock to buy assets that had real value. In this way they created value for the original AOL shareholders, but at the expense of the Time Warner shareholders. It didn't take long for the market to find its way back to intrinsic value. Prior to the merger announcement Time Warner had a market value of about $84 billion. By the time the deal closed a year later, the value of the combined entity had fallen to approximately $109 billion, not much more than the original value of Time Warner all by itself. Absent the acquisition, the original AOL shareholders may have had nothing in terms of future cash flows. As it stood, they owned 54 percent of the new entity—and the original Time Warner shareholders, who used to own 100 percent of the valuable part of the new entity, now owned only 46 percent. On 2/3/2003, the merged AOL Time Warner had a market value of only $52 billion, much to the chagrin of the original Time Warner owners.

From a practical perspective, how can we address the issue of potential wealth distributions resulting from a company trading in its own stock? We should always be aware of significant deviations between the current market value of a stock and our estimate of its intrinsic value. If a company's market price exceeds its intrinsic value, we should consider whether the company is likely to issue new shares of stock. These issuances can take the form of seasoned equity offerings or stock-for-stock acquisitions of other companies. If such issuances are likely, then we should try to quantify their impact on stock values for ongoing stockholders. If a company's market price is below its intrinsic value, we should consider whether management is likely to undertake stock repurchases. If repurchases are likely, then we should try to quantify their impact on stock values for ongoing stockholders. You may have noticed that our guidance is somewhat vague on this issue. This is no coincidence. A company's ability to create and destroy value for ongoing stockholders by transacting in its own stock is one of the most difficult valuation issues to grapple with. Trying to forecast how much value will be created or destroyed is like trying to forecast when a Ponzi scheme will collapse.

The creation and destruction of value through financing activities is not restricted to transactions in a company's common stock. If companies are able to issue debt or preferred stock at inflated values, then they will likewise create value for existing stockholders. But there is one key difference for these non-common equity forms of financing. We explicitly forecast these events in our eVal model. Hence, as long as we correctly forecast the favorable or unfavorable terms of this non-equity capital, their impact on the value of common equity will be incorporated by eVal.

Contingent Equity Claims

Issuing contingent equity claims is another way to create or destroy value through financing transactions. Contingent equity claims take many forms, including company warrants, employee stock options, and the conversion options on bonds.

These contingent equity claims give their holders the right to purchase shares of common stock at prices that may differ from intrinsic value and in many cases well below intrinsic value. If such rights are exercised, then wealth is transferred between the ongoing stockholders and the new stockholders exercising their contingent equity claims. The accounting for contingent equity claims is currently in a state of flux, but neither the existing accounting rules nor any of the new proposals will correctly reflect the impact of contingent equity claims on the intrinsic value of a share of common stock.

We can give you a simple (but admittedly crude) procedure for dealing with contingent equity claims. To the extent that a company has *existing* outstanding contingent equity claims, you should simply value those claims and incorporate them into your eVal computation using the procedure described in Chapter 10. To the extent that you forecast a company will issue contingent equity claims in the *future*, capture the economic effect of this by forecasting that the company will instead engage in a "plain vanilla" transaction that has a similar effect to issuing contingent claims. For instance, with warrants you should simply assume that the company will issue common stock of equivalent value. For employee stock options, simply assume that the company will pay cash compensation of equivalent value. For the issuance of convertible bonds, simply assume that the company will issue plain bonds at the market interest rate. Note that these alternative transactions are not exactly economically equivalent to issuing contingent equity claims. But the key differences hinge on changes in the future stock price of the company. And if we knew how the future stock price was going to change, we wouldn't need to do a valuation in the first place. By replacing the contingent claim transactions with their "plain vanilla" equivalents, we obtain an estimate of intrinsic value that abstracts from the circularity of trying to determine a firm's current value by forecasting its future stock price.

12.4 CONCLUDING COMMENTS

This chapter has introduced you to some of the key complications arising in performing equity valuations and provided you with some pragmatic solutions. There are, however, many other potential complications. Your best means for dealing with these complications is a good understanding of valuation theory combined with common sense in its practical application. Always keep sight of the fact that a financial security is only ever worth the net present value of its future cash distributions. A good equity valuation involves bringing all the data and ingenuity you can muster in order to forecast these future cash distributions.

12.5   LINKS AND REFERENCES

AOL–Time Warner Merger

This case is an advanced valuation case covering one of the most phenomenal mergers of the "dot.com" craze. It illustrates how AOL created value by issuing its overvalued stock as consideration in the purchase of Time Warner. The case also illustrates how acquisitions can be either accretive or dilutive to the consolidated earnings-per-share. The case comes with an eVal input file and is available on the eVal website.

The Valuation of Amazon

This is an advanced valuation case. It illustrates how seemingly reasonable forecasts can actually be quite unreasonable after one examines the financial ratios that the forecasts imply. The case uses an actual DCF model developed for Amazon by a famous Wall Street firm, showing that even the big dogs can make big mistakes. Second, the case illustrates how to compute the abandonment option for Amazon.com. The case includes an eVal input file for Amazon and is available on the eVal website.

- eVal website—www.mhhe.com/eval

Getting Started with eVal

The eVal software is an integral part of this book. While you can definitely read each chapter without sitting next to your computer, we assume that you will be using eVal to construct your valuation models and therefore will need a bit of instruction on how to interact with the software. Unlike many other valuation software programs, eVal is *not* a black box. This book and the software are woven together to teach you exactly why your valuation model produces the answer that it does. Of course, we think eVal is much more than an instructional tool—we think it is a great general-purpose valuation program that will vastly improve the quality of your life (or, at least, the quality of your valuations). But even if you ultimately use some other valuation software, it will be much easier to learn another program after having first learned eVal.

INSTALLING AND RUNNING eVAL

Insert the eVal CD into your computer. If the installation program doesn't launch immediately then navigate to the CD drive for your computer and double-click the setup.exe file. Because there is a ton of financial data included with eVal the installation can take several minutes to run and require up to 20 MB of space on your hard-drive. If you need to uninstall eVal for some reason then go to your Control Panel (usually found under the Settings sub-menu on your Start menu) and select Add/Remove Programs.

Once eVal is installed on your computer, it can be started by double clicking the eVal icon on your desktop or by navigating to the eVal program icon using the Start menu. If you have the security level for Microsoft Office set to Medium or High, a warning message will appear notifying you that the program file contains Macros authored by Russell Lundholm and Richard Sloan, but that these macros have not been authenticated. We have skipped the whole authentication process because Microsoft wants to charge all of us a lot of money to use it. YOU MUST ENABLE MACROS for eVal to function! If your security level is set to High then you will have to check the box "Always Trust Macros from this Source" to proceed; if your security level is set to Medium then you can enable them without checking the "Always Trust . . ." box. In either case, if you check the box to "Always Trust Macros . . ." from Russell Lundholm and Richard Sloan you can avoid generating this dialog box in the future. If you want to change your security settings in Excel, you can find them by going to the Tools menu, then to the Macros sub-menu.

USING eVAL

The first chapter gives you an overview of eVal and the rest of the book shows you all the beauty and nuance that it contains. But if you want to start clicking buttons right now that's fine—you can't break anything. The program is really just a customized Excel file, so if you are familiar with Excel then everything should look pretty familiar. You can change only the yellow cells; everything else is copy-protected so that you don't accidentally mess up the program. The main eVal file is "Read Only" so to save your work you must pick another file name.

Media General Industry and Sector Codes

Sector Code	Sector Name	Sector Code	Sector Name
MG1	*Basic Materials*	MG314	Electronic Equipment
		MG315	Toys & Games
MG11	**CHEMICALS**	MG316	Sporting Goods
MG110	Chemicals—Major Diversified	MG317	Recreational Goods, Other
MG111	Synthetics	MG318	Photographic Equipment & Supplies
MG112	Agricultural Chemicals		
MG113	Specialty Chemicals	**MG32**	**CONSUMER NON-DURABLES**
		MG320	Textile—Apparel Clothing
MG12	**ENERGY**	MG321	Textile—Apparel Footwear & Accessories
MG120	Major Integrated Oil & Gas	MG322	Rubber & Plastics
MG121	Independent Oil & Gas	MG323	Personal Products
MG122	Oil & Gas Refining & Marketing	MG324	Paper & Paper Products
MG123	Oil & Gas Drilling & Exploration	MG325	Packaging & Containers
MG124	Oil & Gas Equipment & Services	MG326	Cleaning Products
MG125	Oil & Gas Pipelines	MG327	Office Supplies
MG13	**METALS & MINING**	**MG33**	**AUTOMOTIVE**
MG130	Steel & Iron	MG330	Auto Manufacturers—Major
MG131	Copper	MG331	Trucks & Other Vehicles
MG132	Aluminum	MG332	Recreational Vehicles
MG133	Industrial Metals & Minerals	MG333	Auto Parts
MG134	Gold		
MG135	Silver	**MG34**	**FOOD & BEVERAGE**
MG136	Nonmetallic Mineral Mining	MG340	Food—Major Diversified
		MG341	Farm Products
MG2	*Conglomerates*	MG342	Processed & Packaged Goods
		MG343	Meat Products
MG21	**CONGLOMERATES**	MG344	Dairy Products
MG210	Conglomerates	MG345	Confectioners
		MG346	Beverages—Brewers
MG3	*Consumer Goods*	MG347	Beverages—Wineries & Distillers
		MG348	Beverages—Soft Drinks
MG31	**CONSUMER DURABLES**		
MG310	Appliances	**MG35**	**TOBACCO**
MG311	Home Furnishings & Fixtures	MG350	Cigarettes
MG312	Housewares & Accessories	MG351	Tobacco Products, Other
MG313	Business Equipment		

Sector Code	Sector Name	Sector Code	Sector Name
MG4	*Financial*	**MG52**	**HEALTH SERVICES**
		MG520	Medical Instruments & Supplies
MG41	**BANKING**	MG521	Medical Appliances & Equipment
MG410	Money Center Banks	MG522	Health Care Plans
MG411	Regional—Northeast Banks	MG523	Long-Term Care Facilities ✓
MG412	Regional—Mid-Atlantic Banks	MG524	Hospitals
MG413	Regional—Southeast Banks	MG525	Medical Laboratories & Research
MG414	Regional—Midwest Banks	MG526	Home Health Care
MG415	Regional—Southwest Banks	MG527	Medical Practitioners
MG416	Regional—Pacific Banks	MG528	Specialized Health Services
MG417	Foreign Money Center Banks		
MG418	Foreign Regional Banks	*MG6*	*Industrial Goods*
MG419	Savings & Loans		
		MG61	**AEROSPACE/DEFENSE**
MG42	**FINANCIAL SERVICES**	MG610	Aerospace/Defense—Major Diversified
MG420	Investment Brokerage—National	MG611	Aerospace/Defense Products & Services
MG421	Investment Brokerage—Regional		
MG422	Asset Management	**MG62**	**MANUFACTURING**
MG423	Diversified Investments	MG620	Farm & Construction Machinery
MG424	Credit Services	MG621	Industrial Equipment & Components
MG425	Closed-End Fund—Debt	MG622	Diversified Machinery
MG426	Closed-End Fund—Equity	MG623	Pollution & Treatment Controls
MG427	Closed-End Fund—Foreign	MG624	Machine Tools & Accessories
		MG625	Small Tools & Accessories
MG43	**INSURANCE**	MG626	Metal Fabrication
MG430	Life Insurance	MG627	Industrial Electrical Equipment
MG431	Accident & Health Insurance	MG628	Textile Manufacturing
MG432	Property & Casualty Insurance		
MG433	Surety & Title Insurance	**MG63**	**MATERIALS & CONSTRUCTION**
MG434	Insurance Brokers	MG630	Residential Construction
		MG631	Manufactured Housing
MG44	**REAL ESTATE**	MG632	Lumber, Wood Production
MG440	REIT—Diversified	MG633	Cement
MG441	REIT—Office	MG634	General Building Materials
MG442	REIT—Healthcare Facilities	MG635	Heavy Construction
MG443	REIT—Hotel/Motel	MG636	General Contractors
MG444	REIT—Industrial	MG637	Waste Management
MG445	REIT—Residential		
MG446	REIT—Retail	*MG7*	*Services*
MG447	Mortgage Investment		
MG448	Property Management	**MG71**	**LEISURE**
MG449	Real Estate Development	MG710	Lodging
		MG711	Resorts & Casinos
MG5	*Healthcare*	MG712	Restaurants
		MG713	Specialty Eateries
MG51	**DRUGS**	MG714	Gaming Activities
MG510	Drug Manufacturers—Major	MG715	Sporting Activities
MG511	Drug Manufacturers—Other	MG716	General Entertainment
MG512	Drugs—Generic		
MG513	Drug Delivery	**MG72**	**MEDIA**
MG514	Drug Related Products	MG720	Advertising Agencies
MG515	Biotechnology	MG721	Marketing Services
MG516	Diagnostic Substances	MG722	Entertainment—Diversified
		MG723	Broadcasting—TV

Sector Code	Sector Name	Sector Code	Sector Name
MG724	Broadcasting—Radio	MG775	Shipping
MG725	CATV Systems	MG776	Railroads
MG726	Movie Production, Theaters		
MG727	Publishing—Newspapers	*MG8*	*Technology*
MG728	Publishing—Periodicals		
MG729	Publishing—Books	**MG81**	**COMPUTER HARDWARE**
		MG810	Diversified Computer Systems
MG73	**RETAIL**	MG811	Personal Computers
MG730	Apparel Stores	MG812	Computer Based Systems
MG731	Department Stores	MG813	Data Storage Devices
MG732	Discount, Variety Stores	MG814	Networking & Communication Devices
MG733	Drug Stores	MG815	Computer Peripherals
MG734	Grocery Stores		
MG735	Electronics Stores	**MG82**	**COMPUTER SOFTWARE & SERVICES**
MG736	Home Improvement Stores	MG820	Multimedia & Graphics Software
MG737	Home Furnishing Stores	MG821	Application Software
MG738	Auto Parts Stores	MG822	Technical & System Software
MG739	Catalog & Mail Order Houses	MG823	Security Software & Services
		MG824	Information Technology Services
MG74	**SPECIALTY RETAIL**	MG825	Healthcare Information Services
MG740	Sporting Goods Stores	MG826	Business Software & Services
MG741	Toy & Hobby Stores	MG827	Information & Delivery Services
MG742	Jewelry Stores		
MG743	Music & Video Stores	**MG83**	**ELECTRONICS**
MG744	Auto Dealerships	MG830	Semiconductor—Broad Line
MG745	Specialty Retail, Other	MG831	Semiconductor—Memory Chips
		MG832	Semiconductor—Specialized
MG75	**WHOLESALE**	MG833	Semiconductor—Integrated Circuits
MG750	Auto Parts Wholesale	MG834	Semiconductor Equipment & Materials
MG751	Building Materials Wholesale	MG835	Printed Circuit Boards
MG752	Industrial Equipment Wholesale	MG836	Diversified Electronics
MG753	Electronics Wholesale	MG837	Scientific & Technical Instruments
MG754	Medical Equipment Wholesale		
MG755	Computers Wholesale	**MG84**	**TELECOMMUNICATIONS**
MG756	Drugs Wholesale	MG840	Wireless Communications
MG757	Food Wholesale	MG841	Communication Equipment
MG758	Basic Materials Wholesale	MG842	Processing Systems & Products
MG759	Wholesale, Other	MG843	Long Distance Carriers
		MG844	Telecom Services—Domestic
MG76	**DIVERSIFIED SERVICES**	MG845	Telecom Services—Foreign
MG760	Business Services	MG846	Diversified Communication Services
MG761	Rental & Leasing Services		
MG762	Personal Services	**MG85**	**INTERNET**
MG763	Consumer Services	MG850	Internet Service Providers
MG764	Staffing & Outsourcing Services	MG851	Internet Information Providers
MG765	Security & Protection Services	MG852	Internet Software & Services
MG766	Education & Training Services		
MG767	Technical Services	*MG9*	*Utilities*
MG768	Research Services		
MG769	Management Services	**MG91**	**UTILITIES**
		MG910	Foreign Utilities
MG77	**TRANSPORTATION**	MG911	Electric Utilities
MG770	Major Airlines	MG912	Gas Utilities
MG771	Regional Airlines	MG913	Diversified Utilities
MG772	Air Services, Other	MG914	Water Utilities
MG773	Air Delivery & Freight Services		
MG774	Trucking		

Standardized Financial Statement Data Definitions

This appendix provides general definitions of the standardized financial statement data items used by eVal. These definitions should be interpreted as broad guidelines rather than precise rules. For more precise definitions of the standardized financial statement data items provided by Media General, COMPUSTAT, and Thomson Research, you should refer to the user documentation supplied with these products. There are many subtle differences and ambiguities in the way that these services construct their standardized databases. From a user's perspective, however, it is sufficient that you have a good understanding of how the standardized data for the company that you are analyzing in eVal has been mapped from the as-reported data.

In applying these definitions, recall that eVal follows two important conventions in coding all financial statement data. First, all dollar and share amounts are recorded in thousands. Second all line items that reduce their respective net income, asset, liability, or equity totals are recorded as negative amounts. For example, cost of goods sold, dividends, and an accumulated deficit in retained earnings all represent amounts that would be recorded as negatives in eVal.

Below, we provide definitions for eVal's standardized financial statement data items in the order that they appear in eVal's Financial Statements worksheet.

The cell **Company Name** at the top of the Financial Statements sheet is simply the name of the company, abbreviated to a reasonable length where appropriate.

The cell **Common Shares Outstanding** at the top of the Financial Statements sheet is defined as the total number of common shares issued net of the number of common treasury shares at the most recent fiscal year end (in thousands).

The cells labeled **Fiscal Year End (MM/DD/YYYY)** contain the date of the end of the fiscal year for the financial statement data entered in that column, in MM/DD/YYYY format (for example, December 31, 1999, would be entered as 12/31/1999).

INCOME STATEMENT

The line item **Sales (Net)** represents gross sales reduced by cash discounts, trade discounts, and returned sales and allowances for which credit is given to customers.

The line item **Cost of Goods Sold** represents all costs directly allocated by the company to production, such as material, labor, and overhead.

The line item **Gross Profit** is computed as **Sales (Net)** plus **Cost of Goods Sold,** recalling that expenses we entered as negative numbers.

The line item **R&D Expense** (Research and Development Expense) represents all costs that relate to the development of new products or services.

The line item **SG&A Expense** (Selling, General, and Administrative Expense) represents expenses incurred in the normal operating activities of the company that are not allocated to Cost of Goods Sold or classified as R&D Expense.

The line item **EBITDA** (Earnings Before Interest, Tax, Depreciation, and Amortization) is computed as **Gross Profit** plus **R&D Expense** plus **SG&A Expense.**

The line item **Depreciation and Amortization** represents non-cash charges for the periodic allocation of the cost of property, plant, equipment, intangible assets, and wasting assets.

The line item **EBIT** (Earnings Before Interest and Taxes) is computed as **EBITDA** plus **Depreciation and Amortization.**

The line item **Interest Expense** represents the periodic cost of securing short- and long-term debt. Ideally, this item should be presented gross of interest income. However, in cases where a firm reports interest expense net of interest income without disclosing the gross amounts, this line item will represent interest expense net of interest income.

The line item **Non-Operating Income (Loss)** represents the net amount of any income or expense items that are not directly related to the normal operating activities of the company. This item commonly includes interest and other investment income, earnings from equity affiliates, and charges related to asset impairments, restructuring or other special items.

The line item **EBT** (Earnings Before Taxes) is computed as **EBIT** plus **Interest Expense** plus **Non-Operating Income (Loss).**

The line item **Income Taxes** represents all expenses recognized in relation to taxes imposed by federal state and foreign taxing authorities.

The line item **Minority Interest in Earnings** represents the fraction of the income of consolidated subsidiaries that is attributable to minority stockholders in the subsidiary.

The line item **Other Income (Loss)** represents any miscellaneous non-operating income or expense items that are reported on an after tax basis.

The line item **Net Income Before Ext. Items** (Net Income Before Extraordinary Items and Discontinued Operations) is computed as **EBT** plus **Income Taxes** plus **Minority Interest in Earnings** plus **Other Income (Loss).**

The line item **Ext. Items & Disc. Ops** (Extraordinary Items and Discontinued Operations) represents the income statement effects of extraordinary items, discontinued operations, and accounting changes.

The line item **Preferred Dividends** represents the total amount of the preferred dividend requirements on cumulative preferred stock and the dividends paid on noncumulative preferred stock. If using Thomson Research data, see the discussion of its treatment of preferred dividends in Appendix D.

The line item **Net Income (available to common)** is computed as **Net Income Before Ext. Items** plus **Ext. Items & Disc. Ops** plus **Preferred Dividends.**

BALANCE SHEET

The line item **Cash and Marketable Securities** represents cash and all securities that are readily convertible into cash.

The line item **Receivables** represents amounts of cash due from others, generally within the next year, net of any applicable allowances.

The line item **Inventories** represents merchandise bought for resale and material and supplies purchased for use in operating activities.

The line item **Other Current Assets** represents current assets other than **Cash and Marketable Securities, Receivables** and **Inventories**.

The line item **Total Current Assets** is computed as **Cash and Marketable Securities** plus **Receivables** plus **Inventories** plus **Other Current Assets.**

The line item **PP&E (Net)** (Net Property, Plant and Equipment) represents the cost of tangible fixed property, plant, and equipment used in the production of revenues, less accumulated depreciation.

The line item **Investments** represents long-term investments, including equity investments in unconsolidated affiliated companies.

The line item **Intangibles** represents the cost of all intangible assets including goodwill, less accumulated amortization.

The line item **Other Assets** represents long-term assets other than **PP&E, Investments,** and **Intangibles.**

The line item **Total Assets** is computed as **Total Current Assets** plus **PP&E** plus **Investments** plus **Intangibles** plus **Other Assets.**

The line item **Current Debt** represents the total carrying value of short-term borrowings with an original maturity of one year or less plus the current portion of long-term debt (long-term debt coming due within one year), including the current portion of capital lease obligations.

The line item **Accounts Payable** represents trade obligations due within the next year or the normal operating cycle of the company.

The line item **Income Taxes Payable** represents income taxes that are due and owing to the taxing authorities within the next year.

The line item **Other Current Liabilities** represents current liabilities other than **Current Debt, Accounts Payable** and **Income Taxes Payable** and includes accrued expenses and dividends payable.

The line item **Total Current Liabilities** is computed as **Current Debt** plus **Accounts Payable** plus **Income Taxes Payable** plus **Other Current Liabilities.**

The line item **Long-Term Debt** represents the total carrying value of debt obligations due in more than one year, including the long-term portion of bonds, mortgages, and capital lease obligations.

The line item **Other Liabilities** represents long-term liabilities other than **Long-Term Debt, Deferred Taxes** and **Minority Interest** and includes pension and other postretirement liabilities.

The line item **Deferred Taxes** represents the accumulated tax deferrals attributable to timing differences in income recognition for financial reporting and tax purposes. Where applicable, this item also includes the carrying value of any deferred tax credits.

The line item **Minority Interest** represents the fraction of the carrying value of the common equity of consolidated subsidiaries that is attributable to minority stockholders in the subsidiary.

The line item **Total Liabilities** is computed as **Total Current Liabilities** plus **Long-Term Debt** plus **Other Liabilities** plus **Deferred Taxes** plus **Minority Interest.**

The line item **Preferred Stock** represents the total net carrying value of preferred stock. If using Thomson Research data, see the discussion on its treatment of preferred stock in Appendix D.

The line item **Paid in Common Capital (Net)** represents the total net carrying value of all common equity accounts other than retained earnings. This item regularly includes the net effects of common stock at par, additional paid in capital, treasury stock, unrealized gains and losses, and unearned stock compensation.

The line item **Retained Earnings** represents the cumulative earnings of the company, net of cumulative dividend distributions. In cases where this item is negative, it is typically referred to as the accumulated deficit.

The line item **Total Common Equity** is computed as **Paid in Common Capital (Net)** plus **Retained Earnings.**

The line item **Total Liabilities and Equity** is computed as **Total Liabilities** plus **Preferred Stock** plus **Total Common Equity.**

STATEMENT OF RETAINED EARNINGS

The line item **Beg. Retained Earnings** (Beginning Value of Retained Earnings) represents the ending value of **Retained Earnings** for the previous fiscal year, as defined for the Balance Sheet above.

The line item **Net Income** represents **Net Income,** as defined for the Income Statement above.

The line item **Common Dividends** represents the total amount of cash dividends declared on common stock for the year.

The line item **Clean Surplus Plug (Ignore)** represents the total net effect of all items other than **Net Income** and **Common Dividends** that affected **Retained Earnings** during the fiscal year. Items that regularly enter this category are treasury stock transactions accounted for using the par value method, stock dividends, prior period adjustments, and retroactive accounting changes. Since future treasury stock transactions are assumed to flow through Paid-In-Capital (i.e., the cost method) and since the rest of these adjustments refer to the past, this item is zero in the future forecasted financial statements. That's why we keep telling you to **Ignore** it.

The line item **End. Retained Earnings** (Ending Value of Retained Earnings) represents the value of **Retained Earnings** for the current fiscal year, as defined for the Balance Sheet above.

Importing Data from a Saved File

eVal is shipped with Media General data for over 8000 firms built in. However, there may be times you want to access saved data from another source. There are four options for importing data from a saved file:

- Import Data from Thomson Research (also known as Global Access)
- Import Data from WRDS
- Import Data from a COMPUSTAT Template
- Import Data from a MarketGuide Template

For each option, inputting the historical data is a two-step process. First you access the data from the third party data provider and then save it in the form specified below. This step does not involve eVal directly. Second, you import the data into eVal by selecting the option that matches your data source.

Note: The instructions for how to interact with the third party data provider are correct as of this writing but these parties may change their format or their URL in the future. If you are having trouble, please check the eVal website for updated instructions.

IMPORTING DATA FROM THOMSON RESEARCH (ALSO KNOWN AS GLOBAL ACCESS)

Thomson Research, a division of Primark (also known as Global Access), provides access to the Disclosure Inc. SEC Database. This service is accessible through the electronic libraries of many leading business schools and also offers individual subscriptions. A key advantage of using Thomson Research is that the data is provided in preformatted Excel spreadsheets. Thus, all you have to do is download the appropriate spreadsheet to your computer. Thomson Research provides a number of preformatted "Spreadsheet Financials" and the "U.S. 10-K (10 Year) History Spreadsheet" provides the data required by eVal. If you have a subscription to Thomson Research, then you can save this spreadsheet for the company of your choice by following these steps:

1. Log on to the Thomson Research service at http://research.thomsonib.com/. (Note: This is a subscription database that is password protected. If your institution has a subscription to Thomson Research, then you will probably have to enter the website through the appropriate proxy server at your institution in order to gain access.)

2. Find the company you would like to analyze in eVal by entering the company name or ticker and clicking the Search button.

3. Click on the link to "U.S. 10-K History (10-Year) Spreadsheet."

4. A 10-year history of financial statement data should be returned in an Excel spreadsheet. From within your browser, save this file on your PC's hard-drive. Some browsers do not allow you access to Excel's Save function. If you encounter this situation, fire up a new Excel spreadsheet and then cut and paste the entire contents of the Thomson Research spreadsheet to your new spreadsheet, being very careful to paste the data to exactly the same cells as in the original Thomson Research spreadsheet. We recommend saving your files in the Thomson Research folder that we have provided in the eVal2 program folder. We also recommend using the naming convention ticker_TR_data.xls for Thomson Research spreadsheets, where "ticker" refers to the company's ticker.

5. Before you try to load the saved data into eVal, send your browser to some other location (Home, for example). If you don't do this, then Excel will be running in the browser window, which may interfere with eVal's import routine.

You can read this data into eVal by selecting the "Import Data from Thomson Research" data input option and following the prompts to tell eVal where the Thomson Research spreadsheet is located. Once this is done, eVal will automatically import all available historical data, and you will be ready to start analyzing this data. eVal is shipped with a sample Thomson Research Excel spreadsheet for Kohl's Corporation.

IMPORTING DATA FROM WRDS

WRDS (Wharton Research and Data Services) is a division of the Wharton School of Business. Most leading business schools subscribe to WRDS, and access is often given to students through "class accounts." Like Thomson Research, WRDS offers preformatted financial statements for downloading. WRDS obtains the financial statement data from the COMPUSTAT database and downloads it in HTML format. If you have a subscription to WRDS, then you can save the required financial statement data for the company of your choice by following these steps:

1. Access the WRDS server at http://wrds.wharton.upenn.edu/ and log in. (*Note:* This is a subscription service that is password protected.)

2. Click on the Financial Statements link on the left-hand side of the screen.

3. In Step 1, select Complete Financial Statements from the combo box.

4. In step 2, select the most recent five years of annual data. For example, if data is available through 2001, select a beginning date of 1997 and an ending date of 2001. *User's Note:* It is important that you select exactly five years' worth of data, otherwise eVal will not import the data into the correct columns.

5. Select the Submit Request button, wait for the data to load in a separate window, and then save the resulting HTML file. We recommend saving your files in the WRDS folder that we have provided in the eVal2 program folder. We also recommend using the naming convention ticker_WRDS_data.htm for WRDS spreadsheets, where "ticker" refers to the company's ticker.

You can read the data in this HTML file directly into eVal by selecting the Import Data from WRDS data input option and following the prompts to tell eVal where the WRDS HTML file is located. Excel takes care of converting the HTML file to Excel format. Once this is done, eVal will automatically import all available historical data, and you will be ready to start analyzing this data.

As mentioned above, WRDS uses data from the COMPUSTAT database, and so is subject to the various pros and cons associated with COMPUSTAT data (described below). However, WRDS also introduces a couple of new wrinkles of its own. First, the data provided by WRDS is rounded to the nearest $10,000. As a result, you may observe rounding errors relative to what is reported in the company's actual financial statements, and these rounding errors may cause the balance sheet not to balance! However, these rounding errors are usually insignificant and can generally be ignored. Second, the WRDS COMPUSTAT data is currently updated only on an annual basis, and so the data COMPUSTAT data provided by WRDS can be up to 18 months out of date. The best fix to this problem is to save only the latest four years' worth of data from WRDS and to then enter the most recent year manually. eVal is shipped with a sample WRDS HTML spreadsheet for Kohl's Corporation.

IMPORTING DATA FROM A COMPUSTAT TEMPLATE

The data import options that we have described for Thomson Research and WRDS import data from a preformatted file. Unfortunately, many other services that provide access to standardized financial statement data do not provide suitable preformatted files. Moreover, it is just not feasible to make eVal compatible with the preformatted financials of every service. Fortunately, most services now come with Excel Add-Ins that allow you to build your own preformatted Excel data templates for downloading data. An Excel data template is an Excel worksheet in which data downloading codes are entered in to the cells. These downloading codes specify which data items from the standardized database are to be entered in which cells of the worksheet. Armed with the appropriate template and data subscription, you simply provide a company ticker to the Excel Add-In, and that company's data is returned in a preformatted spreadsheet. We have designed customized data downloading template formats for both the COMPUSTAT and MarketGuide databases that can be imported directly into eVal.

There are a number of vendors that allow you to build your own Excel templates using COMPUSTAT data. Two of the most widely used are S&P's Research Insight service and FactSet Research Systems. We do not endorse or support any of these services. However, to accommodate experienced users of such services, we have provided a standardized Excel data template for importing COMPUSTAT data into eVal. If you use this option, it is critical that you download the precise data items from COMPUSTAT into the precise cell addresses in Excel that are indicated in our standardized template. The exact format of the standardized template is illustrated in the spreadsheet named "Compustat" located in the Compustat Saved Data folder inside the eVal2 program folder.

On opening the sample Kohl's spreadsheet, you will see that annual Sales (COMPUSTAT item number A12) for the most recent fiscal year is entered in cell B4. Thus, you must create an Excel template in which this item also appears in cell B4. You should also carefully distinguish between cells containing imported data and cells containing formulas that aggregate data. Only import data into the data cells and do not write over any of the formula cells. Note that we use the naming convention ticker_COMP_data.xls for COMPUSTAT data spreadsheets, where "ticker" represents the company's ticker symbol. We encourage you to follow this naming convention. We also encourage you to save COMPUSTAT data spreadsheets in the Compustat Saved Data folder that we have provided in the eVal2 program folder.

IMPORTING DATA FROM A MARKETGUIDE TEMPLATE

This option is for importing MarketGuide data from a third party data service. If the third party data service enables you to download MarketGuide data into a pre-formatted Excel spreadsheet, then you can use this option. This option works in a manner similar to the COMPUSTAT template option described above. The exact format of the standardized template is illustrated in the spreadsheet named MG_Data located in the MarketGuide Saved Data folder inside the eVal2 program folder.

Note that we use the naming convention ticker_MG_data.xls for MarketGuide data spreadsheets, where "ticker" represents the company's ticker symbol. We encourage you to follow this naming convention. We also encourage you to save MarketGuide data spreadsheets in the MarketGuide Saved Data folder that we have provided in the eVal2 program folder. On opening the sample Kohl's spreadsheet, you will see that annual Revenue for the most recent fiscal year is entered in cell B11. Thus, you must create a spreadsheet in which this standardized MarketGuide item also appears in cell B11. You should also carefully distinguish between cells containing imported data and cells containing formulas that aggregate data. Only import data into the data cells and do not write over any of the formula cells. If you have trouble creating such a spreadsheet and importing it into eVal, then we recommend that you input the data manually or subscribe to one of the services for which we have shipped templates with eVal.

LIMITATIONS OF COMPUSTAT DATA

We begin our discussion of the limitations of the three commercially available standardized databases with the COMPUSTAT database. Overall, COMPUSTAT is considered to be the leading (and is certainly the most expensive) source of financial statement data. However, users should be aware that COMPUSTAT often collects data from the footnotes to the financial statements and then uses this data to determine how to map the published data into COMPUSTAT's standardized database format. As a result, you may have difficulty reconciling the as-reported data to the standardized data if you don't also read the footnotes. A common example is in the coding of depreciation and amortization expense for the income statement. Many companies do not report depreciation and amortization expense as a separate line item on their income statements. Instead, depreciation and amortization is either absorbed into inventory and expensed as part of cost of goods sold, or included as part of selling, general, and administrative expense. In order to report depreciation and amortization as a separate line item, COMPUSTAT attempts to recover this amount from the notes, and then deducts this amount from cost of goods sold so that it can be shown as a separate line item. Note that COMPUSTAT may do this even though some or all of the depreciation may have actually been expensed as part of selling, general, and administrative expense.

It is therefore important that you understand how COMPUSTAT has mapped the as-reported data into their standardized database, and this may require you to read through the notes to the financials.

LIMITATIONS OF THOMSON RESEARCH (GLOBAL ACCESS) DATA

There are two major drawbacks to using Thomson Research data in eVal. First, the U.S. 10-K History Spreadsheet does not provide Preferred Dividends and Common Dividends as separate line items. Instead, they provide only a line item described as Dividends, Other Distributions. We therefore make the assumption that this entire line item relates to common dividends and that preferred dividends are zero. This assumption is correct if the company has no preferred stock. However, in cases where you see preferred stock carried on the balance sheet, this assumption is probably false. In the latter case, we recommend that you retrieve the actual amounts for common dividends and preferred dividends from a copy of the published financial statements and manually adjust the amounts for common and preferred dividends on the Financial Statements worksheet accordingly.

The second drawback of using Thomson Research is that relatively little attempt is made to use information from the notes to the financial statements to provide more detailed information in the standardized data. For example, if a company includes R&D expense as part of SG&A expense on its balance sheet, Thomson Research will make no attempt to reclassify this amount to the R&D expense line item of their standardized financial statements, even if this amount is broken out in the footnotes.

LIMITATIONS OF MARKETGUIDE DATA

The MarketGuide data tends to be very similar to the Thomson Research data. As with Thomson Research, relatively little attempt is made to incorporate data from the footnotes. However, MarketGuide does provide separate information on common and preferred dividends, so this limitation of the Thomson Research data does not apply.

Index